THE THEATRE OF

I

-

THE THEATRE OF
MARTIN CRIMP

Aleks Sierz

Methuen Drama

First published 2006
A & C Black Publishers Limited
38 Soho Square
London W1D 3HB
www.acblack.com

ISBN-10: 0–413–77588–7
ISBN-13: 978-0-413-77588-7

A CIP catalogue record for this book is available from the British Library

The extract from *The French Lieutenant's Woman* by John Fowles, published by Jonathan Cape, is reprinted by permission of the Random House Group Ltd

Typeset in Dante MT by SX Composing DTP, Rayleigh, Essex

Printed and bound in Great Britain by MPG Books Ltd, Bodmin, Cornwall

This book is produced using paper that is made from wood grown in managed, sustainable forests. It is natural, renewable and recyclable. The logging and manufacturing processes conform to the environmental regulations of the country of origin.

It is, of course, its essentially schizophrenic outlook on society that makes the middle class so peculiar. We tend nowadays to forget that it has always been the great revolutionary class; we see it much more as the heartland of reaction, for ever selfish and conforming. Now this Janus-like quality derives from the class's one saving virtue, which is this: that alone of the three great classes of society it sincerely and habitually despises itself.

John Fowles, *The French Lieutenant's Woman*

CONTENTS

ACKNOWLEDGEMENTS

My greatest debt of gratitude is to Lia Ghilardi, who discovered and appreciated the work of Martin Crimp long before I did, and who met him in September 1994, when he played harpsichord at a Sunday concert at Orleans House, on the Thames riverside in Twickenham. She subsequently interviewed him, introduced me to him and encouraged me to write this book. I would also like to acknowledge the kindness and patience of Martin Crimp, who not only participated in several interviews, but also answered dozens of queries.

A book like this depends on the enthusiasm and good humour of numerous interviewees: many thanks to Tim Albery, Luc Bondy, David Bradby, Anthony Clark, Jude Kelly, Ed Kemp, James Macdonald, Katie Mitchell, Joe Penhall, Lindsay Posner, Auriol Smith, Sam Walters, Graham Whybrow and Gerhard Willert. Anne Tipton talked to me about her production of *Attempts on Her Life* (2004) and Lucy Taylor about her production of *The Country* (2005). Heiner Zimmermann generously photocopied his collection of Crimp's early plays, interviews and reviews. And provided soap during a theatre conference in Bremen. Graham Saunders helped by providing useful material; Dan Rebellato was generous, encouraging and informed. Penny Black helpfully translated Nils Tabert's 1998 interview with Crimp after the original transcript had been lost, and then did the same for Crimp's interview with Stefanie Carp and Stephan Wetzel. Nils Tabert answered several queries;

Clara Escoda Agusti shared her knowledge of articles about Crimp. Finally, a special thanks goes to my guests for a panel discussion on 'Reputations: Martin Crimp' at the Theatre Museum on 13 May 2005 for TheatreVoice (www.theatrevoice.com): Lindsay Posner, Dan Rebellato, Auriol Smith and Anne Tipton. And to Kate Graham, who transcribed the session.

I was also helped by Micky Albl, Elisabeth Angel-Perez (Sorbonne), Mireia Aragay (Barcelona), Anna Arthur, Steve Barfield (Westminster), Gavin Barker, Joanna Biggs (*London Review of Books*), Nicole Boireau (Metz), Els Boonen (BBC Archives), Robin Booth (Nick Hern Books), Nick Budden (Orange Tree), Harriet Cruickshank, Maria Delgado (Queen Mary), William Dixon, Lisa Fleming, Fin Kennedy, John Ginman (Goldsmiths), Howard Gooding (Judy Daish), Rod Hamilton (British Library Sound Archive), Andie Hawkes (Stephen Joseph Theatre), George Hunka, Emma McDermott (Theatre Royal, Bath), Alex Mangold, Anne Mayer, Martin Middeke (Augsburg), Etela Pardo, Peggy Paterson (Script), Marco Piferi, Lyndsay Roberts (Royal Court), Anneliese Rose (Young Vic), Juliet Rufford, Robert Tanitch, John Thaxter, Ewan Thompson (Royal Court), Merle Tönnies, David Tushingham, Ken Urban (Harvard), Trevor Walker (St Mary's, Strawberry Hill), Stephan Wetzel, Dinah Wood (Faber), Nada Zakula (RSC) and Pilar Zozaya (Barcelona). The staff of the Theatre Museum in London were extremely helpful and efficient. Finally, I would like to thank my excellent publisher, Mark Dudgeon, editor Katherine Fry, and all the staff at Methuen Drama. Any remaining mistakes or misunderstandings are entirely my own responsibility.

Aleks Sierz, London, 2006

INTRODUCTION:
'AT TWO SHIFTS FROM
REALITY?'

At the start of the new millennium, playwright Martin Crimp was
interviewed for a broadsheet newspaper, and when the article was
published its headline branded him an 'enigma'.[1] It's not hard to
see why: all over mainland Europe, from Berlin to Paris, from
Milan to Lisbon and from Copenhagen to Ljubljana, his name can
be glimpsed on the billboards of the best theatres, yet, in his own
country, most theatregoers have scarcely heard of him. This is odd
because, by 2000, Crimp had written more than ten plays in a
career that had already lasted twenty years. For a decade, he'd
been in the vanguard of new writing for the British stage, and it's
no exaggeration to say that his 1997 masterpiece, *Attempts on Her
Life*, is one of the very best plays of the past quarter-century. Actors
of the calibre of Tom Courtenay, Juliet Stevenson, Ken Stott,
Charlotte Rampling, Chiwetel Ejiofor and Uma Thurman have
starred in his plays. Directors such as Katie Mitchell, Simon
McBurney and Luc Bondy have staged them. And, as well as being
an important influence on some leading British playwrights,
Crimp is also an exceptionally gifted translator of French plays. Yet
he is not a resident writer at the National Theatre, nor has he been
a regular at the Royal Shakespeare Company. Little wonder that
arts journalists describe him as a mystery. That old cliché about a
prophet being without honour in their own country hangs in the
air like a bad smell.

The key to the puzzle is simple: Crimp's work is difficult. He

1

doesn't write crowd-pleasing social comedies, gritty council-estate dramas or easy plays about 'me and my mates'. He doesn't do West End hits, soap operas or lyrics for pop musicals. His plays are hard work. Typically, they are experimental in form and unsettling in content. Although animated by a playful delight in subverting dramatic conventions and often exuberant in their wordplay, they rarely encourage audiences to identify with any of the characters. Instead, they challenge them to exercise a certain detachment. And to think. His work is characterised by a vision of society as a place of social decline, moral bad faith and imminent violence, with the result that it offers audiences neither a sense of consoling optimism nor a feelgood high. Instead, they get moral ambiguity and riddles about motivation. Crimp's subjects, moreover, are hardly the stuff of light entertainment: he's tackled a fistful of cruel situations, from abduction to child abuse; his characters are often unpleasant people; his political targets range from media manipulation to consumer culture; he's deconstructed gender and he's criticised the War on Terror. Not really your typical good night out. Finally, his theatre is challenging because it questions the British tradition of naturalism and social realism. As director Dominic Dromgoole says, 'Martin Crimp is a truly European writer [. . .] His work drips with a cool formal sense of theatrical possibility.'[2] Yes, Crimp has been outstandingly innovative, but the insularity of many British audiences has meant that he has also been consistently undervalued.

With some writers, their biography explains their work. In Crimp's case, the life seems much less eventful than the career. Martin Andrew Crimp was born on 14 February 1956 in Dartford, Kent. His mother, Jennie, and his father, John, a British Rail signalling engineer, moved to Streatham in south London when Martin was four. He was obviously a bright child because, after attending a local primary school, he won a scholarship to nearby Dulwich College – a centuries-old public school. After a year, however, the family moved to York because his father was transferred there. Crimp went to Pocklington Grammar School, just outside York, which some years before had educated play-wright Tom Stoppard. At school, he showed an aptitude for languages, especially French, Latin and Greek. And for music, particularly keyboard playing. He was also interested in English literature and theatre: 'I was definitely the kind of pupil who loved acting, directing, adjusting the focus of the lamps, creating sound cues on an old tape recorder at home.'[3] He read the plays of Samuel Beckett and Eugène Ionesco, 'but it never really occurred to me that I would actually become a writer'.[4] Unlike his parents, who hadn't been to university, Crimp passed the Oxbridge entrance exam and went to St Catharine's College, Cambridge (1975–8). There, he read English, did some acting, and his first play *Clang* – influenced by Beckett and Ionesco – was staged by fellow student Roger Michell, who would later enjoy a successful career as a film and theatre director. At the time, Crimp was interested in psychological disorders 'and a clang disorder is when people pick up words by rhyming association, which figured in the play's language'.[5]

After graduating, Crimp moved to London, determined to be a writer. At first, he worked in various dead-end jobs – filing clerk in the local social security office, worker in a factory, transcriber of market-research interviews – punctuated by periods of unemployment. At the same time, he wrote *Still Early Days* (a novel), which was, as several rejection slips from publishers informed him, 'defiantly uncommercial'.[6] He also put together *An Anatomy* (a short-story collection). Then, in 1981, he rediscovered the possibilities of theatre when he joined the writers group at the Orange Tree Theatre, in Richmond, which produced his first six plays over the following decade. At the same time, Crimp also performed as a professional musician, playing piano and harpsichord, and earned money teaching music and as an accompanist to the Canonbury Chamber Choir. As well as writing for the Orange Tree, he wrote numerous radio plays, including the award-winning *Three Attempted Acts* (1985) and *Definitely the Bahamas* (1987). Eventually, he became Thames TV Writer-in-Residence at the Orange Tree in 1988–9. Then, in 1990, he got an Arts Council theatre-writing bursary, and the Royal Court Theatre staged his *No One Sees the Video*. A year later, he was a writer-in-residence at New Dramatists, in New York, and the resulting play, *The Treatment*, won the prestigious John Whiting Award in 1993. Gradually, Crimp became a central figure on the new-writing scene, an important influence on young playwrights such as Sarah Kane and Mark Ravenhill. In 1997, his career reached something of a climax when his masterpiece, *Attempts on Her Life*, was staged at the Royal Court, where he was writer-in residence that year. Since then, his reputation has grown both in Britain and abroad, especially on the Continent, with high-profile productions of his work appearing in Germany and France.

For most of his adult life, Crimp has lived in Richmond with his wife, Maggie, who has had a highly successful career in the medical profession. The couple have three daughters. Part of the reason for his enigmatic image stems from Crimp's reluctance to make his plays easy for journalists by making facile connections between his life and his work. Yet, despite his low profile, he has been interviewed on several occasions, although he usually finds the experience distinctly uncomfortable. In his first newspaper interview, he told a local journalist: 'It's sometimes a bit hard on the writer seeing his play, as it were, from the outside,' and joked about his prime inspiration: 'You couldn't call Beckett exactly commercial and yet, since *Waiting for Godot*, there is even a price on his socks.'[7] Other articles give glimpses of the life of a working writer. In 1990, he appears as a bit self-conscious, with his conversation described like this: 'He takes his time and speaks carefully, anxious not to let a careless word slip by.'[8] In 1993, his writing habits are sketched out: 'He writes "daily and fully sober" from 10am to 3pm.'[9] By 2000, he's matured into 'an elegantly cadaverous, grey-haired figure', and, as 'an intense-looking, bony faced 44-year-old with a greying bob, he certainly comes across as a man possessed of a strong, lonely sense of vocation and a perfectionist's temperament, but the attitude he adopts throughout our meeting is gentle, alert and affable'.[10] Typically, in the early 1990s, he began every interview by criticising the interview format: ' "Whatever I say to you," he tells me, nervously trawling his fingers through his hair, "you will go away and make a shape from it. That shape will be definitive in the way that the relationship between you and I can never be. [. . .] You will undertake a shaping process . . . in which I as a person will be misrepresented. It's inevitable." '[11] A few years later, and he'd relaxed a bit, explaining that 'at the time [of the previous interview] I had just finished writing my play *The Treatment*, which came out of a rather unhappy encounter with the film and TV business. In the meantime my sensitivity has calmed down somewhat, but at the time I had considerable doubts about the substance of interviews.'[12]

In 2000, Lisa Fleming photographed some of the writers at the Royal Court, including Mark Ravenhill and Joe Penhall, focusing on their hands instead of their faces. When it was Crimp's turn, she photographed his inky fingers, which appear slightly blurred, the soiled hands carefully held at arm's length. As an image of a writer's life, it seems to suggest fastidiousness about a dirty business. More revealing, however, are the short pieces of prose that Crimp has written during his career, a reminder that he's never confined himself to the stage. In 1982, he won a short-story competition, run by the London listings magazine *Time Out*, for 'The Statement', and his fragmentary 'Stage Kiss' appears in one of his earliest published playtexts. This is accompanied by a characteristic note: '*Stage Kiss* is a fiction about the theatre. How else should a writer deal with himself, if not at two shifts from reality?'[13] Obliqueness, distance is all. Then, in the published collections of his plays, Crimp has excelled in creating allusive and metaphorical pieces which capture something of the experience of being a writer. His 'Four Imaginary Characters' opens with a vision of international celebrity: 'The theatre has strapped me into planes, welcomed me at airports, driven me into strange cities. The theatre buys me drinks and takes me back to my hotel at 2 a.m. Three hours later it turns on a bright lamp close to my eyes, tells me to wake up and vomit.'[14] In 'Four Unwelcome Thoughts', the bitter rivalry between writers is frankly acknowledged: 'Each of us looks at the fool opposite, and wonders what that smile means.'[15] In these short prose pieces, there's an enjoyment of language and an embrace of self-irony: at one point, a director suggests to Crimp: 'I think you should steer clear of that kind of metaphorical stuff.' And adds, 'What people want is a flavour of what it's like to write plays – not a flavour of the plays themselves, because hopefully the plays will do that job for you.' The punch-line comes when the director advises Crimp to let the reader 'inside your head, that's right. Give them a little tour.'[16] The joke is that while Crimp has assiduously tried to avoid letting anyone into his head, his work reveals exactly what he's like – as you'd expect. And these prose pieces give a perfect impression of the persona that Crimp likes to project: cool, ironic and self-critical.

But although Crimp has emerged as an innovative and experi-mental playwright with a large body of work, it's difficult to find traces of his substantial career in most reference books. The more you search, the more the mystery deepens. If you look at best-sellers about British theatre, the attention paid to him is very slight. Richard Eyre and Nicholas Wright's *Changing Stages*, to take but one example, mentions him only in passing, as one of the new writers 'who are cracking the old theatrical templates'.[17] And while Dominic Dromgoole's recent book on contemporary new writing, *The Full Room*, includes three pages on Crimp, much of it is about Dromgoole's own experiences of European theatre. Other sources are equally silent. Not one production of a Crimp play is recorded in the video archive of the Theatre Museum in London, although his translation of Ionesco's *The Chairs* is included. And when in 2006 the National Portrait Gallery mounted an exhibition, *Royal Court Theatre: A Celebration of Fifty Years*, Crimp was excluded. Even worse, when the Court chose fifty plays for readings to celebrate its anniversary, there was not one Crimp among them. Nor does the academy have a better record. Magisterial as it is, *The Cambridge History of British Theatre* only mentions him once in passing, and brands his *Attempts on Her Life* as a 'post-modern "extravaganza"'.[18] In Dominic Shellard's comprehensive textbook, *British Theatre Since the War*, Crimp's name doesn't appear at all.[19] He does better in a new survey of post-war British drama, which rightly sees the blind taxi driver in *The Treatment* as providing an image of the 'social decay, severed isolation and degradation into aimlessness' of the 1990s, but the rest of Crimp's work isn't discussed.[20] And although he is included in one companion, you'll search in vain for his name in most of the standard theatrical guides and encyclopedias.[21] In fact, the longest entry on his career is in *British Dramatists*, an American publication.[22] Apart from a handful of articles buried deep in academic journals, that's about it. Little wonder that he's seen as an enigma.

Before examining Crimp's work, it's worth remembering that he began his career in the early 1980s, the Thatcher era. After becoming the first woman to lead a major political party in Britain in 1975, Margaret Thatcher was elected Conservative prime minister on 4 May 1979, and her manifesto trumpeted a new beginning. In many ways, it was a different world. Imagine life without mobile phones, cordless phones, email, texting, videos, CDs, DVDs, minidiscs, and digital cameras or camcorders. Or PlayStations. Or personal computers. Or the Internet. No laptops; no iPods. Few people had faxes. There was no need to memorise countless PIN numbers. There were only three television channels (BBC1, BBC2 and ITV). No MTV; no satellite; no cable. Come to think of it, no Ecstasy; no Aids. It was hard to buy a good cappuccino, even in central London. Lattes were unheard of. There were no sushi bars. Most supermarkets had a limited range of foods. There were no cheap airlines; no Eurostar. The trade union movement was strong, and industrial disputes often featured on news bulletins. There was a state monopoly on telephones, electricity, gas, railways, steel, mining. Inflation was high, house prices low. In the public mind, feminism meant bra-burning. In 1979, Princess Di was plain seventeen-year-old Diana Spencer. Tony Blair was an unknown twenty-five-year-old.

Singer Robbie Williams was five. And Crimp was a young Cambridge graduate.

In the course of Crimp's early career, Britain was transformed in many ways. Thatcher won three resounding election victories in a row for the Conservatives – a twentieth-century record. Her political ideals were patriotism, balanced budgets, low taxes, private ownership and individual initiative. Her morality was expressed in the phrase 'a return to Victorian values'. Adopting the economic creed of monetarism – which aims to reduce inflation by lowering government spending – she aimed to use economics to change the soul of Britain. In addition, for an age increasingly obsessed by the media, Thatcher had to adapt her personal image. And theatre played its part in her transformation. She was coached 'by a tutor from the National Theatre, to lower her voice and to speak more slowly in order to appear less shrill and aggressive'.[23] Playwright Ronald Millar wrote many of her speeches.

On the national level, Thatcherism changed the economic, social and political face of the country for more than a quarter of a century. This coincided with enormous international changes: the fall of the Berlin Wall, the abolition of regimes such as apartheid in South Africa, and the creation of a new world order, culminating in the War on Terror which followed the 9/11 attacks on New York in 2001. On the intellectual level, this period saw the struggle between traditional modernist ideas and postmodernism, the new kid on the university block. This confrontation, played out in millions of books, articles and university essays, also affected almost everyone who worked in the arts. Finally, on the most parochial level, both Thatcherism and postmodernism had a direct effect on British theatre during the 1980s and 90s, the period in which Crimp's career developed.

British theatre in the 1980s may have been a cultural backwater, but it too was hit by Thatcherite commercialisation. By 1985, theatre critic Michael Billington could point out: 'We no longer talk of subsidy: we speak of investment.'[24] Productions became 'product' and audiences became 'consumers'. In the Thatcher decade, all theatres felt the chill wind of increasing commercial-isation, with a renewed attention paid to 'bums on seats' and 'value for money'. So radical was this change that, by the early 1990s, it became impossible to talk about the arts in anything but economic terms.[25] Theatre changed from being a net contributor to the 'political, social, personal and moral changes taking place' in Britain to being just part of 'an entertainment industry'.[26] Worse still, the great exponents of modernism in the arts found them-selves increasingly marginalised in a public culture that valued enterprise, the heritage industries and an aggressive populism. It was a time that cried out for blockbuster musicals, such as Andrew Lloyd Webber's *Evita* (1978) and *Cats* (1981), and another fifty-seven varieties of insular, often nostalgic, crowd-pleasing fare. Definitely an odd time to embark, as Crimp did, on a career whose inspirations were difficult, often foreign – in a word, modernist.

In our postmodern age, the word modernism already sounds like something out of a history book. It reeks of discomfort: hard chairs, hard walls, hard art. Its most obvious public icon is the decaying tower block. But, as a cultural movement which began just after the First World War, modernism has transformed our world, from the design of cutlery to the aims of high art, so it's worth taking seriously. In its love of the new, it was utopian, idealistic and a force for good: reject the old, it insisted, and create new forms. The old forms are suffocating; new forms are necessary. And this has been as true for theatre as for architecture. But although British culture has been suspicious of modernism as a foreign, and extreme, solution to a whole variety of twentieth-century problems, it's hard to imagine contemporary theatre without the modernism of Beckett, Bertolt Brecht or Antonin Artaud. Without their influence, audiences would still be watching country-house, drawing-room comedies and light thrillers. Agatha Christie's *The Mousetrap* (1952) – the most popular play in the history of world theatre with a West End run that has continued for more than fifty years – would be the norm rather than an aberration. Not only did modernism liberate theatre from the old form of the well-made, three-act play, but it also revolutionised stage dialogue. Modernism proved that dialogue doesn't have to be naturalistic. If you listen to Beckett's teasing circumlocutions, Ionesco's absurdism, Jean Genet's poetic flights, or Harold Pinter's repetitions, you can hear stage language being reinvented.[27]

From the start, Crimp's project has been the modernist one of experimenting with language and form. The familiarity of traditional theatre forms merely lull the audience to sleep; the writer has to wake them up. Clearly, Beckett, the arch-modernist, ranks high on Crimp's artistic agenda. But although Crimp started out as a modernist, the cultural context in which he wrote was one in which postmodernism loomed large. When, during the Thatcher decade, postmodernism became a buzzword, it generally referred to the philosophical criticism of absolute truths or unchanging identities or grand narratives. And it usually meant a style that was eclectic, using pastiche, parody, different voices. Its sensibility seemed to be cool irony, a knowing detachment and a dive into subjectivity. Yet, as many commentators have pointed out, all these are also the characteristics of modernism. So, despite its name, postmodernism not only comes after modernism, but also coexists with it: different attitudes to the contemporary. For the modernist, the tone is often pessimism, despair, lament. For the postmodernist, it's exhilaration, celebrating excess, gaudiness and bad taste. The typical modernist artist is a fierce ascetic who practises high art. The typical postmodernist rejects the distinction between high art and pop culture. Anything goes. Postmodernism does what modernism does, but with a giggle rather than a frown. Politically, modernism comes from a leftist tradition which seeks to improve the world, while postmodernism often prefers to query the age-old certainties of political belief. So one question worth grappling with is whether Crimp really is a stern modernist – or a just postmodern prankster?

One corner of theatre modernism is occupied by absurdism. A good definition of absurdism would be: the show is over. The audience get up to leave. Time to collect their coats and go home.

They turn round – no more coats and no more home. Yes, there's a nihilistic side to the absurd. Beginning just after the Second World War, the Theatre of the Absurd includes such experimentalists as Beckett, Ionesco, Genet, Friedrich Dürrenmatt, Arthur Adamov and Fernando Arrabal. As a tradition, it was big in Eastern Europe, and influenced Václav Havel. Nearer home, Harold Pinter and Edward Albee have sometimes been labelled absurdist. The Theatre of the Absurd derives from Albert Camus's notion of humankind looking for meaning in a senseless universe.[28] It emphasises the absurdity of human existence by employing disjointed, repetitive and meaningless dialogue, purposeless and confusing situations, and plots that lack realistic or logical development. Absurdism freed theatre from the prison house of naturalism, realism and rationality, its purpose being to criticise the ideology of reason that dominates the machine age. Alienation is conveyed through surreal comedy which parodies conventional mores. Language breaks down, accelerating, repeating itself, nonstarting. In defiance of mainstream British culture, Crimp's early work was written under the sign of the absurd. *Clang*, for example, has a visual image reminiscent in its futility of the absurdist Ionesco: a man rearranges the furniture in his room until he has created a mirror image of how the room had originally looked.

But, apart from questions about Crimp's identity as a modernist or absurdist, the story of his relative obscurity on the British theatre scene has a familiar ring. Haven't we been here before? In the 1950s, the arrival of Beckett and Pinter – writers whose work has had a direct influence on Crimp – was greeted with incomprehension and derision. It seems as if, in Britain, every playwright who pushes out the envelope pretty soon meets with antagonism from the critics, and risks being ignored by the wider theatre-going public (unless, of course, you're lucky enough to be Alan Ayckbourn). Of course, the blame lies less with individuals and more with Britain's culture, which values familiar naturalistic and social-realist work rather than modernistic experiments or innovations, all of which smack of the foreign and the Continental.

CRAVEN COLLEGE

Actor Zabou Breitman once 'made the perceptive remark that the French were suspicious of serious plays which were also funny and that the English were suspicious of serious plays which were not'.[29] Like a spoonful of sugar, comedy helps the modernist message go down. This kind of insular culture leads to the great originals of the British theatre being at first ignored, then under-valued and finally belatedly, and often rather grudgingly, more or less admired. Respected rather than loved. For example, in 2005, Pinter's seventy-fifth birthday was celebrated more in Dublin than in London, his home town. Still, if Crimp ever felt that breathing the air of British culture in the 1980s was stifling, parochial or inimical to his creativity, he didn't make a fuss about it – he just got on with writing. And as for being an enigma, he might not have been surprised to find that the word comes from the Greek for 'to speak allusively'. Which is exactly what his work does.

1 'A KNOCK AT THE DOOR'

Living Remains, Four Attempted Acts, A Variety of Death-Defying Acts, Definitely the Bahamas, Dealing with Clair, Play with Repeats

Martin Crimp started his writing life on the fringe. During the 1980s, the Orange Tree Theatre, a small venue not far from his home in Richmond, produced six of his plays and, despite its small subsidy, even paid him for them. Set up in 1971 by Sam Walters, who has been its artistic director ever since, this was at first a lunchtime theatre showing a mix of new plays and revivals, with an eye on both the local community and wider European politics, especially those of Eastern Europe.[1] True to its origins as part of the alternative theatre movement, its political radicalism was expressed through its promotion of writers such as Václav Havel, who set up Charter 77 as a forum for democracy in Communist-ruled Czechoslovakia. By the early 1980s, despite pressure on alternative theatre from Margaret Thatcher's Conservative government, whose arts policies were distinguished by cost-cutting and subsidy-slashing, the Orange Tree managed to survive as one of three London venues which produced 'their own lunchtime shows as opposed to renting out their space'.[2] Later, it also staged plays in the evening. But chance also played a part in kick-starting Crimp's career. In 1981, Walters employed Anthony Clark as an assistant director, and one of his jobs was to read the backlog of plays that had been submitted – including an unsolicited manuscript from Crimp. Walters remembers that 'My first glimpse of Martin was in our office in Hill Street. There was a knock at the door and this man with burning eyes came in and said, "I'm a writer, I live locally and I've got a play." And I remember this man handing in his play. And that went straight to Tony [Clark].'[3] Clark set up a writers' workshop in 1981, invited Crimp to join, and planned his first season of new plays for summer 1982.

Crimp's professional debut, however, was actually a translation which reflected the theatre's concern with Eastern European dictatorships. In April 1982, the Orange Tree staged *Love Games*, by Polish playwright Jerzy Przezdziecki, in a version co-written by Crimp and Howard Curtis from a feeble translation by Boguslaw Lawendowski. This two-hander examines the domestic strains on one young couple – He and She – imposed by the chronic housing shortage in Communist Poland. In order to meet in private, they have to borrow the flat of one of their friends. At one point, He says that living in Poland is so absurd that it's 'like living in a play'; to which She replies, 'I just want a life of my own.'[4] Partly a marital comedy, partly a political metaphor for a country in turmoil, the ninety-minute piece was directed by Clark, with actors Sian Thomas and David Moylan. Clark stressed its politics by having a Communist hammer-and-sickle poster on one wall and a Solidarność poster (with the word written as a logo showing a group of striking workers) on another. As well as having lunchtime performances, the play was presented in the evening and attracted national newspaper critics. The *Guardian*'s Michael Billington saw it as 'a refreshingly direct account' and said that while it was 'very good on domestic in-fighting, the piece becomes heavily prankish when it lapses into fantasy'.[5] Still, there's something prescient about Crimp starting his career with a play which made its political points by means of metaphor rather than by preaching, and there's also something just a little bit Beckettian about this parable of people enduring the unendurable.

Living Remains

The same could be said of Crimp's first solo play, *Living Remains*, which came out of the Orange Tree's writers' workshops and was staged as one of 'two new plays for lunchtime' in July 1982.[6] In this monologue, Woman, a bag lady who is 'older rather than younger', and who smokes dog-ends from a tin, visits her hospitalised husband, who is too sick to speak and can only communicate by pressing a buzzer, once for Yes and twice for No.[7] After some banter, Woman tells him that she's met a Mr Cook, a 'corpulent' (p. 4) upper-class gent, in a nearby cemetery, and that he has invited her to visit him at his country estate. She's come to ask her husband's permission. The play ends with her asking again and again, but getting only silence in reply. Written with immense attention to language, it's a short but powerful piece which is suffused with ambiguity: it's unclear whether Woman's meeting with Mr Cook is a fantasy or not, and the full force of her impatience with her husband is concealed in the subtext.[8] Performed by Auriol Smith, Walters' wife, the forty-minute monologue was directed by Clark. *Living Remains* has a distinctly Beckettian feel, with its Woman tramp wearing 'a threadbare black dress which must once have been elegant, shoes which do not match, and an elaborate hat' (p. 1), and there is evidence of Beckett's inspiration in some of the text's repetition, and its word-play. So, after having begun his career with a highly topical play, Crimp turned his back on the contemporary in order to explore a symbolic, or absurdist, landscape of cruel personal relationships.

Meanwhile, beyond the Orange Tree, Thatcher's policies were remaking the world in her own cruel image. In terms of economic, social and political change, 1980s Britain was summed up by pictures of burning cars in inner-city riots from Brixton to Toxteth; robots making cars at Dagenham; pitched battles between workers and police during the miners' strike of 1984; City stock-brokers sporting huge mobile phones; increased numbers of beggars and people sleeping rough. Nostalgia was satisfied by the wedding of Prince Charles and Lady Di in July 1981. Abroad, the Falklands War of June 1982 encouraged jingoism and a pugnacious approach to foreign policy. In 1986, the globalisation of the economy got a spectacular boost when, during the Big Bang, the City of London Stock Exchange was fully computerised and integrated into the world financial markets. Share-owning became common. Telephones, airports, gas, oil, electricity and water were privatised. Trade union membership slumped. Thatcherism caused mass unemployment – from 1.3 million to 2 million in her first year of government, rising to 3 million plus in 1982 – and the destruction of heavy industries. As the gap between the haves and the have-nots widened, the social consequences included a massive rise in poverty.[9] Yet, by 1987, two-thirds of the population owned their own home, and liberal intellectuals contented themselves with wryly quoting Yeats: 'The best lack all conviction, while the worst / Are full of passionate intensity.'[10]

Many theatres responded directly to the new climate. Writers such as Edward Bond and Caryl Churchill took the temperature of the times: in Bond's *The Worlds* (1979), a character says: 'Money can do anything. It gives you the power of giants. The real world obeys the law of money,' and Churchill's Marlene in *Top Girls* (1982) expresses a popular view of Thatcher: 'Get the economy back on its feet and whoosh. She's a tough lady, Maggie.'[11] While Thatcherism was attacked by Steven Berkoff's *Sink the Belgrano!* (1986) and Alan Ayckbourn's *A Small Family Business* (1987), the Left was criticised in David Edgar's *Maydays* (1983), and the British love of history indulged in Julian Mitchell's *Another Country* (1981) and Christopher Hampton's *Les Liaisons Dangereuses* (1985). As theatres struggled with funding cuts, a new generation of female playwrights, such as Sarah Daniels, Timberlake Wertenbaker and Charlotte Keatley, took theatre form apart. Others, such as Terry Johnson and Robert Holman, crept on to the scene. At the National, David Hare and Howard Brenton's *Pravda* (1985) satirised the new press barons while at the Royal Court Churchill gave City yuppies the same treatment in *Serious Money* (1987).

Pinter took a political turn, with work such as *One for the Road* (1985) attacking human rights violations around the world. But most lurid of all was Jim Cartwright, in whose *Road* (1986) Carol says: 'Poverty wants me. He's in my hair and clothes. He comes dust on me knickers. [. . .] Nowt's nice around me.'[12] But such overt expressions of economic, social and political reality were anathema to the young Crimp. His early work glanced obliquely, if at all, at the world outside his suburban flat. He had a different agenda.

Four Attempted Acts

Crimp's next Orange Tree outing was *Four Attempted Acts*, a quartet of short plays staged in October 1984, after a successful reading in May.[13] These comprised *The Appreciation of Music*, *Making Love*, *Taking Leave* and *Suicide*. Each of them create an imaginary world which is a far cry from the social realism so common on most British stages at the time. *The Appreciation of Music*, therefore, shows a tweedy Mr Lebrun demonstrating to Mrs Cook how a laboratory guinea pig can be trained through 'trial, and error' (p. 6); *Making Love* is about Mr De A giving dental treatment to a gasping Mrs Lebrun offstage while Lucy, his assistant, lazily leafs through some magazines and half-heartedly attempts some physical exercises; *Taking Leave* features Yvonne, Mr De A's former assistant, telling her lover on the phone that she plans to leave him; *Suicide* sees Mrs De A showing off her daughter Rose's inept musical skills to the conservatory's Dr Lebrun. All of these pieces pun on the word 'attempts': they show their characters attempting to impress others as well as themselves being attempts at telling short stories. Indeed, these playlets, Crimp notes in his stage directions, 'are best attempted on a small stage'. And they all revel in ambiguity. Mrs Cook would like to appreciate music, but she mistakes cruelty for art: 'The exquisite pain of it [. . .] A moment's Mozart and I'm at screaming pitch'

(p. 13). In *Making Love*, it seems at first that Mrs Lebrun's offstage gasps are of sexual pleasure rather than dental pain. And the title refers to an outrageous story about Yvonne, Mr De A's former assistant, who was sacked after being raped by Mr Petley, another patient, in the waiting room, an incident the dentist insists was not a rape because she was giving 'gasps of pleasure'. When she hears this, Mrs Lebrun asks: 'But how can you distinguish?' (p. 27). In *Taking Leave*, the victimised Yvonne is taking leave of her lover by phone, but the absurdism of the conversation also suggests that she's taking leave of her senses. *Suicide* refers both to the death of Mrs De A's husband and to her daughter's self-destructive behaviour.

Directed by Michael Hucks, the cast of *Four Attempted Acts* was Del Henney (the men), Auriol Smith (the older women) and Liz Crowther (the young women). London critics reported that 'Crimp offers us an extremely elegant piece in a form that is to theatre what the essay is to literature; it's commentary rather than the main thing but oddly compulsive for all that', and praised it as 'witty, puzzling and often quite disturbing'.[14] *Four Attempted Acts* is clearly an apprentice work, but it is also a wicked little gem of an entertainment. Originally written for radio, at first it had three scenarios – *The Appreciation of Music*, *Making Love* and *Suicide* – and was broadcast as *Three Attempted Acts* on BBC radio in May 1985. When Crimp created the stage version he added a playlet, *Taking Leave*, which depends on a visual gag: as Yvonne chats on the phone, a man quietly arrives and puts his arms around her, thus proving her lover's jealous fantasies to be true. *Three Attempted Acts* won the Giles Cooper Award for best radio play of 1985, and Crimp was encouraged to continue writing.

By 1985, the spirit of the alternative fringe theatre – which had taken such a battering from Thatcherism – had been quietly dampened, but the theatres that had sprung up in the early 1970s could boast of one achievement: they had survived. 'The London fringe, which had struggled to adapt to an environment where recession and political disillusionment had dulled the appetite for didactic theatre, also began to show signs of revival.'[15] And Crimp's local theatre, the Orange Tree, was part of this revival.

A Variety of Death-Defying Acts

In December 1985, the Orange Tree chose Crimp's *A Variety of Death-Defying Acts* as its Christmas show. The play's full title, reminiscent of the Beatles song 'For the Benefit of Mr Kite' from the *Sgt Pepper's Lonely Hearts' Club Band* album (1967), gives a flavour of its style: *A Variety of Death-Defying Acts performed for the amusement and sensation of the general public by Petley's original travelling troupe without a net and featuring the incomparable Miss Alison*.[16] In this surreal comedy, Petley's Circus comes to town and turns the Grand Guignol café into its home. Characters include bossman Mr Petley, a sleepwalking ex-high-wire act called Miss Alison, a Bearded Lady, a Strongman, and a couple of clowns. A local woman, Miss Kopinski, is attracted to them, and the play ends with the Bearded Lady and Strongman leaving the circus to get married, while the clowns butcher Petley in an illusionist's knife box. If the circus is a metaphor for the theatre, the play's highlights are the absurdist clowns who, dressed as policemen, spend their time philosophising about the nature of crime and guilt.

Directed by Sam Walters, the cast of *A Variety of Death-Defying Acts* included Crimp regulars Auriol Smith and Liz Crowther, plus some hectic clowning by Barry Killerby, who in 1993 was to find fame as the children's TV character Mr Blobby. *City Limits* said: 'This odd-ball comedy by talented local writer, Martin Crimp, juggles mataphysics [*sic*] with farce to achieve an unusual seasonal show with a serious edge that examines the thin dividing line between the normal and the freak,' while *Time Out* pointed out that when Crimp lobs lines such as 'What does it all mean?' and 'It's a little contrived' at the audience, 'it's tempting to lob them back'.[17] Despite some satirical moments, such as the 1st Clown's discussion about the way life resembles a play, *A Variety of Death-Defying Acts* was an experiment in blatant absurdism and knock-about comedy that Crimp never pursued again. On the other hand, the production did him no harm, and he was evidently making his mark within the theatre – the programme lists him as a member of its 'artistic committee'.[18] Despite this, he was absent from the stage in 1986, although his next radio play, *Six Figures at the Base of a Crucifixion*, influenced by Beckett's 1957 radio drama *All That Fall*, was broadcast on the BBC in December. Clearly, 'his early work for radio sharpened his sensitivity for the rhythm and music of the language'.[19]

Definitely the Bahamas

If *A Variety of Death-Defying Acts* was an artistic dead end, Crimp returned to form in September 1987 with a trilogy of pieces called *Definitely the Bahamas*. The origins of the stage version emphasises how important radio was to his developing career. Crimp wrote *Definitely the Bahamas* as a radio play in spring 1986, when it won the annual *Radio Times* Drama Award. Then, as he prepared a stage version, he got an unexpected boost from actor Alec McCowen, who agreed to direct it. At the height of his career and about to star in Beckett's *Waiting for Godot* at the National Theatre, McCowen knew Crimp's work because he had been in his first radio play, *Three Attempted Acts*. He 'liked [Crimp's] style of writing', and so accepted Walters' invitation to direct *Definitely the Bahamas*.[20]

The trilogy comprises *A Kind of Arden*, *Spanish Girls* and *Definitely the Bahamas*. In the first of 'this group of three plays for consecutive performance', Mrs Tighe is relaxing 'beside a pool in a hot country' (p. 1), chatting to Poppy – a younger woman who is watching her husband Max swimming.[21] The quiet humour of Brits abroad darkens as it emerges that Mrs Tighe's husband – who thinks this land is 'a kind of Arden' (p. 4) – is ill in bed, and when

Mrs Tighe finally plucks up the courage to ask Max, who claims to know the local language, to call a doctor, he refuses. Selfishness of an even more sinister kind is explored in *Spanish Girls*, in which Schmidt, an ex-Nazi in his eighties, is visited by Singer, who is investigating his host's part in war crimes. As Schmidt's wife silently does her needlework, Schmidt parries every question by telling Singer how much he enjoys sunny Spain, where he now lives, and how much the local girls used to attract him. In *Definitely the Bahamas*, Milly and Frank, an older couple in the south of England, talk about their son Michael and daughter-in-law Irene, while their au pair, Marijka, pops in and out. The title comes from a running joke: the older couple can't agree about where Michael and Irene went on holiday when their mansion was burgled (p. 37). Gradually, despite the inconsequential chatter, it emerges that Michael is really not a very nice person. When Marijka gets the chance to talk, she claims – in a long outburst – that he's sexually harassed and humiliated her, threatening her by pointedly saying: 'Don't think I don't know your game. My wife was raped. I know that game' (p. 67). Other snatches of conversation reveal that Michael and Irene used to live in apartheid South Africa, and that Irene has had a hysterectomy.

The radio version of *Definitely the Bahamas* was broadcast by the BBC in April, and the stage play was put on in September. The cast was Heather Canning, Amanda Royle, Rob Edwards and John Moffatt, who together played all the parts. McCowen's involvement guaranteed media attention. The major critics welcomed what the *Sunday Times* called 'a writer who is so good both at the comedy of crass nouveau riche smugness and at the black terror of recent history'. Under the headline 'A New Pinter?', the *Telegraph*'s Charles Spencer said that McCowen 'captures both the subtlety and the richnes [*sic*] of these original and beautifully written plays' while Billington argued that for all their stillness, they 'suggest Mr Crimp has a marked and precious talent for discovering the spiritual ugliness that often lurks under the civilised veneer'. Sheridan Morley summed up: 'Sam Walters's Orange Tree in

Richmond has long been among the best and bravest of London's fringe theatres, and with *Definitely the Bahamas* he establishes Martin Crimp as a dramatist of considerable promise.'[22]

In the programme, Crimp quoted Pinter's *One for the Road* (1985): 'You know, old chap, I do love other things, apart from death, so many things. Nature. Trees, things like that. A nice blue sky. Blossom.' But fine weather can't cancel out atrocity. Each of these short pieces plays with the theme of what the Sex Pistols called, in the 1977 single 'Holidays in the Sun', a 'holiday in other people's misery'.[23] The sunny image of the Caribbean, Spain or South Africa contrasts with the chill horrors of terminal illness, genocide and sexual violence. At the time, Crimp had been reading the work of Federico García Lorca, and about his fate at the hands of the Fascists, and this evidently coloured the plays. Their sly comedy of manners gradually reveals a world of pain. Although the dialogues constantly shift ground, the sense of threat underpins every exchange; and there's an openness to experimenting with form. Despite some clumsiness – for example, the device of having Milly and Frank talk to a family friend, who is onstage but remains silent – these accomplished pieces show Crimp finally hitting a mature, suggestive style where words are fugitive and evasion speaks volumes. But while his focus until now had been on imaginary worlds and foreign locations, his next play saw him finally coming home – and beginning to explore the social landscape of Thatcherism.

Dealing with Clair

In 1988, Crimp's career took a decisive turn for the better when he abandoned the absurdist world of his early plays and began to engage, much more explicitly, with social issues and contemporary situations. So pervasive were the effects of Thatcherism that they seeped right into the texture of his late-1980s work. His next play, *Dealing with Clair*, also displays a new confidence in his playwriting abilities. This full-length piece was commissioned by producer Michael Codron, who knew about Crimp from *Definitely the Bahamas*, and his brainwave was to cast Tom Courtenay in the role of the sinister James. The idea of a star working on the fringe was unusual enough to excite comment. Courtenay, reported the *Evening Standard*, not only rehearsed but also sold tickets: 'as the dressing rooms double by day as the theatre's offices he has been answering the phone during rehearsals and taking bookings'.[24] First staged in October 1988, *Dealing with Clair* has since been frequently revived, and was broadcast by the BBC in 1991.

A young estate agent, Clair, tries to sell Mike and Liz's suburban house to James, a distinguished and charming cash buyer. The upwardly mobile young couple, with their little baby, have put Anna, their Italian au pair, into a windowless box room and describe it as a fourth bedroom. Although they both want to 'behave honourably' (p. 13), their greed leads them to accept James's cash deal, which gazumps an offer they've already accepted from a Shropshire couple, one of whom is disabled.[25] But what starts as a cool comedy of modern manners, a sharp look at how the house-buying mania of the late 1980s encouraged individual greed, slowly turns into a murder mystery. James, at first so debonair, becomes increasingly sinister as he pries into Clair's private life. Despite this, she is drawn to him. By the end, James is in her flat, talking to her mother on the phone. He claims that Clair is taking a shower, but it's clear that he has murdered her.[26] Despite her disappearance, Mike and Liz are soon celebrating with Toby, her replacement – they've sold their house at an even higher price to another buyer. As Liz says, 'Life has to go on' (p. 90). This cliché perfectly captures the way the couple deal with unsavoury reality – and shows that they don't care about anybody apart from themselves. So although the play echoes the unsolved disappearance of estate agent Suzy Lamplugh in 1986, it is not a documentary, but a comedy of manners with a cruel twist.

Directed by Sam Walters, *Dealing with Clair* allowed Courtenay to give a star turn, enjoying his vocal gifts, relishing words such as 'turmeric' (p. 39), drawing florid patterns in the air with his hands, and slapping himself whenever he thought he was giving anything away. Janine Wood's Clair was both repelled and attracted by him. When he persuaded her to play the card game snap, encouraging her to shout 'Snap' at the top of her voice, she was clearly discarding her customary inhibitions (pp. 70–1). As the young couple, John Michie and Julia Hills were nervously giggly, smooth and perfectly smug. But while the violence was often suppressed in the dialogue, it smashed its way to the surface in the scenes set in Clair's flat, where passing trains were so loud that they made conversation impossible.

Courtenay's presence in the cast brought another flurry of reviews. The *Daily Mail*'s Jack Tinker appreciated Crimp's picture of 'avarice that wears away finer scruples, isolates individuals and allows such shadowy figures as Mr Courtenay's bogus buyer to operate'. The *Independent*'s Georgina Brown called the play a cross between 'a delicious satire on yuppie moral and emotional bankruptcy and a bleak, black comedy thriller' and Spencer was impressed by the arrival of 'a new writer of real stature', although he also expressed doubts about the morality of creating an entertainment which evoked the Suzy Lamplugh case.[27]

Clearly, the enormous house-buying boom of the late 1980s both forms the background to the play and is the object of Crimp's satire. The final scene in which Mike and Liz discuss the 'spiralling' (p. 94) price of their home is not only an acidic comment on the sheer greed encouraged by Thatcher's ideology of a property-owning democracy, but also captures perfectly the essence of contemporary English identity. In the dialogue, there's always a whiff of bad faith. Mike and Liz want to behave honourably, but they also want to cash in on their luck. Their guilty rationalisations have a resonance that suggests the bad conscience of England's property-obsessed suburbs. The play also mixes irony with ominous understatement – although the predatory males are more fully realised than the victimised females, ugly emotions lurk beneath the surface of normality. For example, in Mike and Liz's relationship there's a constant suspicion about his sexual attraction to both Anna and Clair. At one point, the couple's drunken conversation takes a dangerous lurch when Liz confronts Mike: 'You mean you want to rape Clair' (p. 58). Although the accusation comes out of the blue, you can see that Liz has reasons to be suspicious. Elsewhere, the language carries dramatic irony: at the start of the play, Clair talks on the phone to her mother: 'Who knows *what* I'll do? Maybe make a killing and just . . . disappear. (*Laughs.*) That's right. Vanish' (p. 6). Which is exactly her fate.[28] Finally, *Dealing with Clair* also shows Crimp's readiness to experiment with form: Clair's opening monologue is mirrored by James's final one, and Crimp refuses the temptation to include a scene which explicitly explains what really happened to her. That remains a mystery. After the play's considerable success, Crimp could have repeated the same formula – but he didn't. Instead, he tried another, more playful, experiment with form.

Play with Repeats

By October 1989, the Orange Tree had really hit its stride, especially in its promotion of international plays, having clocked up seven by Havel, as well as Franz Xaver Kroetz's *The Nest*, Alfonzo Vallejo's *Fly-By* and Jules Romain's *Dr Knock*. And, once again, Walters chose a new Crimp play to kick off his autumn season. 'And I did think,' he remembers, 'am I being awfully boring, always opening seasons with Martin Crimp plays?'[29] Written while Crimp was the theatre's Thames TV Writer-in-Residence, *Play with Repeats* takes a sci-fi idea, that of being suddenly able to relive your life, and confronts it with the truth of character. Anthony 'Tony' Steadman, an earnest inadequate on the eve of his fortieth birthday, is unsatisfied. In the opening pub scene, he buttonholes Nick, a younger man with no regrets, and Nick's girlfriend, Kate. Tony wants to go back in time and use his wisdom to better his lot: 'Yes, we accumulate wisdom, but what use is it to us? Because the events when the wisdom would've been useful, they're over and gone' (p. 188).[30] When, after visiting Mouhamed Lamine – an African holy man – Tony gets his wish, what actually happens is that he fails to live the life he has so often fantasised. We watch his clumsy attempts to make friends, gain promotion at work, assert himself, and seduce a woman at a temporary bus stop. Every repeat is worse than the first attempt. When, finally, the play replays the opening pub scene, Tony is stabbed by Nick. Immediately after, Nick asks, as if in self-justification: 'What makes them [strangers] start conversations? What do they expect to achieve?' (p. 269). Both that scene and the play's title show the influence of Beckett. When Tony is stabbed, Kate tries to take Nick away, and there is a Beckettian moment: 'Move,' she says. Pause. 'Move now.' '*Neither moves*' (p. 269). This stage direction echoes *Waiting for Godot*, and the piece's title evokes Beckett's *Play*, which also uses a repeat.[31]

Directed by Sam Walters, *Play with Repeats* had Thomas Wheatley as the pitiable Tony and Stephen Marchant and Caroline Gruber as Nick and Kate. It was not well received. Billington found it 'a frustrating experience' which lacked an 'internal dynamic': 'a strange play: baffling, repetitive, opaque', while Andy Lavender in *City Limits* said that, after taking so many steps forward, 'Crimp takes an enormous leap back with a play that tries to be profound, and ends up looking pretentious'. Although Spencer championed Crimp's style – 'he is a dab hand at suggesting that things are not quite as they seem, at creating an atmosphere of tension and creepy uncertainty, and his work offers sudden, alarming glimpses of loneliness, spiritual malaise and fear' – he also said that this 'eerily effective' play is 'a little too long for its own good'.[32]

Crimp's teasing 'back to the future' piece feels like a video being replayed, and mixes an appealing sci-fi idea with a portrait of one of life's losers. He tackles the subject of both individual failure and urban anomie with restraint, creating a growing sense of unsettled emotion, with the repetition of events emphasising how Tony has no control over his life. Right from the start, Tony is conscious not only of the desire to 'Live our lives again' (p. 194), but also that, ironically, 'I know I have a habit, I know I've a habit of repeating myself' (p. 191). But his repeated claim that 'I have insight' (p. 184) is hollow. Tony is trapped inside his own inadequate personality and his dream of knowing enough to escape is illusory. Unable to connect with other people, he seems to sleepwalk to his doom. The piece successfully shows that trying to relive your life with the wisdom of experience is pointless because you cannot be other than you are. Taking his epigraph from the occult philosopher Petyr Demianovich Ouspensky (1878–1947) – 'If you go back now, everything will be the same as before or worse' (p. 178) – Crimp satirises the fashionable 'if only' alternative philosophy, and exposes the chilly reality of an impoverished daily life. The play evokes English society in both its settings – pub, small factory, launderette, a temporary bus stop – and in its characters, so-called ordinary people whose ideas are the sum of our common fantasies. From Tony's trite formulations of the wisdom he has accumulated – 'for human beings everything should be possible' (p. 192) – to the holy man's empty aphorisms – 'Christ could appear in the garden' (p. 210) – language is used to fill the sad silences and keep communication going, even if it's going nowhere. In the end, the most truthful, and most unavoidable, form of communication is violence. Although *Play with Repeats* has been condemned for its overt theatricality and its 'striving after effect', its welding of form and content is both apt and thought-provoking.[33]

During its run, there were momentous changes in the world beyond Richmond. On 9 November 1989, the fall of the Berlin Wall marked the disintegration of the Eastern European dictatorships. Shortly afterwards, in December, Václak Havel was elected president of Czechoslovakia and, in the following year, Lech Wałęsa became president of Poland. Meanwhile, the Orange Tree's *Play with Repeats* programme boasted of its new talent: 'And in particular MARTIN CRIMP has recently emerged as a new young writer who has his home at the Orange Tree.'[34] By then, Crimp had spent almost a decade at the theatre. But however productive in terms of his gradual move from an absurdist style to a much more social-realist one, in these years Crimp was just knocking on the door of British drama. It was only when his work was put on at the Royal Court Theatre that he finally arrived.

2 'DENIAL, BRUTALITY AND SHEER HUMAN CONFUSION'

No One Sees the Video, Getting Attention, The Treatment, The Misanthrope

In 1990, Martin Crimp became a Royal Court Theatre playwright. It was the realisation of a long-standing dream: ever since 1975, when he'd visited that venue to see Samuel Beckett's *Not I*, his first experience of professional theatre, his ambition had been to have his own work performed there. That's perfectly understandable. After 1956, when it staged John Osborne's iconic *Look Back in Anger*, the Court gradually became the proud home of 'new writing'. Over the following decades, the notion of new writing – as opposed to the simple fact of a play being new – grew to mean contemporary, original and somehow virtuous. Just as adverts constantly stress newness when selling products, so the arts began to put a premium on the new. '"New" came to stand for a significant, meaningful text that had "relevance" and new plays became the central platform in the emerging theatre.'[1] In a sense, new writing was a type of theatrical modernism. The Court's George Devine, founding father of its resident English Stage Company, argued passionately for state subsidy to stage new plays and for the 'right to fail' when putting on experimental work.[2] Funded by the Arts Council, the theatre could afford to be non-commercial, although box-office receipts became increasingly important during the 1980s.

By 1990, the Royal Court had, despite its subsidy, suffered several years of financial squeeze, and Max Stafford-Clark, its artistic director since 1979, had shut the small Theatre Upstairs studio space for six months in 1989. It was a time when British theatre alternated 'between bursts of glory and inspissated gloom'.[3] At the Court, 'those days of cyclical deprivation of funding or esteem for the arts had a profoundly depressing effect across the board. It was impossible to create a policy, let alone a consistent view, when a place like the Court appeared to lurch from one financial blow to another.'[4] In November 1989, left-wing playwright Caryl Churchill resigned from the theatre's Council when it accepted sponsorship from Barclays Bank. A year later, when Crimp made his debut, the main crisis had passed. The Arts Council recognised that the theatre was a 'vital resource for new writing', and the Theatre Upstairs reopened.[5] Elsewhere, however, there was a general crisis in new writing. 'The late 1980s saw a precipitate decline in the amount of new work presented. From 1970 to 1985, new work formed roughly 12 per cent of the repertoire of the main houses of the regional and London repertory theatres. From 1985 to 1990 it dropped to 7 per cent. [. . .] Hardly a week passed without the *Guardian* and the *Independent* having some sort of stab at new theatre writing.'[6] Artistic directors had become suspicious of new plays, fearing they were hard to market, and the most successful ones were by older writers at the National, such as David Hare (*Racing Demon*) and Alan Bennett (*The Wind in the Willows*). Despite the gloom, the Court soldiered on.

No One Sees the Video

Advertised as 'a new play which casts a cold eye on the world of market research', Crimp's *No One Sees the Video* opened in November 1990 at the Court's Theatre Upstairs.[7] Based on his own experiences as a transcriber of market-research interviews in 1980–3, the play was unexpectedly timely. A journalist who interviewed Crimp wrote: 'Market research usually only comes to light at politically interesting times like these, when the news is full of opinion polls.'[8] She was referring to the fall of Margaret Thatcher, whose colleagues had decided she was now a liability because of her increasingly strident views and unpopular policies. On 22 November 1990, she left office and John Major became Tory leader and prime minister six days later. Thatcher's fall was 'the main drama of the year', but her legacy for theatre was 'a siege-mentality, excessive prudence and the sanctification of the box-office as the ultimate arbiter [of taste]'.[9] It was a good time for a play that was critical of the market economy.

No One Sees the Video is not only about market research, but also, said Crimp, 'partly a play about language, about acquiring the language to do a job', and about people's 'search for happiness and meaning'.[10] It begins when Liz, a middle-aged woman just left by her husband Paul, is stopped in the street by a market researcher, and asked whether she buys frozen pizzas. She is persuaded to take part in a video-recorded interview about her lifestyle and shopping habits. The interviewer is Colin, a married man with an eye for other women. At first Liz lies to him about her family, then confesses that Paul has left her. Although Colin is irritated because this makes the interview worthless as part of a family sample, he sees Liz's potential, and offers her work as a market-research interviewer. Liz starts by quizzing women about their preferences in sanitary products, and enjoys her new-found power. Meanwhile, her rebellious sixteen-year-old daughter, Jo, is appalled when her mother decides to burn Paul's possessions, and when Colin visits Liz at home, he is drawn towards Jo. However, as her mother becomes a workaholic, Jo joins an anarchist commune and becomes pregnant. Then, on a business trip to the north-east, Liz finds herself in a hotel room with a casual pickup. She tells him a story about interviewing local women, one of whom was uncooperative. When he reveals that the woman is his wife, Liz throws him out. In the end, Liz and Jo tacitly exclude Colin from their lives, and look forward to Jo's baby.

As staged by Lindsay Posner, then artistic director of the Theatre Upstairs, the play had a bare set, designed by Simon

Vincenzi, with a simple, hygienic white cyclorama. Playing Liz, Celia Imrie mixed delicate irony with a cool imperiousness while Neil Dudgeon as Colin swung between ingratiating smiles and outbursts of temper as he conveyed his character's restlessness. Emer McCourt as Jo was innocent, sulky and dreamy. There was one particularly haunting image: while Colin talked to Liz on the phone, he put out his hand to touch the television screen, where her video image was freeze-framed, embodying in one gesture the longing for human contact in an alienating world, for warmth in a time of cold screens.

No One Sees the Video had mixed reviews. Michael Billington thought the play showed how market research 'turns nosiness into a bogus science and demeans people by pigeon holing [*sic*] them according to class and social type' and that 'our consumerist culture conceals a deep unhappiness', before adding: 'while I see what Mr Crimp is driving at, I wished he dramatised the argument as well as the conclusion'. Charles Spencer was exasperated with Crimp's technique of showing 'lives of quiet but none the less profound desperation' because 'he has been doing this for three or four plays now and it doesn't seem to be getting him any further'. *Time Out*'s Jane Edwardes argued that 'Crimp's real strength lies not in his manipulation of plot but in the atmosphere of individual scenes and in the edgy, rhythmic dialogue in which not a word is wasted', and Sheridan Morley thought that 'sketchy dialogues of Pinteresque pointlessness are interrupted by the occasional good East European joke', a reference to Crimp's oblique nod at Václav Havel: 'People who have a playwright running the country, these must be people whose mission in life it is to suffer' (p. 16).[11] Michael Coveney saw Crimp as part of a trend towards 'stylistic ellipsis, angst and the whole European modernist bag of moral ambivalence', but several critics, including the veteran Milton Shulman, were unsympathetic to the play's politics. The most telling criticism was that Liz's transformation from vulnerable housewife to ruthless executive was too sudden to be convincing.[12]

Clearly, *No One Sees the Video* argues that market research is a parasitic activity that is at best of questionable value and at worst positively intrusive. Although each interviewer assures their interviewees that 'No one sees the videotape apart from myself' (p. 26), this is blatantly untrue since they are shown to the researchers' clients. One of them, Roger, has distinctly voyeuristic tendencies: when an interviewee, Sally, is asked about her choice of sanitary products, she asks: 'I mean does Roger get off on this or something?' (p. 52). Market research is shown to categorise individuals as objects of consumer society, creating desires for commodities and normalising opinions. But the interviewees' suspicion of the camera's voyeuristic eye conflicts with their narcissistic desire to be filmed, and the interviewers' manipulative skills corrupt their own morals. Yet, although sceptical about the use of market research, Crimp is also interested in the way the job affects its employees. 'There is a line in it,' Crimp said, 'where the man [Colin] is trying to persuade the woman [Liz] to take a job in market research and he says, "Just acquaint yourself with the vocabulary and the rest will follow." [p. 45] Once you have acquired the tools, then that becomes set in your mind and you behave in a certain way.'[13] The play explains the difference between a 'prompt' (which tells the interviewee what to think) and a 'probe' (an open question). The trouble with probes is that they easily turn into intrusions. And they are addictive. Gradually, the researchers become victims of their work. There's also an emotional, and sexual, aspect to probing. In the beautifully observed scene between the awkward Colin and the precocious Jo, Colin explains the difference between probes and prompts, advising 'Trust the former, avoid the latter' (p. 57), and then allows Jo to question him, revealing the name of his wife (Jennifer). Colin's advice to Jo – 'I'll tell you something: we all turn, Jo, into the kind of people we used to despise' (p. 61) – captures perfectly both the tone of an older man lecturing a teenager and encapsulates the play's main theme: the vaguely lefty Liz becomes a businesswoman. These question-and-answer techniques, so suggestive of police interrogation, give the play an air of manipulative power games with uncertain outcomes. On the other hand, Crimp's repeated references to the 'void' in modern life (pp. 36, 73–4), and the need to fill it, are perhaps a touch unsubtle.

At the time, Crimp thought of the play as 'not a satire or a harangue against market research. If you want a label for it, I suppose it is a post-consumer play, dealing with the idea that markets and aspects of business are like the air you breathe. The characters don't really have the strength to bring anything to bear against it, like they might have done 10 or 20 years ago.'[14] Although the play has a sense of subdued rage against market research, and the way it manipulates consumers, Crimp was clearly aware that the social and political climate was one in which most people naturally equated happiness with commodities. And felt powerless to do anything about it. Since one party, the Conservatives, had been in power for eleven years, this feeling reflected, however indirectly, the times.

Getting Attention

Crimp's next play, the deeply disturbing *Getting Attention*, was written before *No One Sees the Video*, and received a public reading at the Court at the end of October 1989, while *Play with Repeats* was at the Orange Tree. But it wasn't produced until March 1991, when Jude Kelly, artistic director of the West Yorkshire Playhouse in Leeds, directed it there. The play then transferred to the Theatre Upstairs in May. Crimp says that he got an image for the play through a chance encounter. In May 1987, while he was travelling on the London Underground, he looked at another passenger's newspaper and, under the headline 'Relatives in Mask Protest', saw a photograph of 'two adults wearing grotesque rubber masks': 'The previous day I'd written a few pages of dialogue in which I'd tried to map out passages of denial, brutality and sheer human confusion – the emotional labyrinth surrounding child abuse. The photograph showed the relatives of a man accused of precisely this crime.'[15]

At first glance, *Getting Attention* seems like a gritty social-realist council estate drama: a young couple, Carol and Nick, live with her four-year-old child, Sharon, and their neighbours include Milly, a woman in her fifties, and twenty-something Bob. When Nick and Carol quarrel, the neighbours listen in. When Nick and Carol have sex, the neighbours listen in. But when Nick and Carol abuse Sharon, no one notices. The abuse starts gradually, with stepfather Nick's initial irritation slowly turning into violence. Meanwhile, their neighbours miss all the clues to what's happening. For example, Sharon's desperate scratching on the wall for help is audible to Bob, but he doesn't know what it is. During Sharon's birthday party, Nick and Carol put on grotesque masks, then they smash the child's birthday present and pour beer on her cake. In the second act, Crimp breaks up the narrative with Milly and Bob's monologues, testimonies at a future investigation in which they recall how, 'knowing what we do now' (p. 151), they failed to spot the signs of abuse.[16] It emerges that Sharon has been starved, scalded with boiling water and murdered. In a final scene of unbearable bleakness, a social worker visits Carol and Nick. As she notes their apparent progress in looking after Sharon, the little girl is already dead in her room, with the bedcovers pulled over her head. Carol says, 'Calls that doing a tortoise doesn't she Nick' (p. 173). The social worker leaves, oblivious to the child's fate.

Not many critics saw *Getting Attention* in Leeds. The *Guardian* pointed out that it was the second in the West Yorkshire Playhouse's Lifelines season about child abuse, and said that 'what baffles and appals is that even when the worst happens, Carol's first concern is not for her baby's suffering but that someone might find out [. . .] Apparently based on an actual case, *Getting Attention* rings true – as far as it goes.' The *Independent* felt that 'not only do the characters not know what to say, neither does the play as a whole' while *The Times* opined that 'somewhere a scene is missing'. When the play opened in London, it also received a battering, although most critics understood its meaning: Peter Kemp said that 'the play's point, though, is that despite all this snooping, something appalling can go unnoticed' and Billington observed that, while 'Crimp is sometimes too oblique for his own good', he 'is partly saying that we have lost any sense of communal life: that we dump people down in bleak modern estates where they lead solitary, cellular lives'.[17]

What baffled some reviewers was Crimp's experimental attitude to form. At first, *Getting Attention* seems to be a social-realist play, part of the genre of British housing-estate dramas, a Royal Court tradition that stretches from John Arden's *Live Like Pigs* (1958) through Edward Bond's *Saved* (1965) to Leo Butler's *Redundant* (2001). The usual naturalistic conventions of the council-estate drama, which are based on the idea that working-class life is more authentic than middle-class life, are reproduced here, but then Crimp wrong-foots the audience by adding the final monologues, and subverting – through dramatic irony – the form of the play. He also tricks our expectations by keeping Sharon offstage, a device that focuses our attention on the relationship between Nick and Carol, and the way that their neighbours fail to see what's taking place. With Sharon invisible, Crimp underlines the central horror of the story, leaving it to our imaginations to come up with a picture of her suffering. With brutal irony, the play's title refers not only to the way inquisitive neighbours pay attention to the wrong things, but also to the fact that Milly mistakes Sharon's agony for attention-seeking: 'It's attention isn't it. [. . .] The more you give them the more they want' (p. 144). But Crimp never judges his characters; he simply shows how they behave, from the nosy Milly to the uncertain and finally distraught Carol. A distinct feeling of unease oozed from the production, which featured committed performances from Nigel Cooke as the muscular Nick and Adrienne Swan as the scantily dressed and barefoot Carol. This unease was partly due to the way that Crimp both challenges the audience to consider what they know about their own neighbours and manages to suggest that there are understandable limits to all our knowledge of other people.

At the same time, Crimp was also responding to the way the

British media discuss violence, and how it turns the perpetrators of abuse into monsters. By doing so, he anticipated the hysterical attacks on horror videos that followed the murder of the toddler Jamie Bulger in 1993. When Milly watches the film *Evil Dead*, she explains, 'Well . . . you know . . . company isn't it.' Then: 'Oh I'm afraid I like a bit of violence. Keeps me awake a bit of violence. (*faint nervous laugh)*' (p. 137). Typically, this is both an acute observation of the social role of horror films and a comment on the real violence visited on the hapless Sharon.

When the play transferred to the Court, Crimp gave an interview in which he talked about how theatre can make public the private anxieties of an age. He also pointed out that one of the reasons why child abuse happens is because these things 'remain private'. He offered no explanation for the actions of Nick and Carol except that they are isolated individuals with no one to help them. So although *Getting Attention* is deeply troubling and reflects anxieties about child abuse, it never offers easy answers to difficult issues. In the interview, Crimp also mentions working for film: 'A play is like being a painter of pictures; writing a film script is like being an interior decorator. You can paint the room blue and then the producer comes along and says, "Actually I think green would be better." '[18] Obviously, writing for film was not a happy experience, but it did feed into his next play.

The Treatment

In 1993, Max Stafford-Clark left the Court, and was succeeded as artistic director by Stephen Daldry. Although he initially programmed Irish and American plays, plus some experimental work exploring masculinity, there were signs that new writing was beginning to revive.[19] At the Bush Theatre, a small fringe venue in West London, artistic director Dominic Dromgoole was putting on new plays such as Philip Ridley's *The Pitchfork Disney* (1991) and Jonathan Harvey's *Beautiful Thing* (1993). At the National, work such as Tom Stoppard's *Arcadia* and David Hare's epic trilogy was inspiring younger writers. From the United States came Tony Kushner's monster-sized *Angels in America* (1992–3). In response, Daldry programmed an American Season, whose publicity leaflet announced: 'Welcome to the decade of Fear'.[20] The season included the British premieres of Howard Korder's *Search and Destroy* (1990) and David Mamet's controversial *Oleanna* (1992), a play whose politically incorrect account of the sex war divided audiences, and couples.

Significantly enough, the American Season did not start with an American play, but kicked off with Crimp's main-stage Court debut, *The Treatment*, which opened in April 1993 and could be seen as a home-grown response to American playwright John Guare's *Six Degrees of Separation*, which had been a hit in 1992. According to one newspaper, Crimp's play was 'originally titled the rather less cine-specific Playwright in New York (Broadway Boogie Woogie)'.[21] This refers to its painful gestation. After *Getting Attention* and *No One Sees the Video*, Crimp suffered writer's block. Unwilling simply to repeat a formula, he got stuck. 'I'd written the first scene of this play but I didn't see what it was part of,' he told one newspaper. 'I had some bits of dialogue but they didn't have a home.' Then in 1991 he went to New York on a three-week trip as part of a Court exchange programme with New Dramatists, an American new-writing organisation. 'New York was for me filled with a kind of terminal energy,' he said. But he wasn't about to write a piece of literal Americana. 'There is almost a sense that I have used New York as a convention, in the same way that certain Jacobean writers use Venice as a convention. They took their own decadence, sexual anxiety and violence and distanced it by setting it in Italy.' Crimp was also defensive about the bleakness of his writing. 'There is definitely a feeling that this [style] is wrong and that we need something uplifting. But, for me, confronting the dark is positive and uplifting.' He was irritated by an interviewer who couldn't imagine having any of the relationships shown in *The Treatment*. 'I found that a very strange remark. Would you want to have any of the relationships, for instance, in *Madame Bovary*?' He pointed out that 'commercial success is the overriding criterion now of art in general' and 'success is the criterion by which we are measured'. Typically, he also argued against the clichéd new-writing dictum of 'Write what you know', pointing out that he'd only spent three weeks in New York and that 'Kafka wrote *Amerika* without going there'.[22] 'The writer writes to imagine,' Crimp told another interviewer. 'I'm sceptical about having to write what you know. Writing is an investigation, a pushing back of barriers. I believe that's how you discover things.' It follows that the notion of using your life as material is ethically suspect: 'I think that would be deeply disturbing. And horrible. I think the idea of selling things about yourself is terrifying.'[23]

This anxiety permeates *The Treatment*. Set in New York, the play tells the story of Anne, a young woman whose husband, Simon, likes to tie her up, silencing her with a piece of tape across her mouth, and talking to her about 'the beauty of the world' (p. 285).[24] She decides to leave him, and meets two film producers, Jennifer and Andrew, who become interested in making a film of her story. Clifford, a professional writer who was big on Broadway in the 1950s, is hired to write the script, and turns reality into a voyeuristic fantasy: when Andrew seduces Anne, Clifford watches their curt sex act. Meanwhile, John, a famous black film actor who was once in love with Jennifer, is invited on board, and he takes over the project, becoming its producer. Nicky, the company secretary, adds her suggestions to the script. As the film develops, it becomes less and less like Anne's life. John uses his financial muscle to sack Clifford, while Andrew finds himself increasingly drawn to Anne. For her part, Anne is so upset by Clifford's voyeurism that she contacts Simon and, in revenge, they tear out Clifford's eyes with a fork. A year passes, and the all-powerful John now leads the celebrations for the launch of the film, in which Nicky plays Anne. Leaving the party, Andrew goes in search of Anne, finding her once again bound and gagged in her apartment. He frees her, her husband arrives, and, as she suddenly makes a run for it, she bumps into Jennifer, who in a panic shoots her dead.

Directed by Lindsay Posner, *The Treatment* – the title means the outline of a film, medical care and, crucially, the way we treat others – was a thrilling theatrical experience, with a cast which included Larry Pine as Andrew and the late Sheila Gish as Jennifer. Anne was played by Jacqueline Defferary and Simon by Mark Strong. On Julian McGowan's neon-lit set, with a soundtrack that mixed menacing sirens, blaring jazz and power chords, it felt like a vivid cocktail of Martin Scorsese, Jim Jarmusch and John Guare. Showing a world of sushi bars, hotel rooms, subways, city parks, street encounters and script meetings, the production sizzled with energy and excitement. Gish and Pine ably suggested how the human heart can be distorted by the ambition of media vultures, with Gish especially good at masking predatory moves with superficial smiles. By contrast, Defferary conveyed Anne's vital mix of lip-quivering vulnerability and vengeful aggression. The cover of the published playtext, which doubled as the production's programme, featured a fork – a reference both to an early scene when Clifford sells Simon a fork (p. 291) and to a latter one when '*Simon stabs the fork into Clifford's eye*' (p. 368).

The critics readily appreciated the play's cry of dismay at how art is judged by commercial rather than aesthetic criteria. They also noted Crimp's leap, in Billington's words, 'from genuine promise to rich fulfilment' as a writer whose work could set a main stage ablaze. John Peter said that 'the writing is harsh, elegant and sardonic: a tapestry of ruthless social comedy, harrowing violence and cold and repugnant sexuality', while Benedict Nightingale said that 'Crimp's play is most alive when he gives eccentricity and outrageousness its head'. Some critics, however, were less convinced. Nicholas de Jongh argued that 'Crimp finally steers the play towards melodrama's gulf, exalting sensationalism at the expense of explaining and justifying behaviour', while Ian Herbert enjoyed it 'but hated myself for doing so'.[25] Still, Crimp had the public support of his actors. Larry Pine, who was the only American in the cast, was not new to the Court, having acted there in Wallace Shawn's *Aunt Dan and Lemon* five years previously. He said: 'I read the play and discovered they [the Court] have found a playwright I would class with Wallie Shawn – and I've done four of his plays.'[26]

The Treatment is first and foremost a city drama. Not only is it full of urban cacophony, but its dialogues are alive with ideas. At one point, Andrew describes his and Jennifer's role as that of 'facilitators', and then metaphorically as a chip making connections or as a grid: 'Like the city itself exactly a *grid* into which things feed' (p. 313). In several scenes, people speak across each other, creating a traffic jam of verbiage, with ideas colliding and images proliferating in an exciting commotion of impressions. Here, Crimp captures the American confessional mode; there, he lampoons mediaspeak. Typical of his style is the contrast, exemplified by Andrew, between a surface coolness and subterranean passions. Or, as Simon says in a moment of typical quirkiness, 'the city goes down as far maybe farther than it goes *up*. Down down down it goes, which is why we must stay pure' (p. 357). And Crimp's by now characteristic themes – the way language creates reality, media manipulation, exploitation of women – are all here. Above all, there's a sense of metaphoric density. In his vision of a hellish if exhilarating urban experience, there are symbolic eyes everywhere. When Andrew begins seducing Anne, he says: 'You have the eyes of the city' (p. 297). From the theme of voyeurism to the play's final image, when the blinded Clifford and a blind cab driver drive together through New York, there are constant references to sight, insight and seeing. In this way, *The Treatment* rewrites *King Lear*.

The play's epigraph is Paul Auster's comment that 'Life as we know it has ended, and yet no one is able to grasp what has taken its place . . . Slowly and steadily, the city seems to be consuming itself' (p. 274). Not only is New York consuming itself, but Anne's life is being cannibalised. As Andrew tells her: 'no one's story is theirs alone' (p. 298). Anne finds her life consumed and regurgitated in an unrecognisable form, and this theme is stressed by various references to eating, from scenes set in restaurants to oral sex; obliquely, by the use of a fork as a weapon and, meta-phorically, by the characters' hunger for success. At the centre of the play, Anne's character is deliberately mysterious, perhaps unknowable. Anne is a cipher, a woman who allows men and other women to define her character, and her significance. Compared to Nicky's strident certainty, Anne is tentative, unclear, uncertain. Her account of Simon's treatment of her is vague, allusive, strange. At first she volunteers the fact that Simon 'has a knife and calls me a bitch' (p. 280), then, when questioned, she says, 'The knife isn't visible', 'It's more the sense, the *sense* of a knife' (p. 281). Every suggestion made by Andrew and Jennifer – who see her experiences as a straightforward case of sexual abuse – she parries with a puzzling comment. So when Jennifer assumes that Simon abuses Anne physically, she responds, 'No. I'm sorry. He's abused no one' (p. 284). Her torture is the torture of the mundane; her husband, she insists, is no weirdo: 'He is profoundly ordinary' (p. 286). Near the end, she confesses, 'I was lonely' (p. 351). It's as good an explanation as any other. Perhaps it is Anne's elusive quality, her unusual nature, that attracts the 'disenchanted' (p. 352) Andrew to her, an attraction some critics found difficult to understand. Finally, Anne's treatment is typical of 1990s British theatre in that it poses an ethical problem: how is it possible to object to her life being stolen when she insists on giving it away? She is a victim, certainly, but also a complicit one. After all, she not only approaches Andrew and Jennifer willingly, but she equally willingly returns to Simon. At the end, her sudden death is merely the final of several robberies of her experience.

Although set specifically in New York, *The Treatment*'s satire on film-makers and the media is universal. For example, John makes a pointed 'joke' about getting involved 'in the kind of degrading shit that has become her [Jennifer's] trademark' (326). In the final scene, the blind writer travels by taxi, but the wind keeps snatching the pages of his script, a satirical image of the transience of writing. The play is about art, its social construction and its power to convey meaning. Near the end, John says: 'art changes *everything* [. . .] It is the enduring reflection of our transient selves. It is what makes us *real*' (p. 374). Once again, this feels like both a wicked satire and a provocative truth. A metatheatrical irony is that this satire on filming is offered as a stage play, a medium that can't compete with cinema's trendiness nor with its audience size. At one point, Simon observes: 'I have no interest in the theatre' and 'I will not pay good money to be told that the world is a heap of shit' (p. 292). As Sheila Johnston commented: 'Once all the world was a stage, now it's a screen.'[27] Finally, the play's last lingering vision of a blind cab driver provides 'an abiding image', typical of 1990s drama, of the 'bleak (arguably nihilistic) observations of social decay, severed isolation and degradation into aimlessness'.[28]

The Treatment is an outstanding play, amazing to read and wonderful to see performed. It won the 26th John Whiting award, and Crimp was given his cheque for £6,000 by actress Frances Barber at the Hampstead Theatre on 7 September 1993. One newspaper reported that the play 'was a critical, but not a box office, success, but was admired by US producers and opens at the Newman Theatre in New York in October'.[29] Yet, despite this success, Crimp again found himself blocked. Not for the first time, he was finding it hard to produce a follow-up.

The Misanthrope

Meanwhile, the British new-writing scene was beginning to generate excitement. In 1994, the iconic *Trainspotting* and Anthony Neilson's shocking *Penetrator* toured Britain, and Philip Ridley's controversial *Ghost from a Perfect Place* was staged at the Hampstead Theatre. A new sensibility was emerging in British new writing: in-yer-face theatre. Then, in January 1995, the tipping point came when Sarah Kane's debut, *Blasted*, opened at the Theatre Upstairs, and rapidly became a cause célèbre, attracting some of the most hostile reviews of the decade.[30] In response, senior playwrights such as Harold Pinter, Edward Bond and Caryl Churchill defended her. On 23 January, the *Guardian* – whose critic had called *Blasted* 'naive tosh' – published one of several letters of protest. Attacking Billington's social-realist criteria as 'an aesthetic which denies a writer the right to create his or her own imaginative world', the letter states that 'the power of Ms Kane's play lies precisely in the fact that she dares to range beyond personal experience and bring the wars that rage at such a convenient distance from this island right into its heart'. It ends by asking, 'Who is being "naive" here? Who is writing the "tosh"?'[31] It was written by Crimp and signed by him and three other writers. Clearly, they were angry at the banal definition of theatre as naturalistic realism based on personal experience. From a modernist standpoint, Crimp must have felt that this was an intolerably narrow view of theatrical possibility.

Still, the controversy over *Blasted* proved that theatre was buzzing. By 1996, Billington was upbeat: 'I cannot recall a time when there were so many exciting dramatists in the twenty-something age-group: what is more, they are speaking to audiences of their own generation,' and in *The Times*, Nightingale talked about a 'buzz in the air'. A year later, he characterised the new wave as 'a Theatre of Urban Ennui, marked by its abrasive portraits of city life'.[32] Playwrights such as Martin McDonagh and Conor McPherson lit up the West End. Plays such as Joe Penhall's *Some Voices* (1994), Judy Upton's *Ashes and Sand* (1994), Kevin Elyot's *My Night with Reg* (1994) and Patrick Marber's *Dealer's Choice* (1995) all grappled with the crisis of masculinity. Above all, the success of Jez Butterworth's *Mojo* (1995) and Mark Ravenhill's *Shopping and Fucking* (1996) proved that new writing was coming on strong.

But Crimp, who was absent from the new-writing scene for two years, showed no desire to jump on the rolling bandwagon of in-yer-face theatre. After all, he'd already written a child-abuse play set on a council estate (*Getting Attention*) and a play which featured explicit sex and violence (*The Treatment*). His immediate problem was writing something different. This time, his solution was to sidestep the block by journeying back in time and updating a European classic. Instead of trying to squeeze out a new play, he turned Molière's 1666 classic, *The Misanthrope*, into a contemporary play. '*The Misanthrope*, which is my first text based on a French text, was written entirely for my own amusement and enjoyment, just to get me out of a kind of black hole – if you like – of writing.'[33]

Crimp's version updates the play by setting it in a contemporary London of theatre and media folk, and giving it a dazzling blank-verse language that is hilariously, enjoyably savage. The misanthropic Alceste is the only character who retains their original name; his love, Célimène, is renamed Jennifer, an American film star. The object of playwright Alceste's mockery, at the start of the play, is Covington, a theatre critic who has written a wincingly bad play. The rest of the cast includes a journalist, an actor, an agent and an acting teacher. Among the targets satirised are celebrity journalists, anti-smokers and artist Damien Hirst. What's immediately striking is the wonderful freshness of the language. For example, an early speech of Alceste's begins: 'What total bollocks. Nothing's more effete / than the moral contortions of the self-proclaimed elite. / The slobbering over the ritual greeting, / the bullshit spoken at every meeting / makes me vomit' (p. 107), while John's following joke emphasises Crimp's self-irony: 'I have to say that this so-called rage / would make more sense on the seventeenth-century stage. / And surely as a playwright you're aware / of sounding like something straight out of Molière' (p. 109). The final rejection of Alceste by Jennifer is characteristically quizzical about contemporary mores: 'You're seriously asking me to join you in some kind of suburban nightmare? / Shop? Cook? Clean? What? Do the dishes? *Sleep*? / Drive the kids to ballet in a Japanese *jeep*?' (p. 194).

The Misanthrope was staged at London's Young Vic in February and March 1996. Lindsay Posner's production was quick, elegant and amazingly funny. The verbal shocks came fast and furious through the deliciously barbed and rhythmic text. Superbly bitchy, this rasping satire hits out at false friendship, treacherous ambition, naked opportunism, journalist malpractice, postmodern clichés and the whole media circus. Alceste, played by the bulky but nimble Ken Stott, contrasted nicely with the fleetness of Elizabeth McGovern's Jennifer. At the time, one journalist revealed that, a week before the start of rehearsals, McGovern had replaced first-choice Rachel Weisz, who preferred 'to co-star in her first Hollywood film [*Going All the Way*, 1997, with Ben Affleck]'. McGovern saw her character as 'Madonna-esque': 'She's comfortable with that facade of "I'm in control of my career, my choice, my sexuality, my life." She projects the in-vogue way to be that Madonna taught us.'[34] Here, it sounds as if reality aims to outbid satire.

With its bright final scene, when the cast don clothes from the era of the Sun King, the show was really well loved. Spencer welcomed the way that Crimp 'has dragged Molière, crudely at times, into the 20th century', while Morley called Crimp's language 'crisp, scatological and often blindingly funny'. Although Billington liked the writing, he complained that while in the original, 'Alceste risks arrest through his blistering attack on a court versifier', in Crimp's version 'nothing vital seems at stake'. Some critics recognised themselves. For example, Michael Coveney said that Crimp's Alceste 'is a dramatist with a bad word for everyone from Andrew Lloyd Webber to Alan Bennett and David "fucking" Hare. He even hates critics, especially a middle-aged, menopausal white male specimen named Michael Covington. Not an amalgam, surely, of myself and Michael Billington? Pretentious, badly dressed – *nous*?'[35] Actually, although Crimp does belittle Bennett and Hare (p. 161), he points out in the published text that '*C'est un scélérat qui parle*' (It's a scoundrel talking). But his example of a bad play is a wicked parody of Hare's *Skylight* (1995):

MAN: Let's dine out at my restaurant. The limousine is ready.
WOMAN I'd rather stay at home and cook my own spaghetti.
[. . .] They kiss beneath the leaking skylight. (p. 122)

Crimp himself publicised the show by writing a spoof encounter between himself (Mart) and the play's original author (Mol). It ends with Mol gracing us with a piece of writerly advice: 'Respect the text. Avoid workshops and play-doctors. / Stay away from shows with helicopters. / Love and support the theatre. And fight as / hard as you can for living writers.' Then, as an antidote to excessive seriousness, Crimp continues: '*Mart wipes away a tear.*'[36]

The success of *The Misanthrope* – later revived at Chichester in a multiracial production directed by Indhu Rubasingham (2002) – also had one unexpected result: Crimp was asked to translate more French plays. He went on to study the language again and to work on texts by modernists such as Ionesco, Genet and Koltès, and by the classical Marivaux (see Chapter 4). However useful as a way of earning money, Crimp's straight translations were nevertheless a stopgap. It was with his next original play that he made another definitive leap in his project of pushing theatrical form as far as it would go – and this time it made him an international star.

3 'PRIVILEGED DISTANCE FROM DEATH AND DISMEMBERMENT'

Attempts on Her Life, The Country, Face to the Wall, Cruel and Tender, Fewer Emergencies

In 1997, Martin Crimp's masterpiece, *Attempts on Her Life*, was staged at the Royal Court Theatre, an event that secured his reputation as the most innovative, most exciting and most exportable playwright of his generation. For a play which satirises, among other things, media hype, it is fitting that it was produced in a cultural atmosphere that positively reeked of overstatement. In 1996, the media – led by *Newsweek*, *Le Monde* and London's *Evening Standard* – rebranded London as the 'capital of cool'. Within a couple of years, even Tony Blair was talking about Cool Britannia, the name given to this putative cultural renaissance.[1] Britain was being hyped as a Young Country, and the inevitable assortment of scene-creamers was led by Culture Secretary Chris Smith, whose love letter to the creative industries, *Creative Britain*, sported a glossy Damien Hirst cover. But while Cool Britannia was principally about cultural industries such as Brit pop and frock flicks, traditional art forms such as theatre were soon swept up in the excitement. Whether on the superficial level of marketing, or because of a genuine creative upsurge, theatre was suddenly newsworthy again. Wherever you looked, there was a young dramatist eager to make a splash. As playwright David Edgar put it: 'Five years on from all the obituaries [of new writing], theatre is listed along with pop, fashion, fine art and food as the fifth leg of the new swinging London.'[2] But while the arts media were busy looking for the next Sarah Kane or hot twenty-something writer, the best play of the decade was written by an experienced playwright who had spent nearly two decades honing his craft.

Attempts on Her Life

In the dying days of John Major's Tory government, a sorry tale of sleaze and continuous xenophobic clamour, *Attempts on Her Life* appeared as both a brilliantly original and a distinctly European play, both a comment on the late-twentieth century and a vision of what the theatre of the future might be.[3] With its punning title – which also recalls Crimp's Orange Tree plays – the piece advertises itself as 'Seventeen scenarios for the theatre'. These seventeen scenes, which vary between extreme brevity and lengthier dialogue, each explore a different aspect of a woman called Anne (also Anya, Annie, Anny and Annushka) – who appears to be a complete enigma. She is the recipient of a variety of telephone messages, the heroine of a film, a victim of civil war, a typical consumer, a megastar, a tourist guide, a make of car, a physicist, an international terrorist, an American survivalist, an artist, a refugee's dead child, a victim of aliens, the girl next door, the object of a police investigation, a porn star, and the subject of a conversation among friends. During the play, the people talking about her include Mum and Dad, art critics, official interrogators, border guards, advertisers, film-makers, spin doctors, showbiz performers, abusive stalkers, lovers and friends. In geographic range, she skips across the globe, with mentions of distant continents, as well as European capitals and North African countries. Her age fluctuates between teenage and forty; she's both a single woman and a mother. In 'Girl Next Door', the idea of her fluid identity reaches a hilarious climax when she is described as everything from 'a cheap cigarette' to 'a dyke with a *femme*' (pp. 263–4).[4]

The play is the culmination of Crimp's quest to marry form and content. With enormous imaginative flair, his text indicates where one speech begins and ends, but doesn't assign them to named characters, leaving it to the director and actors to distribute the lines. Although the cast 'should reflect the composition of the world beyond the theatre' (p. 202), the number of actors is not specified. Nor is their gender indicated, although in some scenes, such as 'Mum and Dad', it can easily be inferred. Similarly, the scenes are not random: they refer to each other and quote each other, and some motifs occur again and again. Above all, the play's daring form is symmetrical: two scenarios, both played in a foreign language with a translation, occur near the beginning and the end of the play; and there are two rhymed scenes, 'The Camera Loves You' and 'Girl Next Door'. Two scenarios, 'Faith in Ourselves' and 'Strangely!' are episodes from the same story. Some scenes, such as the car advert and 'The Occupier' involve using words from real advertisements or those printed on products, a kind of *objet trouvé*. But although the play does include a diversity of voices, most notably that of the mother of the American survivalist in Scenario 10, the recurring tone is that of today's art-makers, creatives and commentators – who all sound the same.

Attempts on Her Life begins with 'All Messages Deleted', which consists of eleven answerphone messages, most of which relate to one or more of the subsequent scenarios. For example, one from 'Sally at Cooper's' says 'the vehicle *is* now in the showroom and ready for your collection' (p. 204), which clearly prefigures Scenario 7, 'The New Anny', a parody of car adverts. The definitive text's note that in performance the first scenario may be cut allows directors to omit material which is just a prelude to the main play. The other cut – of the original stage direction: 'Let each scenario in words – the dialogue – unfold against a distinct world – a design – which best exposes its irony' – was made to discourage versions which too obviously underline the play's irony.[5]

The original production was staged in a makeshift space at the Ambassadors Theatre in the West End, where the Court, an early recipient of the National Lottery bonanza, had rented two theatres – the other was the Duke of York's – as temporary bases while its crumbling Sloane Square building was being refurbished. Director Tim Albery cast four men and four women, including a Bosnian and a Nigerian. In defiance of the Court's tradition of austere staging, *Attempts on Her Life* was overtly theatrical, a richly entertaining event despite its tiny budget. Images of Albery's production that stick in the mind include the two long lines of red lights that converged at the back of the stage, suggesting an airport runway; a black frame reminiscent of airplane windows, conference venues or a television screen; the passing images of X-rayed luggage on an airport carousel in 'Mum and Dad'; bleak cityscapes and a violent TV movie. In Scenario 5, Hakeem Kae-Kazim performed a rap song while a film projection showed a girl's legs dangling – which suddenly twitch as blood starts running down them, soaking her white socks – and Scenario 14 was a showbiz song-and-dance routine. Bosnian Etela Pardo played the 'New Anny' scene with Howard Ward translating; Kacey Ainsworth was the naive 'Pornó' girl and her Portuguese translator was Danny Cerqueira. In 'Untitled (100 Words)', the critics were seated around a table in a parody of *The Late Show*, BBC2's arts review programme. In the final scenario, which looked like a dinner party, the actors appeared not in character but as themselves, in their ordinary clothes: with the play over, the cast enjoy a meal; wine has been poured and the smokers have lit their cigarettes. The atmosphere is relaxed, untheatrical.

The critics struggled to impose a coherent explanation on the play, some more successfully than others. Nicholas de Jongh began his review by seeing *Attempts on Her Life* as a suggestion of 'what the brave new theatre of the 21st century will look like – both on stage and page', but ended it with the putdown: 'Just heartfelt pretension.' Paul Taylor said: 'One does end up congratulating the play for the wit and agility with which it disappears up its own self-reflexive futility.' John Peter correctly saw it as 'a private drama whose heroine is defined by her absence', while the *New Statesman*'s Susannah Clapp praised the 'visual creativity' of the production, describing the play as 'a blow on behalf of bewilderment'. Alastair

Macaulay made the most sustained case against what he saw as a 'terrible' play, calling it postmodern – 'post-civilisation, post-truth, post-feeling, post-teeth, post-everything' – and accusing Crimp of playing 'repulsive', manipulative games with terrorism, family, art and media. Michael Billington saw Anne as 'basically a vehicle for the writer's moral rejection of a selfish, materialist civilisation based on consumer fetishism' and argued that Crimp has 'proved that the act of theatre can still survive if propelled by moral fervour'.[6] In general, what threw the critics was the idea that Anne could have so many different identities. But, as the scenario in which she is presented as a make of car makes clear, Anne is a vehicle.[7] Like a metaphor, she carries meanings that aren't literal. Indeed, the piece's playful approach to serious issues is signalled by the original playtext's back-cover blurb: 'Attempts to describe her? / Attempts to destroy her? / Or attempts to destroy herself? / Is Anne the object of violence? / Or its terrifying practitioner?' The answer, of course, is all of these, and more.

Crimp has said that *Attempts on Her Life* was the play he was 'happiest writing', partly because he felt free from the obligation to create naturalistic characters and a linear plot.[8] Anne's contradictory character indicates that she's an absurdist notion, an absence filled by other people's opinions and ideas. In fact, in Scenario 6 Crimp nimbly parodies this view: 'An absence of character, whatever *that* means . . .' (p. 229). Yet, although he has liberated himself from the conventions of the traditional well-made play, he also makes sure that the piece has a satisfyingly symmetrical form, and that its kaleidoscope of scenes is based firmly on narrative. The whole play, Crimp has pointed out, is held together by the fact that people are 'telling stories all the time'.[9] Each of the stories draws attention to its own telling, so the story of Anne the suicidal artist is told by means of a discussion among critics about the merits and demerits of her life and art. At the same time, passages of concrete poetry, groups of free-floating words, punctuate the discussion – it is, after all, a scene about art. And when one of Crimp's characters claims that the artist Anne 'should instead be compelled to undergo psychiatric treatment' (p. 253), it's a knowing reference to a real-life event: Charles Spencer's review of Kane's *Phaedra's Love*, in which he wrote, 'It's not a theatre critic that's required here, it's a psychiatrist.'[10]

One of the most ambitious and thrilling new plays of the 1990s, *Attempts on Her Life* is Crimp at his iciest and satirical best. A tension between the characters of the play, who are recognisable individuals even if they don't have names, and the extreme fragmentation of the play's overall form gives the work its contemporary edge. But its formal daring also suggests a future kind of theatre in which the conventions of naturalism are subverted and reinvented. This is a recipe for an avant-garde theatre which both represents reality and simultaneously deconstructs it. The result is a series of paradoxes, both playful and horrific, in which the play's audiences are voyeurs of a satire on voyeurism, find meaning in critiques of meaning's social construction, and create a character out of the fragments of her fugitive absence. Wisely, Crimp refuses to finally offer a comfortable explanation. As in *The Treatment*, the border between life and art is trampled, leaving lingering images of terror and suicide, violence and violation. His characteristic themes – the social construction of images of women and the relationship between art and life – come at you with a dizzying speed, yet always with a sense of linguistic pleasure and with tantalising intelligence.

Attempts on Her Life has been the most often performed, and most often studied, of Crimp's works. David Edgar rightly sees it as both an experiment in form and as a critical questioning of audience expectations:

> Crimp's purpose is not only to question whether we can truly know another human being, but whether we can regard other people as existing at all independent of the models we construct of them. And he does this not by a bald statement, but by playing an elaborate and sophisticated game with the audience's expectations of how scenes connect within narrative.[11]

Other reactions have been less coherent. For example, academic Mary Luckhurst enthusiastically sees the play as 'the most radically interrogative work in western mainstream theatre since Beckett', and then gives an account of her York University production in 2002. Focusing on the politics of Crimp's 'fascination with the sexual objectification of women and women as victims and perpetuators of violence', she points out that Anne can be 'a fantasy-repository for extreme kinds of wish-fulfilment'. But since her reading of the play is so appreciative, her conclusion that its content is 'limited' is odd, as is her criticism that its suggestion that women are complicit victims remains unquestioned and that its representation of men is 'so excessively negative'.[12]

By contrast, Dr Heiner Zimmermann sees Anne as 'a gallery of mirrors in which the play satirically reflects the multitude of contradictory images of postmodern woman'. For him, the play is an example of post-dramatic theatre, in which images of Anne try to render her presence while simultaneously emphasising her absence:

> The speakers evoke reflections of Anne in various media such as photographs, videos, film scripts, recordings on an answering machine, a commercial, trial proceedings, her suicide notes and personal objects such as her medicine bottles or her ashtray – in short an archive of the absent central character.

Zimmermann rightly stresses that Crimp not only satirises the male gaze but also the response to it of feminist body art. The piece, he convincingly argues, parodies discourses about women, and its politics are precisely a denunciation of 'the absence of woman in a culture in which male projections of her conceal her reality'.[13] Reviewing the American premiere, playwright Ken Urban sums up:

> The play is after the big question: how is it that we come to know the other? Crimp suggests that the process of knowing is never a neutral one, and in fact, that the subject perpetuates a violence on

the object that it seeks to know. It is no coincidence that the object of investigation in this play is a woman, since the female other has been the object of the male gaze since time immemorial.[14]

Finally, Dr Merle Tönnies sees *Attempts on Her Life* as Crimp's reaction to the more headline-catching in-yer-face playwrights of the 1990s. He 'opposed a deliberately low emotional temperature to the general mood of sensational excess'.[15]

Attempts on Her Life was not only an international hit, with productions in many European countries and beyond, but it has also gained resonance following the events of 9/11 and the War on Terror. In a production at London's BAC in 2004, directed by Anne Tipton – winner of that year's James Menzies-Kitchin award for young directors – the play's references to terrorism and violence felt, if anything, even more timely than in the 1997 original. In common with *The Treatment*, the worst productions are those in which the media element of the play is excessively highlighted, drowning its satire with noisy video images or the like.

On 1 May 1997, Tony Blair was elected prime minister and the era of New Labour, with its spin doctors and politically correct control freaks, began. About eighteen months later, the *Guardian* ran a feature in which British playwrights were asked to describe their favourite playwright. Crimp chose Caryl Churchill:

> While most of us inch forward like pawns, she leaps about the board with the strange freedom of a knight. She always dares to imagine. She is never guilty of what Beckett once called 'that dismal conservatism of form and fatal journalism of content' that is still frequently found masquerading as theatre.[16]

In what reads like a personal manifesto, he also praised her ability to realise the 'playfulness of the play'. In the same article, Kane chose Crimp:

> He's remorselessly unsentimental and has some very hard edges. His work doesn't scream for attention, but he's one of the few genuine formal innovators writing for the stage. He's constantly

refining his language to find more accurate theatrical expression, marrying rhythm and skill with real beauty. His precision compels.[17]

This suggests something of the mutual regard that these two playwrights had for each other. However, despite her professional success, Kane was deeply troubled, and, in February 1999, she committed suicide.[18]

The Country

As the new millennium began, British culture sent out mixed messages. On the one hand, there was the Millennium Dome, a white elephant which symbolised all that was wrong with New Labour's ignorant and philistine attitude to the arts. On the other hand, British film, television and media – as well as theatre – entered the new era with its fair share of creative and innovative clout. When, in 2000, the Royal Court moved back into its refurbished Sloane Square base, it staged plays by talents such as Conor McPherson, Jim Cartwright and, of course, Crimp. But, having pushed the boundaries of theatrical possibility to the limit with *Attempts on Her Life*, his next play, *The Country*, ostensibly took a more traditional form. As he said, '*Attempts on Her Life* was a play that pulled plays apart, so this is a play where I attempt to put a play back together again.'[19] As well as its form, it also tackled that staple of mainstream theatre, 'an adulterous relationship' which symbolises 'the problems of modern marriage'.[20] *The Country* was originally broadcast on BBC radio in 1997, and when it was put on the main stage of the Court in 2000, the *Independent* quoted Crimp as saying that 'after the chilliness of much of his preceding work, *The Country* is his first stab at a "hot" play', and that 'at a very simple level [it] is about fidelity and infidelity and the different kinds of pain that both might entail and it explores, or it plays with, the relationship between the urban and the pastoral'.[21]

The Country is about a forty-something couple, Richard, a GP, and Corinne, his wife, who have moved to the country with their children. Despite his respectable job, he is a recovering drug addict and they're trying to start a new life. One night, he brings home Rebecca, a twenty-something American, whom he claims to have found unconscious by the roadside. Corinne is suspicious, and, while Rebecca sleeps, she examines her expensive watch. Then, while Richard talks to Morris, his senior partner, on the phone, she discovers Rebecca's bag. When Richard leaves to visit a patient, Corinne questions Rebecca, who turns out to be Richard's lover: he brought her home to recover when she overdosed on the drugs Richard had given her. For her sake, he has neglected another patient. After that man's death, Richard has to face Morris's anger, although the senior doctor covers up the negligence. It also emerges that Richard has brought his family to the country because Rebecca moved there first. She tells Corinne that he bought her the watch. In the last scene, two months later, Richard celebrates Corinne's birthday by giving her an expensive pair of shoes. She then tells him that, the night before, she visited the same place where Rebecca overdosed and that she met Morris. Morris had just found Rebecca's watch there. 'What if I have to spend the rest of my life simulating love?' she asks (p. 366).[22]

Directed by Katie Mitchell, the cast was Juliet Stevenson, playing Corinne with clenched suspicion, balancing a chilly sarcasm with a deeper warmth, Owen Teale, plausible, slippery and finally sinister, and Indira Varma, whose Rebecca had a subdued sensuality and cruel confidence. Casting a non-white actor like Varma also gave her character an otherness that contrasted well with the Anglo-Saxon Englishness of the main couple. Vicki Mortimer's dark, bare and brooding set radiated discomfort, with its crepuscular lighting indicating a night of fear, and only blossomed into sunlight at the end. The noise of the telephone which interrupted Richard and Corinne as Morris phoned to check up on Richard added to the tension. And two rows of rootless, bare trees were suspended above the room. Their presence conveyed a sense of menace, as if they might crash down at any moment, and their wintry sterility suggested stunted feelings. As Stevenson asked the question about 'simulating love', pain radiated from the stage. In the playtext, Crimp mentions the children's game of scissors, paper and stone, an echo of the power games of these unhappy adults.

The play had mixed reviews. Billington saw it as 'an assault on the pastoral myth: the Virgilian idea of the country as a place of order, harmony, continuity', and as 'deeply disturbing'. In *Country Life* magazine, he aptly noted that the play was about 'a sickness at the heart of modern man which we cannot expect the countryside alone to cure', while Taylor said, 'Like Crimp's compelling, microscopically calculated script, the production transmits a powerfully [*sic*] sense of the abyss gaping under this precarious middle-class marriage.' Spencer was more sceptical, observing that Crimp's dramas 'may generate interest, but they never generate warmth' as he 'combines the unsettling menace of the early Pinter plays with the sexual anxiety that informs his mid-period masterpieces'. The metaphor of surgery appealed to some critics: Georgina Brown said that 'Crimp detects the tumour of betrayal with a specialist surgeon's precision and accuracy' while Sam Marlowe praised the 'razor-sharp linguistic precision of these exchanges'. Finally, de Jongh commented on the play's wider resonance: 'At a time when doctors have lost their old aura of sanctity and too many are being dramatically exposed as incompetent, delinquent and heartless, *The Country* hits raw nerves.'[23] As well as being a play about a marriage, it also offered a passing comment on a decaying health service.

One of Crimp's richest and most subtle plays, *The Country* is oblique and disturbing. It is divided into five scenes, each of which has two speakers. Although none of the speeches is ascribed to a named character, the combinations are clear: Richard and Corinne in the first two scenes; then Corinne and Rebecca; then Rebecca and Richard; and finally, Richard and Corinne again. The plot unfolds through a series of stories they tell each other, with important characters – such as Morris, Sophie, the part-time nanny, and the couple's children – kept offstage. The central theme is that modern urbanites tend to see the country as a refuge from the evils of city life. But all their attempts to escape fail – they have simply brought their misery with them. At one point, Rebecca and Corinne talk about the difference between the words 'country' and 'countryside', and this underlines Corinne's alienation. The theme of a rural idyll is repeated with variations. In the first scene, Corinne tells Richard of how Morris visited her in the afternoon, at one point 'chanting to me in another language' (p. 303), which turns out to be a poem by Virgil, the Latin poet of the *Georgics* pastoral. Other references to him follow. And there's also a touch of fantasy. Early on, Corinne says she feels like 'a goat-girl' from a fairy tale (p. 301), then later she's like Cinderella, trying on new shoes. Rebecca uses the language of a bedtime story to describe how Richard gave her drugs and had sex with her:

> The treatment was wild, children. It could take place at any time of the day or night. In any part of the city. In any part of her body. Her body . . . became the city. The doctor learned how to unfold her – like a map.
>
> Until one day the bright young girl decided the treatment would have to end – because the more medicine she took, the more medicine she craved – and besides, she was leaving for the country. (p. 342)[24]

The play is suffused with an enigmatic feel and emotionally raw undercurrents. Often the devices Crimp uses are simple, such as Richard's reiterated reply of 'I have kissed you' to Corinne's request for a kiss. Although there is no doubt about the emotional devastation of Corinne's line about simulating love, Morris's reply – 'I'm sure the two of you will simulate love immaculately' (p. 366) – feels like a judgement on both of them. And his discovery of Rebecca's watch is typically ambiguous: it shows either that Richard is still meeting her, or it is simply a reminder of her existence. What happens between the lines is as significant as what is said. On one level the play shows how language can be used to evade responsibility and to elude reality, on another it packs a satirical punch in its account of urbanites seeking rural bliss, and echoes Cavafy's poem 'The Town': 'New places you will not find, you will not find another sea. / The city will follow you.'[25] Wherever you go, you take your problems with you. Gradually, Richard and Corinne's marriage erodes, and Rebecca, who at first seems to be a victim, emerges as manipulative and forceful, a bearer of truths no one wants to hear. In a house where sharp objects – such as scissors – echo the hard clarity of the language, an oppressive feeling of evasion and of the banality of evil mingles with issues of trust and truth. 'Scissors meet stone; metal meets flesh; stone meets flesh. The country is full of the contention of elements. It has, Corinne explains, "nothing whatsoever to do with Virgil".'[26]

The year 2000 also saw the publication of the first volume of Crimp's collected plays. This collection included a preface which, instead of interpreting the plays, offered a portrait of 'the writer' under the title 'Four Imaginary Characters'. With delightful self-irony, Crimp describes, for example, meeting the actors of his plays: 'The room becomes a tiny theatre in which we improvise delight, modesty, anxiety, mutual respect, with varying degrees of success' (p. vii). Reminiscent of Franz Kafka and Jorge Luis Borges, these short pieces are beautifully written and wonderfully evocative of a writer's life. With their ironic tone, and their slippery slide from autobiography into fiction, and back again, they are characteristically Crimpian.

Face to the Wall

Crimp returned to the Royal Court in March 2002 with *Face to the Wall*, a powerful slice of theatrical minimalism about the media, mass murder and domestic violence. It was, he said, a 'kind of footnote to *Attempts on Her Life*', the result of an attempted but abortive *Attempts on His Life*.[27] This fifteen-minute short begins with three nameless characters discussing a massacre: 'He shoots her through the mouth' (p. 25). Character 1 elaborates on the story, which involves schoolkids being killed, while characters 2 and 3 add suggestions. Although this seems like a private script conference for a film, it suddenly becomes apparent that the characters are performing in public. As the emotional reality of violence hits home, it puts such a strain on 1's memory that he forgets his lines and needs prompting from character 4. Then 1 loses his temper, there's a pause and he resumes, answering questions from 2 and 3 about the killer's motives: he has none of the usual motives. When 1 says that a late postal delivery makes him feel 'angry', the others suggest he might kill the postman. No, replies 1: 'It's not the postman's fault' (p. 33). Then he imagines the postman waking up, as his child brings him a cup of tea, 'but the postman just pushes himself harder against the wall' (p. 34). Now the play flips over completely and a twelve-bar blues song is performed, telling the postman's story. It ends: 'Woke up this morning / Heard my son call / Turned away from the window / Turned my face to the wall. / Son son, I hear what you say / But there just ain't gonna be no deliveries today . . . / (No way)' (p. 36).

Face to the Wall was directed by Katie Mitchell. At the time, she was also directing an experimental production of Jon Fosse's *nightsongs*, with the main stage of the Royal Court reconfigured into a traverse setting. On the same minimalist set, Crimp's play was performed by actors from the *nightsongs* company, and tickets were free if you booked for either *nightsongs* or the Theatre Upstairs show. Peter Wight was the lead, with Sophie Okonedo, Paul Higgins and Gillian Hanna in support. At the end, through the gloom, you could see Crimp himself, pounding the ivories as he accompanied Wight in the thumping twelve-bar blues whose refrain, 'Turned my face to the wall', summed up the loneliness and anger at the play's core. Not many critics reviewed the play. Lyn Gardner in the *Guardian* said that 'the distinction between performance and story, actor and reality are entirely blurred' and, at the end, 'The song curls through the auditorium and into your brain like a whiff of smoke from a still-warm gun', while Ian Johns in *The Times* wrote: 'In Crimp's typically absurdist style, he summed up a media-saturated, pop psychologising age that tries to warp up complex horror in neat packages.'[28]

Crimp's play is utterly simple but profoundly resonant. He gives a vivid snapshot of feelings so awful they are almost beyond words. Then he neatly subverts all the usual explanations of psycho-killing – domestic violence or abuse – and suggests that representing these horrors can put an intolerable strain on writers, actors and directors. Little wonder that most media images of horror are sanitised. During the twelve-bar blues, the most shocking event is when the postman responds to his child's waking him with a cup of tea by throwing it 'RIGHT IN HIS FACE', and then advising him: 'Don't rub on butter / When your skin is all burned' (p. 35). The postman has become a man possessed and his savagery raises troubling questions: are aggressive feelings towards children normal? And, in an age saturated by violent media images, what is normal anyway? With its self-subverting structure, which keeps audiences on their toes by constantly surprising them, this is a gem of a play, as hard and disturbing as a piece of grit in the eye.

By now, Crimp was also responding to global events. After 9/11, world politics were transformed by President George W. Bush's declaration of a War on Terror. One result was the war in Iraq, an invasion led by the USA and Britain that resulted in the fall of its dictator, Saddam Hussein. The invasion began in March 2003 and, in the following month, the Royal Court staged 'War Correspondence', a series of protests which included poems by Tony Harrison, a documentary piece by Caryl Churchill, and short plays by Rebecca Prichard and Crimp. Crimp's *Advice to Iraqi Women* is a savagely satirical piece which lists some domestic dos and don'ts starting with 'The protection of children is a priority. Even a small child on a bike should wear a helmet' and concluding with advice about sunburn: 'Your child will not burn if you are liberal with a reliable [sun]cream.' The contrast between worrying about your child in a safe Western country and the pointlessness of protecting your child in a land bombed by missiles was stark. The piece was read by Stephen Dillane and Sophie Okonedo, who 'solemnly delivered household tips as if addressing westernised bourgeois women. In the context of the week's pictures of maimed mothers and children, the idea of the home as a potential "minefield" moved from metaphor to grisly reality.'[29] But Crimp's response to the War on Terror was not limited to this short piece; it was also the subject of his next play.

Cruel and Tender

The War on Terror soon provoked 'a significant body of theatre work in London'.[30] Nicholas Hytner's inaugural production as artistic director of the National Theatre in 2003 was a contemporary version of Shakespeare's *Henry V*, whose stage images recalled the war in Iraq, and verbatim documentary dramas a year later included David Hare's *Stuff Happens* (National), as well as *Justifying War* and *Guantánamo: Honor Bound to Defend Freedom* (Tricycle Theatre). All this went hand in hand with a renewed interest in Greek tragedy, exemplified by a rare revival – by Katie Mitchell – of Euripides' *Iphigenia at Aulis* (National, 2004), plus two versions of his *Hecuba* (Donmar and RSC, 2005). Arguably, the most interesting of these Greek projects has been Crimp's *Cruel and Tender*, which like *The Misanthrope* was a radical rewriting of a previous play, in this case the *Trachiniae*, Sophocles' 'ancient story of marriage and violence'.[31] Also known as *The Women of Trachis*, the original Greek tragedy tells the legend of Deianeira and Herakles (Hercules), her vainglorious husband. He sacks a city to get his hands on the king's daughter and sends her home as booty. To regain his affections, Deianeira sends him a shirt soaked in the centaur Nessus's blood, but this turns out to be fatally poisonous.

Crimp began by collecting photographs of child soldiers from current wars. He says: 'I couldn't imagine writing a play that wasn't cut, linguistically, culturally, from the material of contemporary life. [. . .] As for the background of terror, political hypocrisy, and a city destroyed for a lie, I didn't have to look very far to discover a congruent universe.'[32] In Crimp's version, Herakles has become the present-day General fighting a War on Terror and his wife is called Amelia. Set in what the stage directions call 'the General and Amelia's temporary home close to an international airport', the play starts with Amelia talking to her chorus: a housekeeper, a physiotherapist and a beautician. She's in trouble. The General, who has been away for a year, has tried to eradicate terror but has overstepped the mark and is now under investigation for war crimes. He sends home the only two survivors of the siege of an African city, which he has reduced to dust. One of them, Laela, is the daughter of an African leader. As Amelia soon discovers, from Richard (a journalist) and despite the spin-doctoring of Jonathan (a politician), she is the General's mistress – and he has destroyed the city to possess her. To get him back, Amelia sends what she imagines is a love potion concealed in a pillow. In fact, it's a small chemical weapon, and when her son James describes its effects, Amelia commits suicide. The General returns, severely disabled, so James takes over the family's affairs, giving up his father to justice. In a final irony, the soldier who makes the arrest is the same man whose life the General once heroically saved.

Commissioned by the Wiener Festwochen, the Chichester Festival and the Young Vic, *Cruel and Tender* was staged by Swiss director Luc Bondy in a co-production between the Young Vic, Bouffes du Nord and Ruhrfestspiele Recklinghausen. Bondy had been fascinated by Sophocles' rarely performed tragedy and encouraged Crimp to take 'the original subject in a new direction'.[33] 'Behind my reason for asking him to translate Sophocles was a desire to provoke him into writing a new play. On the phone he said to me, "You know, I like the play because the constellation of two women and one man in *The Country* is a little bit like this story, because here you also have one woman visited by another who is taking her place." '[34] Working for the first time on an English-language production, Bondy cast the New Zealand film actor Kerry Fox as Amelia. The production, which opened in May 2004 at the Young Vic before its European tour, was notable for the way in which Fox's pent-up anguish and hysteria broke through her worldly cynicism, and for its stage picture of the muscular General, played by Joe Dixon, with his catheter, tubes and urine bag, and his skin blistered by chemicals, staggering onstage, ravaged by gross injuries and a raving mind. You also remember the small touches: an illuminated toy globe, a marble relief of Pan copulating with a goat, the way the women accept the children into their home by stroking their plaited hair, Fox crushing a wine glass in her hand. Designer Richard Peduzzi evoked contemporary icons – gym equipment, stability ball, drinks cabinet, television – while giving the set the colours of an ancient site.

The critics were generally positive. While expressing doubts about Kerry Fox's performance, de Jongh pointed out how the play was part of a trend: 'Classical Greek tragedy is all the rage just now in London' – 'the barbarous warfare and murders, the terrorising and violence [. . .] now strike familiar chords.' Spencer was enthusiastic: 'Nothing I have seen in the theatre to date so resonantly and provocatively captures our bewildering post-9/11 world, with its alarmingly amorphous war against terrorism and the ghastly aftershocks coming out of Iraq.' And Billington located the play in a century-long tradition, that includes Jean-Paul Sartre and Jean Cocteau, of reworking Greek myths: 'Crimp shows that global terrorism is a reality: his point is that it is a hydra-headed monster that cannot be defeated by conventional means.' Although sceptical of the play's politics, John Gross pointed out how 'it's a forceful, carefully worked-out play, and it has been given a brilliant, tightly focused staging [. . .] your nerves are so wound up that every detail counts, down to the smallest gesture or grimace'.[35] Director David Farr sums up: 'I loved the strangeness of Bondy's vision – I thought it described our world in a curious way really extremely well.'[36]

Crimp's subversive modernisation of a Greek tragedy was written in a heightened style and shot through with images, violent, spiky, lyrical, shocking. Although there are numerous references to the War on Terror – such as the General's comparison of terror to a Hydra: 'for every head I have ever severed / two have grown in their place' (p. 58) – the play also tilts the global axis of world politics, substituting an African location for the war in Iraq. Yet it remains thrillingly of the moment. At one point, Amelia tells Jonathan that 'I'm starting to find the way you speak / an atrocity which makes cutting a man's heart out / seem almost humane' (p. 21). That 'almost' speaks volumes. There are many political references: when the dying General sees Laela, he says: 'She thinks I'm a cockroach' (p. 62), the term used for Tutsis by Hutus during the Rwandan genocide of the mid-1990s. At the end of play, Laela reads from Hesiod's *Works and Days*: 'Father will not respect son and the son will despise his father and hurt his father with cruel words' (p. 70). As she does, an African song is sung, and an aircraft passes overhead.

As Crimp says, emphasising his 'own privileged distance from death and dismemberment', the horrific events we hear about from distant lands are 'reflections of our own anxiety. The darker it gets outside, the blacker a window becomes, and the more it turns into a mirror.'[37] As this metaphor suggests, Crimp was becoming increasingly conscious of his ability to articulate current anxieties. In 2005, he told an interviewer that he'd been reading *The War for Muslim Minds*:[38]

> Even the so-called 'new terrorism' has at its root plain old-fashioned social injustice. I've been reading for example how the Saudis first encouraged *Wahhabism* (or *Salafism* – a kind of strict letter-of-the-law fundamentalism) as a way of suppressing unrest in a society with such extremes of poverty and wealth. How can theatre cope? By constantly reminding us that human beings are

more contradictory and strange than any ideologue could ever imagine.[39]

In 2005, the second volume of Crimp's collected plays came out. In his introduction, 'Four Unwelcome Thoughts', he returned, among other things, to the subject of Sarah Kane. In 'When the Writer Kills Himself', he tells a story about how a playwright's suicide affects his fellow writers. Although the writer is male, the comments obviously apply to Kane: 'The texts are short and few in number – after all, the writer was very young, so the body of work is small' (p. xi). Despite their support for the dead writer, the playwrights begin – in an echo of *Attempts on Her Life* – to get annoyed: 'The dead writer is getting on their nerves. This monstrous self-promotion!' (p. xii). In the end, they attend a celebration of the suicide's work but can't help eyeing each other as competitors, and thinking, now that the genius is dead, *'there is no longer any competition'* (p. xiii). It's both a satire on the pieties that follow a real sorrow, and a heartfelt expression of a writer's fiercest instincts. Typically, it crosses the uncertain territory between public appearance and secret feeling.

Fewer Emergencies

The playtext of *Face to the Wall* is published with *Fewer Emergencies*, another short play which has three unnamed characters. This time, they chat: character 2 asks, 'And how are things going?', to which character 1 replies, 'Well things are improving' (p. 41).[40] These improvements include brighter weather, better boating, more confident smiles and a cleaner neighbourhood. Then, suddenly a boy called Bobby is introduced into the conversation. He has a cupboard full of useful things to cope with emergencies, and bizarrely this includes the cities of the world in miniature, tiny trees and a mountain lake. Although Bobby might be threatened by riots and civil unrest, he is safe indoors. Still, even if things are improving, and 'there are fewer emergencies' (p. 46), this safety is illusory: Bobby is wounded by a stray bullet. The original playtext was dated 10 September 2001, the day before 9/11.[41]

Fewer Emergencies, says Crimp, 'was written on one of those very rare days when writing seems effortless. I was renting a room, and in the distance I had a glimpse between the buildings opposite of the river, where boats were gliding by . . . The following day the twin towers in New York were destroyed.'[42] The short play received its first productions in 2004, at the Théâtre National du Chaillot and the Schaubühne in Berlin. A year later, both plays, plus a third – *Whole Blue Sky* (written in order to make this a theatrical outing of acceptable length) – were staged at the Court. All three plays – an hour-long trilogy under the title *Fewer Emergencies* – have the same theme, a radical scepticism about the 'culture of contentment' that pervades the middle classes, making them indifferent not only to the suffering of those in distant lands, but also to the poor of their own country. Although two of them were written before 9/11, they predict the states of emergency that have gripped Western nations during the War on Terror, and their British premiere came two months after the 7/7 terrorist bomb attacks in London.

Director James Macdonald and designer Tom Pye turned the black box Theatre Upstairs into a white box, with white seats, and further subverted expectations by putting the house lights up at the start of the show. Performed by Tanya Moodie, Neil Dudgeon, Paul Hickey and Rachael Blake, the production was very still, with the actors coolly changing position for each scenario. At one point, Moodie doodled; at another, Blake played with a pen. Each speech had the hesitancy of a thought forming in the air. Critic Sam Marlowe praised the production as 'very elegant' and the writing's 'intricate reverberations of its imagery, its tinder-dry humour and above all its overriding sense of acute anxiety', while John Peter got the sense that 'perhaps Crimp is dramatising the eerie feeling you sometimes have that someone out there is imagining your life', and Dominic Cavendish described the show 'as theatre for the iPod generation'. Most reviewers found the evening both mysterious and oddly compelling.[43]

Crimp always seeks to avoid the obvious, a process which he reveals beautifully in these texts, which suggest how the writer's mind thinks up a fictional scenario. As well as being about how suburbanites fend off the emergencies taking place in the wider society, the playlets are also about how narratives are created, and the text can be interpreted – as Macdonald did – as the voices in one person's head.[44] They could also be about different situations, a script meeting perhaps, or a rehearsal, or a party game, or an acting workshop or a publisher's brainstorming session. They show how ideas morph out of each other, out of control – in the words of Beckett, 'always going, always on'. Each story has a twist in the tail: the first subverts the idea of the voice in Bobby's brain; the second, under the pressure of horror, slides from the perpetrator of the massacre to the violent frustrations of his postman; and the third follows Bobby into the wonderland of his possessions – which include 'a shelf full of oak trees', 'a wardrobe full of uranium' and 'souvenir life-size Parthenons' (p. 45) – before wounding him in a freak shooting. In *Whole Blue Sky*, Crimp plays with the audience's expectations about how much a writer knows about their own character; part of *Face to the Wall* is taken up with negating the obvious psychological explanations of violence; and *Fewer Emergencies* takes the theatrical innovations of *Attempts on Her Life* and recreates them in a minor key. These playlets not only seek to make form and content one, but are a sustained satirical attack on some of the platitudes of life at the turn of the new century. Together, they confirm Crimp's position as a radical innovator who articulates some of the central anxieties of British suburban life: a strand of dread – about violence towards women and children, international terrorism, war – runs through his work like a dark stain.

4 'FRENCH IS MY FILM OR TV'

The Chairs, One More Wasted Year, Roberto Zucco, The Maids, The Triumph of Love, The False Servant

As well as writing original dramas, Martin Crimp has also enjoyed a parallel career as a translator of French plays. At times this sideline has threatened to eclipse his main work. 'Here,' wrote a British journalist in 2000, 'he is best known as a wizard of French translation, with a brilliant sequence of adaptations of classics staged over the past four years – Molière's *Le Misanthrope*, Jean Genet's *Les Bonnes*, both at the Young Vic, and a knockabout version of Ionesco's *Les Chaises* for Theatre de Complicite.'[1] Crimp divides his translation work into two categories: complete rewrites and straight translations. *The Misanthrope* and *Cruel and Tender* are 'a rewriting of the original' in which his 'sense of ownership is very strong', while his straight translations are 'owned' by their original writers. His translating career began in 1996 when he adapted *The Misanthrope* 'for my own amusement – it was the first piece for many years which hadn't been commissioned'. Although Crimp originally wrote it in order 'to refresh my brain', soon people 'proposed French texts to me and I became a French translator by default'. If his first translation was a bit of a bluff – he was by no means a fluent French speaker – he soon started to study the language and literature again. His two-track career also had an economic imperative. 'I always say, "Unless you're a genius or mediocre you're not going to write a play a year so you have to do something else." Many people write for film or TV; I translate from French. French is my film or TV.'[2]

The Chairs

After Crimp's enormous success with his sparkling version of *The Misanthrope* (see Chapter 2), it's fitting that his first straight translation should be of an absurdist classic he had known for many years: Eugène Ionesco's *The Chairs* (1952). The play is about an nonagenarian couple, Old Man and Old Woman, who live in a tower on an island. The Old Man is a janitor, and the couple set up chairs for distinguished guests who have come to hear his message to the world, the fruit of a lifetime's experience. When the guests arrive, they are invisible to the audience, and instead the stage fills up with chairs. After an Orator, who will deliver the message, arrives, the couple commit suicide. But the Orator turns out to be a deaf mute. As Martin Esslin pointed out in his account of post-war European modernism, *The Theatre of the Absurd*, the play's theme is 'the incommunicability of a lifetime's experience': it dramatises 'the futility and failure of human existence' and satirises 'the emptiness of polite conversation'. Typically enough, however, Ionesco insisted that the play's subject was 'the chairs themselves'.[3]

Invited to translate the play by Simon McBurney, artistic director of Theatre de Complicite, Crimp accepted because he thought, '"Ah, this would be fun, it would be great fun to work with Simon", and, of course, it was.' Crimp had been 'fascinated by Ionesco when I was younger and it was very interesting to return to him after a long break'.[4] 'One of the strengths of *The Chairs* is the improvisatory nature of the play: Ionesco took two people, a couple of chairs, and waited to see what would happen.' From 'the way that the characters tell stories or try to tell stories, you can see that the text comes from this improvisational spirit'. He'd also read that the Old Man and the Old Woman jump out of the window at the end 'because Ionesco had had enough of them and didn't know how to end the play. So he simply let them jump out of the window.'[5]

The Chairs opened at the Theatre Royal, Bath, in October 1997, before touring and ending up at the Royal Court, at its temporary base in the Duke of York's theatre, the following month. As directed by Complicite's McBurney, it began with a cinematic camera pan, giving the audience the illusion of approaching the old couple's island by boat. Then, the slow accumulation of chairs was accompanied by a cacophony of buzzing flies, water shooting up from the floorboards, orchestral chords, farting, creaking limbs until – in a dazzling *coup de théâtre* – the King arrived and took his place in a box above the stalls (a stunning blaze of light picked out two white gloves on the box's edge). The filling of the empty stage by chairs of all shapes and sizes took place to the music of wild doorbells and buzzers, and was choreographed to mad perfection, with a slow avalanche of chairs appearing from doors and ceiling. By the end, they were hanging off the set and cluttering the stage, making Ionesco's point that the absence of people focuses our attention on life's nothingness. As the 'master of the mop and bucket', Richard Briers, dishevelled in an open-neck shirt, was all toothless grins and childish self-pitying supplications, while Geraldine McEwan was a sag-mawed, shock-haired Mrs Mop, with angular, animal movements and a voice of wailing lamentation. Her falling stockings hugged her fluffy slippers. Even as you laughed at their antics, you felt compassion for these lost souls. When Mick Barnfather's grotesque Orator arrived, he scribbled – a garbled version of 'God is gone' – on a door and grunted repeatedly. Finally, all that remained onstage were empty chairs – a powerful metaphor of theatre itself.

Benedict Nightingale hailed the production as 'a rediscovery of real importance' while Paul Taylor joked that 'for 90 unbroken minutes, *The Chairs* keeps you glued to your seat'.[6] The critics agreed that the production, for all its virtuoso effects, brought out the essential humanity of the play. Just as Ionesco's method was partly an 'attack against fossilised forms of language' so Crimp's translation combined a fresh contemporaneity with respect for the original.[7] As Alastair Macaulay pointed out, 'his translation partly transposes the play into English references ("Henry VII" for

"François I") and into 1990s parlances ("spindoctors") without jarring its essence. As the Old Woman resists her new admirer, she tells him "Find some other path to happiness. Time's wingéd chariot has passed us by."[8] Similarly, the Old Woman's familiar 'poppet' contrasts with the Old Man's 'elevated nonsensical parlance': 'Where are the snows of yesteryear?'[9] Crimp's Ionesco pokes fun at pompous property owners, randy top brass, faded society beauties, arrogant media types, middle-ranking celebrities, royalty and 'the inevitability of progress with the occasional hiccup of genocide'.[10] All in all, it was a fun evening, but a fun evening with bite.

The Chairs was part of the French Theatre Season, which ran from 30 September to 30 December and was an eclectic mix of classics, such as the Comédie-Française's elegant production of Marivaux's *Les Fausses Confidences* at the National, and newer work, such as an English version of Michel Vinaver's *Overboard* at the Orange Tree. *The Chairs* was not the only instance of Crimp's participation in the event – three of his translations were staged that year.

One More Wasted Year

As well as translating *The Chairs*, Crimp was also involved in a project to make other, less familiar, French authors available to the British public. As part of the French Theatre Season, the Royal Court put on a week of new work, 'New Voices from France', in November 1997. These were mainly readings, but included – as part of the Court's first ever New European Writers' Season – a production of Crimp's *One More Wasted Year*, his translation of *Encore une année pour rien* (1997) by Christophe Pellet. The Court's involvement had started in 1996, when Pellet – who had been recommended by the Société des Auteurs et Compositeurs Dramatiques – attended its international summer school, and worked on his play with Crimp and director James Macdonald.[11]

In his introduction to the published playtext, Professor David Bradby pointed out that while the new French writers of the 1990s had a similar bleak view of life to that of British writers, the main difference was their rejection of naturalism and their desire to experiment in form. 'However down-to-earth their subject matter, their writing demonstrates the enduring influence of Beckett and of Genet, of Duras and of Sarraute [. . .] their work seldom tells a linear story, but juxtaposes different time-scales, different viewpoints of the same event.'[12] This emphasis on the theatricality of live performance means that French playwrights tend to avoid using words in a naturalistic way, and leads them to write in a carefully structured manner which embeds clichés of everyday conversation in a poetically layered texture which only really resonates when spoken out loud. Playwright Noëlle Renaude put it well: 'My characters ARE their words – they only exist as they speak – it is through their words that they are present to themselves.'[13]

Pellet's *One More Wasted Year* comprises thirteen short scenes, which begin with childhood friends Antoine and Pierre, who are now twenty-something, meeting, as is their habit, in a café in a town by the sea. Both are equally introspective, with Antoine particularly obsessed with the way he appears to other people, especially Clarisse, their mutual friend. Soon Pierre gets a job and Antoine has a brief fling with Clarisse, who doesn't love him enough to leave her boyfriend. Then Pierre introduces Antoine to a middle-aged Man, a foot fetishist who pays him for indulging his fantasies. Meanwhile, Pierre has a brief fling with Clarisse. Antoine walks in on the couple, leaves, and then quarrels with the Man, after demanding more money for his services. In the end, he is alone.

Commissioned by the Court, the play opened in November 1997, before its French premiere at Criel the following month. Directed by Mary Peate, it was a brightly lit, coolly stylish production with the characters talking over a simple metal café table, and with a square black screen opening and closing between scenes like the blinking eye of a camera while thumping house music covered the scene changes. At other times, the sound of the sea gave an air of solitude to the piece. Paul Bettany was a drawling, plaintive Antoine, Matthew Rhys an egoistically indifferent Pierre and Georgina Sowerby an icily unemotional Clarisse. All three conveyed the essential idea of being obsessed with appearances, dreading being old at the age of thirty, and suffering end-of-millennium angst.

Although the play started off naturalistically, its portrait of self-regarding youth was highly stylised. Antoine's obsession with the sound of his voice, and Clarisse's memory of how her father 'could hear who I'd been with from my voice' (p. 14), both drew attention to the actors' stage presence. At one point, Pierre and the café waitress discussed a cat that's disturbed his sleep. 'What,' she asked, 'if what you heard in the cat's cries was actually the cry for help you'd been neglecting just a little earlier during the day' (p. 23). An imaginative moment briefly transformed the narcissistic solipsism of Pierre's life. At another point, Antoine took the cliché of someone 'being nice' and gave it a good thumping (p. 25). Near the end, Clarisse had a poetic speech about 'withdrawing from the world' (p. 28). Gradually, however, the roar of the sea intruded more and more on the *mise en scène*.

The critics had mixed reactions. Michael Billington put Pellet's play in the context of wider European politics by pointing out that 'even as we edge closer to monetary and political union, drama reflects a distinct sense of place'. For him, the play 'deals with the narcissistic introspection, sexual ambivalence and moral drift' of youth, and 'there is something definably French about the use of the coast and the sea as a poetic metaphor, and about the calm acceptance of fetishism'. John Peter noted the similarity of the characters to Antoine Roquentin, the narrator of Jean-Paul Sartre's *Nausea*, 'stranded in the world but detached from it', with the tone being one of 'anxiety expressed as vanity. I think about my age therefore I am.' The case against the play was made by Macaulay, who called it 'posey, cynical, and depressive [. . .] The translation, by Martin Crimp, seems perfect; but, then, I find Crimp's work posey, cynical, modish, detached, and horrid.' In her review, Susannah Clapp noted that ushers called in the audience by shouting: 'The theatre is open for one more wasted year.'[14]

Roberto Zucco

In November 1997, Crimp's translation of Bernard-Marie Koltès's *Roberto Zucco* (1990) opened at the Royal Shakespeare Company's Other Place in Stratford-upon-Avon, a belated British stage debut for the French playwright's masterpiece. Koltès, who had died of Aids in 1989, a week after his forty-first birthday, completed the play shortly before his death. He had been inspired by seeing a Wanted poster in the Paris Métro in 1988: it showed four photographs of the Italian murderer Roberto Succo, looking different in each one. Later, on a TV news programme, Koltès saw how Succo, after his arrest, managed to escape, climb on to the roof of Treviso prison, speak to journalists, take off his clothes and throw roof tiles at the warders' cars. Koltès was struck by the scene's theatricality. When Pascal Froment, a journalist working on Succo's biography, met Koltès, they discussed their shared interest in the man. Froment sent Koltès a recording of Succo saying, 'To be or not to be [. . .] sooner or later we all have to die.'[15]

In the play, Roberto Zucco starts off in prison, jailed for killing his father. He escapes, strangles his mother, has a brief sexual fling with a young woman, stabs a policeman to death, gets himself beaten up, holds 'an elegant lady' hostage in a park and shoots her teenage boy through the back of the head, before finally being arrested again and imprisoned. He then gives his guards the slip, climbs on to the roof and falls to his death. But a mere synopsis doesn't do justice to the way that Koltès's Zucco is 'a mythical character, a hero like Samson or Goliath, monstrously strong, finally laid low by a stone or a woman' (p. 59) or to the way that the play's realistic portrayals of social exclusion blur into its more philosophical passages. Whoever they are, the characters speak a language that mixes street talk with a dispassionate, dreamy eloquence. Zucco can say, 'I'm dreaming about the immortality of the crab, the slug, and the dung-beetle' (p. 24), but equally, 'Come on. Fight. You gutless bollockless bastard' (p. 22).

Directed by James Macdonald, *Roberto Zucco*'s fifteen snapshot scenes lasted about a hundred minutes. Zubin Varla played the self-contradictory Zucco, earnest, uncertain and blinking in bewilderment at a world where, despite his murders, he is shown as not so different from the cynical cops, drunks, pimps and tarts that inhabit this metropolis. Varla's dark good looks explained women's attraction to Zucco, and his detachment suggested Albert Camus's existential Outsider. The production perfectly captured the play's irony and humour. Publicity photographs showed Varla holding Diana Kent, as Zucco's hostage, with a mixture of desperation and eroticism. That scene was particularly memorable, especially when the crowd began to act as if it was watching a TV show, with their voyeurism making even less moral sense than Zucco's behaviour. In general, the feeling was of events happening while the characters talk about those odd, even cranky, things we all feel and think, yet rarely articulate. Here people speak of their hopes and fears, of dying and loneliness, of casual sex and brutal violence, with moments of beauty and bliss jostling with scenes of cruelty and sadness. The minimalist design, by Jeremy Herbert, was a traverse staging on a white strip which retained after-images of footprints or fallen bodies in a unearthly fluorescence. Under a grey light, doorways were represented by brightly lit red lines; clocks ticked in the background; video clips showed grainy street scenes.

Some critics attacked Koltès for glamorising violence, but most admired the production. Although Nicholas de Jongh only awarded it one star, he appreciated how Zucco assumes 'a fresh persona to suit each situation. He is secret agent and Sorbonne student, peace-loving and violent', and described the show as having 'all the menace of a snake slithering remorselessly towards you'. But while Benedict Nightingale spotted the similarities between Koltès's chaotic metropolis and 'the London of our own young chroniclers of urban ennui', Charles Spencer thought that the dramatic style was too wordy, and advised: 'Come off it, mate, let's get on with the shooting and sex.' Similarly, Robert Hanks didn't appreciate Crimp's use of heightened language and accused him of lapsing 'into translatorese, that version of idiomatic English that seems to have been learnt from a dictionary'.[16]

Although based on a real case, Koltès's *Roberto Zucco* is not a docudrama but a fantasy on urban and mythical themes. His play is prefaced by an extract from an ancient ritual of the cult of Mithras. His isolated anti-hero quotes passages from Victor Hugo, and his death is heralded by an explosion which has *'the blinding brilliance of an atomic explosion'* (p. 53). Zucco is a figure of Artaudian 'excess'.[17] In the labyrinth of the city, and driven by forces he doesn't quite understand, he confronts the Minator and shares the fate of Icarus. Not only does his identity change from scene to scene, but his creator also suggests that any of us could become a killer. Instead of a police thriller, or a psychological study, he gives us a fast-moving meditation on society's attitudes to violence. Here, each family encounter is characterised by brute force: Zucco murders both his parents, and the family of the girl he seduces is equally brutal. When her brother hears about her seduction, he pimps his sister. Koltès's language recalls Bertolt Brecht's *Baal*, and crosses the gamut of emotions 'from desire to disgust'.[18] In the scene entitled 'Ophelia', for example, the language speaks not only of one sexual relationship but of all sexual relationships. Crimp's enjoyable translation encompasses all these meanings, and more.

The Maids

If Crimp seemed to disappear from the scene in 1998, he was back the following year. After a tour, *Roberto Zucco* transferred to

London, and his translations of two other plays were put on, including another modernist classic. *The Maids* (1947), Jean Genet's second play, is a study of the relationship between master and slave. It is often played as a flamboyantly theatrical piece where, following the author's suggestion, male actors play the two maids and their mistress. The intention of Crimp's version, which Katie Mitchell directed at the Young Vic, London, was to find a register of language which could convey realistically the subtle shifts in feelings between Claire and Solange, the maids, and their relationship with Madame.[19] While she is out, they spend each evening in her Louis XV bedroom, taking turns at playing the roles of mistress and maid. 'They are bound to their lady, who is younger and more beautiful than they, by a mixture of affection, erotic love, and deep hatred.'[20] Tensions increase due to their rivalry over a local delivery boy, and because they have caused the arrest of Monsieur, Madame's lover, and they fear being found out. So they decide to kill Madame with a cup of poisoned camomile tea. In the end, they fail, and Claire, taking the role of mistress, drinks the poison. The play has two endings, and in one of them Solange's last words are: 'We're beautiful, wild, free and full of joy!' (p. 80)

Mitchell's production, which opened in July 1999, was a tour de force of exploratory naturalism, beginning in half-lit gloom as Claire and Solange spent several minutes scampering about, whispering, hushing each other and behaving like naughty schoolgirls. Vicki Mortimer's creepily claustrophobic set, filled with the funereal scent of lilies, and the sound of distant birdsong, was so naturalistic that it felt as if even the unopened cupboards were full of cutlery and crockery. And of the right period and design. Anastasia Hille's tensely neurotic Claire and Aisling O'Sullivan's tough, argumentative Solange came across as emotionally bruised; both of them towered over the diminutive Angela Clerkin (Madame), whose vulgar accent, fluffy slippers and sexy underwear showed that she was more nouveau riche than the lady of the maids' fevered imaginations. In a production which lasted 140 minutes without a break, their deeply ingrained self-disgust made sense of their increasingly intense death wish.

Billington appreciated how 'Mitchell now treats Genet's *The Maids* not as an arid essay on the absurdity of being but as a moving study of sisterly obsession' and praised the way Claire and Solange 'still get an erotic thrill out of playing mistress and servant', while Spencer summed up the critics' verdict: 'We are unlikely to see a more deeply felt and intelligent production of this play, but I have to admit that there were long stretches when I suffered agonies of boredom.' Robert Butler argued that 'the trouble with Mitchell's painstaking, archaeological approach to directing – digging ever deeper into the text – is that you can bury what's on the surface', losing the piece's vitality. Dominic Cavendish thought that the 'lucid new translation [. . .] embraces the mock-ceremonious vitality of Genet's maidspeak without making it sound as hideously floral as their aprons', while Jane Edwardes observed that Crimp's translation was 'steeped, not so much in Catholicism, but more in the world of the murder magazines that the two women love to read'.[21]

The Triumph of Love

Two months after *The Maids* opened in south London, Crimp's translation of Marivaux's *The Triumph of Love* (1732) had its premiere north of the river. Pierre Carlet de Chamblain de Marivaux (1688–1763) was a man of letters who lived by investing his fortune in foreign markets until he suffered bankruptcy after a financial crash in 1722. Championing the Moderns over the Ancients in the literary disputes of the time, he developed an innovative writing style in which young love is shown sensitively and obliquely through subtle changes in the register of language. This new delicate style was scorned as '*marivaudage*' by those spectators who preferred the heavy sentimentality of his rivals, but has outlasted his critics: Marivaux is now an established classic. In a newspaper interview, however, James Macdonald pointed out that Britain was 'about 30 years behind France' where Marivaux, 'a liberal humanist', had been rediscovered in the late 1950s.[22]

The Triumph of Love is set in the realm of classical mythology and the plot concerns Léonide, a princess, who plans to restore her kingdom to its rightful owner, a young man called Agis. He has been brought up by Hermocrate, an unmarried middle-aged philosopher who lives with his unmarried sister, Léontine. Knowing that she will be seen as a usurper by Agis, Léonide disguises herself as Phocion, a man, and, with her servant Corine, enters Hermocrate's garden. In order to charm Agis, she has to pretend to be in love with both the middle-aged Léontine and with her brother, who soon discovers that she is a woman. Léonide succeeds in the deception long enough to seduce Agis, who – when he finally finds out who she is – willingly forgives her.

Opening in September 1999 at the trendy Almeida Theatre in Islington, *The Triumph of Love* was sensitively directed by Macdonald, again, in another collaboration with designer Jeremy Herbert. Set amid high hedges and on a sandy floor, with a background of formal gardens, this 120-minute game of love and chance was galvanised by Helen McCrory's passionate Léonide and Chiwetel Ejiofor's sweet-natured Agis. Colin Stinton's Hermocrate was amusingly priggish and self-regarding, while Linda Bassett's prim Léontine appeared in the final scene in a silver gown, low-cut dress and a garland of flowers. In the comic roles were Tony Haygarth as a gloved and bearded Scottish gardener and Antonio Gil-Martinez as a goggle-eyed French Arlequin. As the sands of time ran out, symbolised by a huge sun clock, the riot that love makes with reason ended on a long stunned pause as Léonide exited with Agis, leaving Hermocrate and Léontine with their emotions turned upside down.

Before praising the production as 'a palpable hit', Michael Coveney quoted Voltaire's quip about his rival Marivaux 'weighing flies' eggs on scales made from a spider's web'. Billington commented that, 'as James Macdonald's revival shrewdly realises', Marivaux 'attacks the notion that you can treat people as guinea-pigs while analysing the human heart with merciless precision'. Macaulay wrote a heartfelt appreciation of Helen McCrory and also pointed out that the translation included 'a few of the now standard rude anachronisms by which he [Crimp] and other translators like to trash the spirit of the *ancien régime*, such as "piss off out of it"'. John Gross called Crimp's translation 'colloquial but mercifully not too colloquial', and David Benedict praised it as 'exhilarating'.[23]

The False Servant

After the well-received *Cruel and Tender* (see Chapter 3), Crimp returned to Marivaux for his second translation of 2004, *The False Servant* (1724), which opened in the same month as his version of Sophocles. The action is introduced by the servant Trivelin, who lives on his wits, as do his betters, namely the Chevalier, a beautiful heiress disguised as a son of privilege. By chance, she has meet Lélio, a handsome aristocrat, at a costume ball. Realising that he is the man her family want her to marry, she remains disguised in order to find out what kind of man he really is. Lélio is completely duped, and enjoys telling his new young friend about how he is engaged to a rich middle-aged Countess, but plans to ditch her in favour of a better prospect (the Chevalier herself). But since, because of a prenuptial agreement, he stands to lose a great deal of money if he breaks off the engagement, he asks the Chevalier to seduce the Countess so that it is she who ends their relationship. The Chevalier agrees, and enjoys reducing the proud Countess to submission to his (her) desires. In the end, the Chevalier reveals his (her) deception, to Lélio's irritation and the Countess's alarm. As in *The Triumph of Love*, there is a cruel streak in the story, a discrete touch of sadism.

Jonathan Kent – who had left the Almeida in 2002 after twelve years as joint artistic director with Ian McDiarmid – directed *The False Servant* at the National Theatre, where it opened in May 2004.

Paul Brown's candlelit set was a spectacular array of tarnished silvery mirrors, in which the characters could admire their own reflections, and whose glitter recalled the reign of Louis XIV. Dressed in the classy couture of 1930s Paris, the play opened with Adrian Scarborough's Trivelin stumbling down the aisle, complaining that although he'd really wanted to see Alan Bennett's *The History Boys*, he'd been fobbed off with tickets to see Marivaux: 'French? What do I want with a French play?'[24] After this cheeky opening, the play continued with Nancy Carroll as an androgynous Chevalier and Charlotte Rampling as a dignified, elegant and vulnerable Countess. Anthony Calf played the cheating and cynical Lélio, while Scarborough upstaged everyone with his comic turns. 'So here am I,' he said sardonically, 'playing a minor part, as it were, in a delightful comedy.' Crimp's translation touched some taboos, as when the Chevalier says sardonically, 'I see blood on a regular basis' (p. 58), and its register mixed sophisticated wordplay with the ruder idiom of the lowly characters. An erotic, cruel and not very tender classic, this production got a mixed reception.

Gross, for example, said that 'for much of its length the evening has a cold, elegant charm', while Kate Bassett said that 'this staging is not as deeply disturbing as Neil Bartlett's recent productions of Marivaux', and Georgina Brown found it 'lacklustre' and 'never, alas, as good as it looks'. Billington appreciated the production's design, saying that the Chevalier 'is driven by an androgynous narcissism that links her with the cross-dressing Dietrich and Hepburn heroines of 20th-century cinema'. Carole Woddis called the translation 'bleakly acrid', although Taylor thought it was 'marred only by a few aggressively contemporary notes in the translation ("been there, done that, got the T-shirt")'.[25]

Although Crimp has specialised in translating from the French, he has also worked on shows where the original is in another language. In February 2000, his rhymed translation of Franz Lehár's 1905 operetta *The Merry Widow* for the Metropolitan

Opera House, New York, was successfully staged, directed by Tim Albery and starring Plácido Domingo and Frederica von Stade. In June 2006, his translation of Anton Chekhov's *The Seagull* was produced at the National Theatre, directed by Katie Mitchell and starring Juliet Stevenson and Ben Whishaw. The play was advertised as a 'pared-down version' which 'lays bare its comedy and its cruelty. Whether it's love, sex, fame, or simply a trip into town, each character is denied the thing they most crave.'[26] Also relevant is the programme note, at the end of which Crimp talks about his ailing eighty-year-old mother under the title: 'My Mother and Chekhov'. So although Crimp started his career by using strategies of evasion, always keeping himself at two shifts from reality, by 2006 he had become braver, more open, more personal. And, as if to emphasise that his work is characterised by a diversity of output, Crimp also wrote an original libretto for two singers, *Into the Little Hill*, a chamber piece for composer George Benjamin, scheduled to open at the Paris Opéra in November 2006.

With all of these projects, Crimp has confronted the problems of translation head on: 'Either the translator brings the playwright to the audience, that is, the text is Anglicised; or alternatively, all foreign aspects of the play are left intact and the English audience is asked to travel abroad.'[27] A good translation not only has to make literary sense, it also has to suggest scope for both a director's stage sense and an actor's delivery. 'With theatre translation, the problems of translating literary texts take on a new dimension of complexity, for the text is only one element in the totality of theatre discourse.'[28] The eclipse, in the 1980s, of the academic translator by the playwright translator gives audiences better dialogue at the cost of greater distance from the original. As if to underline this, the question of fidelity to the original is a hardy perennial in British arts journalism. In 2003, for example, a feature article included Crimp in 'that band of writers without whom the great works of global literature would never find their way to the British stage'. Crimp was quoted as saying that Macdonald wanted

Roberto Zucco to retain its Frenchness, and that he used 'the markers in the language like "madame" or "monsieur". We weren't trying to create an imitation English play.' Translating, he added, has an invigorating effect on a writer's style: 'It pushes you towards areas of vocabulary that might not be on your usual menu.'[29] For the programme of *The Misanthrope*, Crimp defended, with a typical dash of self-irony, his translation (literally 'move from one place to another'): 'And if, 300 years later, reflecting the contemporary world has meant taking certain "liberties" with the text, this is only in the belief that – at this distance in time – re-invention, re-writing of one writer's work by another is "fidelity" of the truest and most passionate kind.'[30] Thus 'the problem of the transference of plays from culture to culture is seen not just as a question of translating the text, but of conveying its meaning and adapting its new cultural environment so as to create new meanings'.[31] In this way, the best translations are those which reimagine the original in the context of the present.

5 'DIALOGUE IS INHERENTLY CRUEL'

Martin Crimp in Conversation[1]

South-West London

Aleks Sierz: Let's start at the beginning. When you left university, you obviously decided to become a writer. Could you say a few words about how you first approached the Orange Tree?

Martin Crimp: First, let's just clear up this idea of 'deciding to become'. There wasn't a decision involved because writing for me was a given. Even the word 'writer' seems contestable to me for the reason that it implies a profession or career or structure or something equally worldly, and that way of looking at writing as if it was a career option like, whatever – investment banking – would've been anathema to me at that time, and still is to a certain extent. It is therefore unsurprising that I had no idea about how to approach theatres. I had no idea about what went on; I didn't know what literary managers were. So I sent unsolicited manuscripts of my plays to several theatres just as I sent unsolicited manuscripts [of my prose] to several publishers. One of the theatres was the Orange Tree, which by chance was close to where I lived. Then Tony [Clark] decided to call in some local writers, so, since I lived on the doorstep, I was called in.

AS: What was the name of the unsolicited play that the Orange Tree looked at?

MC: It was called *British Summer Time Ends*. A good title, better than the play itself. And it was a satirical play about a topical subject, the nuclear threat. I'm quite grateful that the play wasn't produced, but I'm equally grateful that I had the chance of getting involved with the Orange Tree.

AS: Did the workshops help you learn the craft of playwriting?

MC: No. There wasn't a teaching programme. All we did was read plays, and then discuss them afterwards. But my clearest memory – really – is sitting on church pews, on these little padded cushions, and sizing up the other writers.[2] That's what it was about.

AS: What were your influences?

(*Pause.*)

MC: To me, looking back, it's obvious that I was heavily influenced by Beckett. Of course, that's a really dangerous influence, but in some ways not a bad one. Better than no influence at all. (*Pause.*) At the same time, I think that something more personal to me was already present – I was going to call it satire, but maybe that's not the right word. Jonathan Swift is, of course, another Irish writer I've always admired and continue to read.

AS: *Living Remains* looks like it's gone through several drafts. You were never the kind of writer who arrives at a workshop with a first draft.

MC: (*Laughs.*) The idea of arriving with something half finished wouldn't have occurred to me. It still doesn't. There's nothing wrong with workshops. But you need to be strong and experienced in order to benefit. At the time, I'd seen very little theatre.[3] So when I started at the Orange Tree, I saw a text as a musical score. And I expected people just to get on with it – and do the music.

AS: It's a good analogy –

MC: It's *quite* a good analogy. (*Pause.*) Because obviously actors are more complex than that, they need more than musicians do. With a musical score, if it says *forte* and someone is playing *piano*, it's easy to correct, but acting is more complicated, and the more experienced you get, the more you realise that perhaps *piano* might be a better choice than *forte*.

AS: (*Laughs.*) But what about other influences?

MC: You have to remember that I spent my adolescence in this Yorkshire backwater. And, from the drama library at school, I had Beckett, and lots of Ionesco. I was a big fan of Ionesco, and I must have put on all sorts of weird plays by him at school: *The Lesson*, *The New Tenant*, and a play about the character Macbett.[4] But I was completely unaware of the new wave of –

AS: Kitchen-sink?

MC: No, not kitchen-sink. Bond-type plays. Angry plays. Political plays. Which I discovered much later. So I was coming from a place which seems to me now quite strange and isolated. At that time, I read Ionesco in English, and Alain Robbe-Grillet, Nathalie Sarraute, books which I found in the York Book and Record Exchange. They didn't always make sense to me; but they left a subliminal mark. As far as British drama was concerned there was definitely a ten-year time gap between me and everybody else.

AS: From the beginning, there's an interest in cruelty and control. How conscious were you of this?

MC: I don't think I was. Particularly. The cruelty is instinctive – if you like. (*Laughs.*) For me, dialogue is inherently cruel. There's something inherently cruel about people talking to each other. And I don't know what that is. My parents' constant arguments as a child possibly have something to do with it.

AS: Clearly, radio was also important.

MC: It was fantastic that BBC Radio was, and still is, a huge supporter of new writing. People such as John Tydeman, who directed my *Three Attempted Acts*, had worked with lots of writers I admired. So there was a continuity, and an acceptance of drama which took place in a territory that was not completely kitchen-sink or soap-opera realism. That was obviously a good thing for me.

AS: Looking at *Three Attempted Acts*, why did you choose this playlet form?

MC: Because the first play I sent to the BBC was a bit too difficult. So they said, 'We like your work; send us something else.' So I sent them a portfolio of short plays because I thought that surely they'd do one of them. And they did all three. And, obviously, there's something in my temperament that enjoys constructing relationships between short pieces.

AS: The relationships between the characters in *Three Attempted Acts* are quite surreal, and you've created this absurdist world . . .

MC: Yes, well. I don't know whether it *is* absurd. (*Pause.*) I think I'd rather use this word of yours: cruel. It's a cruel world. If you're looking for an antecedent for this formalised cruelty, maybe Pozzo's treatment of Lucky is pretty close. And the formality extends to the links between the three pieces – the shuffling of character names – the sense of game-playing. It's something I've recently rediscovered in *Fewer Emergencies*.

AS: The games are perverse – the way the dentist justifies not giving his patient an anaesthetic.

MC: Ah yes, but – you see – that is something that my dentist actually told me. I can remember him saying that providing local anaesthetic would be bad because he could do me more damage if I couldn't respond when things got out of control, for instance if the drill went too deep. So these early plays are not all absurd fantasies – there's a core of observation. Recently I lost the filling with which that dentist tortured me all those years ago, and finally the tooth itself – what was left of it.

AS: Ouch. And good riddance. Already, in these plays, the woman's point of view comes across very strongly. Were you conscious of this at the time?

MC: I don't think I was. And, now you mention it, it reminds me that I've often blundered into subjects without being aware of their ramifications. And maybe that's a good thing when you're young. At that point I wasn't even aware that the rape narrative of *Making Love* was possibly contentious. My work was very instinctive. On the other hand, Marijka's monologue, for example, in *Definitely the Bahamas* consciously delivers a woman's point of view. The character, you might say, collaborates with the author. You have this sad couple who believe that their son is wonderful, and that every woman must love him too. And then the au pair has this speech which demolishes their son and shows him to be a very nasty piece of work.

AS: Yes, the words just tumble out. And there's that bit when it emerges that Michael has a gun because his wife has been raped, and Marijka says: 'Would it not be more appropriate, Mr Taylor, for your wife to carry the gun.'

MC: Aha. Elements of *that* story are based on what I was told about a distant relative of mine. The idea that his wife was raped, therefore *he* has a gun is absolutely true. This is another little seed – if you like – or foreign body around which the rest of the text has grown. Those little chunks of reality are like splinters that get stuck into you, aren't they.

AS: Well, it's interesting that your first play was a female monologue, and that there's a female monologue in *Definitely the Bahamas*, and another in *Four Attempted Acts*, all of which are quite convincing. . .

MC: Well, you'd have to ask a woman about that. You have to remember that the female monologue is one of the great male literary forms, of which the most famous example is maybe Molly Bloom's. Then, of course, there's *Happy Days*, *Footfalls* and *Not I*.[5] So the fact that a man chooses to write a female monologue certainly isn't an assurance of good intentions.

AS: (*Laughs.*) Well, I won't accuse you of good intentions. The fourth attempted act is about music and suicide . . .

MC: Yes. The child prodigy who's no longer a child. And the father who's killed himself. And I'm sure you don't need me to point out to you, Aleks, that this connection between attempting to write, and attempting to destroy oneself or others, will eventually resurface as *Attempts on Her Life*.

AS: What else can we say about the imaginary world of these early plays?

MC: Well, it's a fantasy world, the world of somebody who hasn't yet looked or perhaps I should say lived outside of books for their main inspiration, their main spur to writing. These plays are closed and crystalline, aren't they. Closed worlds. Autistic worlds. Someone needs to give the writer a kick.

AS: With *Dealing with Clair*, that's exactly what happens. Did you feel that too?

MC: Yes. While we were recording one of the wacky or – if you prefer – autistic radio plays, Alec [McCowen] said to me: 'Martin, someone you ought to read, I think you'd really like, is David Mamet.' So I thought, 'OK, I'll read some Mamet.' I did so, *Glengarry Glen Ross*, and of course that was the kick. Suddenly I found this different, high-speed way of writing which immediately dragged me away from these absurdist antecedents – if you like – into the real world. If I was writing a thesis about my work – my worst nightmare, by the way – I would say that in *Dealing with Clair* the old style meets the new style, and the old style is typified by James, who is the slightly baroque, emotionally blank character inhabiting an abstract world, and he meets the new characters I've just discovered, the suburban dwellers whose dialogue has got a completely different fuel in it. You could say I let the banal into my work. And the banal is enormously energising.

AS: In terms of form, there's these two long monologues which bookend the action . . .

MC: In fact, it took me a long time to arrive at that form. The first version is constructed in a slightly different way but it never felt right to end the first act with a phone call.[6] It wasn't until the play came to be reprinted that I finally solved the problem, which was to take Clair's phone monologue from just before the interval and place it right at the start of the play.[7]

AS: These monologues are a joy for actors because there's a lot happening under the surface.

MC: Yes, I'd finally discovered subtext, hadn't I? (*Laughs.*) More important, in my process of self-improvement, was the fact that the plot revolves around a cultural phenomenon which is close to many people's hearts in the UK – the buying and selling of their own homes. So the story is – to borrow terms from the visual arts – representational rather than abstract.

AS: The other notable thing is that it's hard to identify with anybody – were you consciously withholding a character with whom the audience could identify?

MC: I think that the satirical impulse was uppermost. Therefore I see the couple, Mike and Liz, as a satirical version of every couple who have the opportunity to make a great deal of money, agonise over the moral propriety, then go ahead anyway. It's a satirical play.

AS: It's also a murder mystery.

MC: Possibly. (*Pause.*) For a long time the play was a series of images looking for a story. The stuff about the Pyrenees and the gravel had been piling up for a while but it needed this story about property to energise it. As for the murder, you'll have to provide me with the evidence.

AS: Well, that's in the text. You also throw in a few hand grenades – like that bit when Liz says to Mike about him wanting to rape Clair.

MC: You mean when a woman pulls the rug from under the man's feet? I wouldn't call them hand grenades – it's more that something subtextual is suddenly articulated explicitly by one of the characters, either Liz or, in *Definitely the Bahamas*, Marijka.

AS: It's interesting that you say pulling the rug because that's the woman's point of view, whereas from the point of view of the man it is a hand grenade in the sense of something exploding in his face.

MC: A Freudian would probably call it castration.

AS: (*Laughs.*) Yes. Probably. But do you still see Clair as a victim?

MC: This cultural notion of woman as victim is something I don't fully deal with until *Attempts*. Clair is obviously a victim here of masculine predation, but perhaps less obviously she also falls victim to the logic of the market forces she herself is promoting.

AS: Now, *Play with Repeats*, did that come from reading Ouspensky?

MC: Yes, it did. And the idea of attempting to relive your life struck me very strongly. And there's also a passage somewhere in Proust about experience, something to the effect that experience is not what people now might call a learning process – and certainly not a process whereby you learn to change – but it is the process by which you learn what you are unalterably like. (*Laughs*.) So that was an influence. The difficulty of *Play with Repeats* is that when you have a central character who's going to fail, it's vital to feel that this person might succeed. That's the challenge. And I only saw that challenge properly met once, with a production of the play in Romania by Cristian Popescu who removed all its social apparatus, and presented it instead as an existential struggle. It was very interesting to see Tony as a powerful figure fighting against destiny. But that certainly means playing against the text.

AS: In the text, Tony meets these obstacles to change.

MC: Yes, there are two obstacles – internal and external. In the scene at the temporary bus stop, he believes he's changed, become more assertive, but meets an external object – the woman, Heather, who resists him. When he meets Franky, the Human Resources person – and refuses the job she offers him – the obstacle is internal: he can't accept the job because he realises he himself is incapable of change. I'm using the coordinates of an observed world to map my invented world. In fact, somewhere, I actually have Mouhamed Lamine's card. In Paris, there are – or certainly were – lots of North African marabouts giving out these cards that make magical claims which are mirrored now by what we've come to call therapy culture. The coil factory is based on my own – fortunately brief – experience of doing really crap jobs. And pubs are just part of life. As are launderettes. Obviously.

AS: And there's the playful element in Lamine's stories, which are like mini-jokes.

MC: They are, in fact, Sufi stories. The one about death is a very famous one.

AS: How many drafts did you use to do?

(*Pause*.)

MC: Normally what happens is that, in the case of *Dealing with Clair*, first of all there is a vague need to write something, to pursue a particular image. So there's a lot of that sort of writing. On my table, you might see piles of stuff like that, brief exchanges of dialogue. But, of course, that is not a play. Once I have an idea of how that might be incorporated into a narrative – because I do believe in narrative – then the process quickens because I know where I'm going. So then I would expect to make – say – three drafts. And then discuss the work with the director and just do a bit of tweaking. As I've become more experienced, I would also expect to tweak during previews. It's the audience that makes a play live – but also the audience that exposes the dead wood – whether that's in the acting or the directing or, obviously, in the writing.

AS: I think that gives a good impression of your working practice . . .

MC: I'm not sure it does actually. I'd say I just picked that thing about three drafts out of nowhere. Don't believe a word of it. (*Pause.*) I also keep lots of notes in notebooks, which to my eternal frustration have absolutely nothing to do with my plays. Notes from the notebooks have occasionally found their way into my prose pieces, but very rarely into my plays. So it's like a separate strand of writing. All the things to do with plays are on loose sheets, and there are lots of them, and I keep these in files. I like scribbling. I like to make marks. I always write freehand and I only use a computer to produce the final draft.

AS: I noticed that in the typed versions of your plays there are no corrections.

MC: You mean the old pre-computer typescripts? Sam [Walters] used to say, 'You always come along with the finished article impeccably typed.' So there you go. The words on the page are one of my concerns: the way something looks on the page is important to me.

AS: Ever since you saw *Not I* at the Royal Court, that theatre has been a magnet. Was the first time your work was shown there a reading of *Getting Attention*?

MC: Yes, it was. Directed by Philip Howard. It was written after

Play with Repeats. It's quite hard to talk about this play, and quite hard to watch it sometimes. (*Pause.*) It was an uncommissioned play and, at the time I wrote it, there were a number of influences. One was all the media reporting about child abuse. The second thing, which got up my nose, was that many well-known British novelists of the 1980s were becoming fathers, and, in response to fatherhood, they were becoming increasingly sentimental. I remember reading an interview with one of them, which talked about his wonderful study overlooking his lovely garden, and how he looked around 'with concern', when he heard his child, which was being looked after by its nanny, not, you will note, by him. My experience of having children was different. It was not sentimental. It was beautiful, but hard at the same time. When I wrote this play, I wanted to confront physical – and I mean physical rather than the more fashionable sexual – abuse and, at the same time, to explore satirically some of the discourse that surrounds it, which is represented in the play by the neighbours. And, unconsciously perhaps, in the relationship between Nick and Carol, there was a desire to write a hot play about relationships, a sexual relationship between two people, and about a child that gets caught between them. The child is the victim – if you like – of that.

AS: But there's nothing satirical in your portrayal of Nick and Carol.

MC: No, there isn't. It is a direct relationship. I've just been to see a wonderful production, directed by Christophe Rauck, which frees the play from its limited social context, which may have diminished it in its first production.[8] This is partly the writer's fault, because I originally specified a particular stage design, and the play has a particular class background encoded in the writing. But when you take the play into another country, away from the linguistic markers of social class, and make the design less concrete, it grows enormously. And becomes much more a play about this difficult central relationship. Here, it can feel as if you're looking through the wrong end of a telescope; in Paris, it feels as if it's through the right end of the telescope: the relationships come right up at you.

AS: In that final scene, when Sal arrives, I assume that Sharon is already dead.

MC: (*Laughs.*) Well, it's up to you what you assume. It's like the ending of *Dealing with Clair*. What these two plays have in common is a strategy that still makes me cheerful as a writer – the false happy ending. Both have a false happy ending. I don't often like my own writing, but I do like that last scene in *Getting Attention*. The brighter and more cheerful it is, the more it hurts.

AS: One of the reviews said that 'somewhere a scene is missing', which probably means that no one stands up and explains what has happened.

MC: If you're in thriller mode, that's exactly what you have to avoid. I love reading Raymond Chandler but the last ten pages are always a fevered explanation of the previous two hundred – and normally I can't understand them anyway. In *Getting Attention*, I instinctively withheld the voice of authority. Even the social worker Sal is functioning at a low level of authority. Which is why the neighbours' testimonies are given lots of space. Authority is absent from the play and can only be inferred. That's very important in a play about abuse because all you ever hear in the media is the voice of authority, isn't it? The expert pundit wheeled on to tell the public what to think. Although, in fairness to experts, I should say that I once found myself taking part in an after-show discussion in Darmstadt with an expert social worker on the panel and, to my great relief, he confirmed the 'accuracy' of the play – psychologically, I mean, and socially.

AS: After this, you wrote *No One Sees the Video*.

MC: That was the first play to be commissioned by the Royal Court. Max [Stafford-Clark] was artistic director at the time and [literary manager] Kate [Harwood] helped get the commission through. *Getting Attention* appears to have been my calling card. It's almost a Royal Court cliché: an abuse play with characters from a lower socio-economic group.

AS: Quite. But Liz isn't an object of satire either.

MC: Liz is a woman who has countercultural values and finds that they crumble under pressure because they don't have any intellectual underpinning. The adults in this play are all disillusioned, aren't they. Colin finds the world of consumption equally unsatisfying, but has no replacement for it. It's tempting to see these characters as people whose values were formed in the seventies, but then have to live in the world of Margaret Thatcher. That's the social context. The epigraph is by Ernest Gellner, who sees rational scepticism as the only useful intellectual tool for apprehending the world, but at the same time recognises that there is something unsatisfying about it. An emptiness. That resonates strongly with me. There's a similar feeling in Colin's outburst about the void – the void is consumer society, which we all enjoy but which also leaves us with feelings of absence. So perhaps it's a bigger play than it was first perceived to be.

AS: Is there any significance in this being a three-act play?

MC: Form follows function, doesn't it. In *No One Sees the Video*, there's a Chekhovian one-year time lapse between Act Two and Act Three so the division into acts is related to time. But the main rule here is one of symmetry: two lots of people watch each other on video, there are parallel interview scenes, the despised frozen pizza of the first scene is accepted in the last scene.[9] And so on. And the original production expressed what I wanted to express. It showed how people, when they are tested, accept to live in this world. The only person who doesn't is Jo. She doesn't accept it. But of course she's young.

AS: Yes, and the ending is quietly optimistic.

MC: It is, it isn't a false happy ending. It's not that happy therefore it's not false. (*Laughs.*)

AS: Now, I know that *The Treatment* came out of a particularly unhappy experience with film. What was that all about?

MC: I have two memories which can be merged into one: at the start of the 1990s, I was approached to write short films. And the scene was just like that scene in *No One Sees the Video* or the opening of *The Treatment*: one person is being asked questions by another and there's a third person who says nothing, just watches. After I wrote the film scripts I would go to a meeting with the person who had commissioned them, and there would be another person in the room. Who were they? It was never quite clear. I was never introduced to them. It was nothing like my experience of writing for the theatre. It was a different kind of conversation. None of this work ever came to anything. And I realised I was being duped. These short films turned out to be calling cards for ambitious young directors who just wanted material they could shoot. I found the whole experience very humiliating. Then, when they were shooting the second film, I was kindly invited to see the shoot. It was taking place in Manchester. I turned up there and I couldn't find it. I had a phone number, but no one answered. This was a quintessential Martin situation: I get off a train and I'm looking for my film in a big city. And I've no idea where it is. I never found them. And they never found me.

AS: The original title was *Playwright in New York (Broadway Boogie-Woogie)*, wasn't it?

MC: Yes. That came from Lorca's *Poet in New York* and Mondrian's painting, *Broadway Boogie-Woogie*, which represents a grid of right angles so characteristic of Manhattan. But I changed that title – wasn't that a good idea?

AS: (*Laughs.*) Well, *The Treatment* is much more Crimpian. What were your experiences of the New Dramatists exchange?

MC: It was July, very humid. New Dramatists is based in a converted church on West 44th Street, and has this warren of rooms at the top. Often, during these three weeks, I found myself alone in this church. I would return at night, open the big oak doors, and the first thing I did was to patrol the building. I would wander through the basement and make my way up to my little room at the top. Two little rooms in fact. It was incredibly hot. I would have a drink and try to sleep. Afterwards I discovered that these rooms were named after writers: mine was William Inge – who had killed himself. It was strange to be there. And afterwards, strange to imagine having been there. And – of course – I'm not the first European to go to the United States. And we always react in the same way – like a child being shown this weird fairyland. All the clichés are true and yet not true. So *The Treatment* is part of that long tradition of non-Americans using America as a –

AS: Like Baudrillard.

MC: Exactly. You can feel his excitement in that book.[10] He wants to hate the place. After all, it represents his worst fears: death of meaning, loss of the real, et cetera, et cetera. But at the same time he's completely in love with it. And that was exactly my experience. The play was very exciting to write because it genuinely was an improvisation. When I started it, I didn't know who Andrew and Jennifer were. It began with the scene of Anne telling her story to one other person, with a third in the room. And then it's not until the next scene that I, and the audience, find out who those people are. The play was made up as it went on. And I used symmetry as a way of constructing it, with the two taxi scenes for example.

AS: What about the eye imagery?

MC: As I was speeding through the play I grabbed a lot of stuff on the way. Because some scenes took place in the street, I thought of Jacobean tragedy. But the Shakespearean references come from a party I went to at New Dramatists. I remember an elderly writer telling me that his plays were continuously rejected because they were seen as old-fashioned, and I put his joke about Shakespeare into the play.[11] Then I thought of Shakespeare in the Park, and of being blinded as in *King Lear*. The process was like that. I would catch an idea and run with it. But my favourite thing in this play, apart from the scenes with the blind taxi driver – which do fill me with joy – is the scene with the three overlapping conversations. And I particularly enjoy it when I hear it in a foreign language. It's like music. It's tremendous. Just for a moment not to be able to hear individual conversations, but just this mixture of conversations . . . The event onstage is brought about by language. But the language itself doesn't need to be understood. The truth of the scene is elsewhere.

AS: Were you stuck after *The Treatment* because you didn't want to repeat the same formula? Were you conscious of that?

MC: Yes, really conscious. Although I wouldn't call it a formula. (*Pause.*) The fact is, we don't have any trustworthy received forms left in the arts, so every time you have to find a way of starting from scratch.

AS: So you came up with *The Misanthrope*, a radical adaptation of a classic.

MC: Yes, that was fun, wasn't it. It's funny because a play that is so full of energy came out of a period when I was feeling very miserable about writing because although *The Treatment* meant that people took me seriously, I found myself unable to write the next play. So anyway, this play was a great way of sounding off through the persona of Alceste and at the same time having enormous fun with language. At first, I was quite nervous about writing verse, and looked at Caryl [Churchill]'s *Serious Money*, which reminded me that you could have free metre and still have rhyme. The problem, you see, with using regular rhyming couplets in English is that it comes out sounding like Alexander Pope.

AS: It's been revived since at Chichester, so what do you think about it now?

MC: Oh, I love it. The fancy-dress scene at the end makes me smile. (*Pause.*) For me, this was a very precise reading or rewriting or whatever you want to call it of Molière's play. Which is that the protagonist says all the right things, has all the right thoughts, but at the same time is completely wrong. My Alceste is in a cage of his own anger, and he's rattling the bars. But he can't get out of that cage. Can't see beyond it. And, perhaps more disturbingly, doesn't wish to.

AS: Some critics thought that nothing was at stake in your version.

MC: I think that a lot matters here. Truth-telling and its consequences matter. The original production showed very well how Alceste storms out and how the others continue to party. It showed the shallowness of the world he's left behind. Maybe it's impossible in a world that sees values as relative for there to be high stakes, but this form of postmodern moral relativity is exactly what Alceste opposes. One of his targets is moral emptiness and another target is aesthetic emptiness.

AS: Let's go back to this idea of being blocked –

MC: Did I say that? I sometimes think that 'blocked' is one of those words, like 'draft', that gives writing a professional vocabulary that is in fact alien to writing itself as I see it. But it's true that part of learning how to be a writer is that there are gaps. Unless you're lucky enough to be a genius. There are no rules for creativity. Writing is bound up with your identity so it's not so much that you can't write that is frustrating, but it is the sense of disappearing when you can't write that's frustrating. It's like being absent, which is something I write about – I mean, where is Anne?

AS: That's a neat segue. Can you tell me how *Attempts on Her Life* originated?

MC: In the gap between *The Treatment* and *Attempts on Her Life*, I reached a point of frustration with – what you might call – the normal way of writing. I was completely bored with doing 'he said' and 'she said' dialogues. I was frustrated with psychological drama, and bored with so-called cutting-edge theatre. Writing is no good unless there's pleasure in it. And for a while after *The Treatment* I had been getting pleasure from writing little short stories in dialogue form. I felt a real urge to write in this way. And that's how *Attempts* came about. I kept writing pieces like this, and then I'd look at them and say, 'Sorry, Martin, this isn't a play.' Then, in the end, I thought, 'Of course it is.' I was pleased with the writing – it felt entirely like me, Martin-like – and it worked.

AS: Yes, I agree. But did any other plays influence you at the time?

MC: I remember talking to a German critic in Amsterdam, at the premiere of *Attempts on Her Life* there, and he asked me this irritating question, Aleks, about which authors have influenced me, and I said, 'Well, I read a lot of James Joyce at university, but I don't see that that has anything to do with my work now.' And the guy said to me, 'Ah yes, I can see what it has to do with your work: it's the fact that when you construct a play you use motifs as a way of linking things,' and I saw that he was absolutely right. So although I am no longer interested in those Joycean formalistic experiments, something from them has percolated into my work. And it's much easier for other people to see these things than it is for me.

AS: But was there a point when you realised that the form and content was becoming one?

MC: Oh yes. The moment that Anny became a car. It's one of those moments when you sit there, smiling to yourself and you realise that although you have invented this structure which appears at first glance limiting, it is actually limitless. It can be opened out in any direction. If Anny can be a car, she can be anything. And I'm free. (*Laughs.*) And, Tim [Albery] encouraged that freedom. I always felt confident about what he was doing, and he encouraged me, in our discussions before I made a final text for rehearsal, to go as far as I wanted. He was also very professional about what he was delivering to the audience. That night in the very special amphitheatre space at the top of the Ambassadors was the first opening night that I'd enjoyed for a long time.

AS: By now, you must have seen a good many productions.

MC: Yes, I've been invited to several productions. They tend to fall into one of two categories: one is the way that Tim did it, which involves inventing a different world – if you like – for each scenario. The other way, which is the way that Gerhard [Willert] did it in Munich, is to have almost no decor at all. This was also Katie [Mitchell]'s approach in Milan. I suppose it depends what attracts a director most to the play: the discontinuity of its structure, or the continuity of technique – I mean, this writing as narration. I should add that in Milan this extraordinary company of actors had all learned the whole text, and in the big ensembles, no one knew who was going to speak next.

AS: It's the play of yours that threatens to be the most misunderstood. You criticise everything, including yourself –

MC: I should hope so too.

AS: – and it allows no resting place, no consolation. But how would you describe the moral foundation of the play?

MC: You can't ask me to tell you what *Attempts* is all about. All I can say is that it's trying to come to terms with contradictory things in the world and also contradictory things about writing about the world. Maybe that's why it's so symmetrical: it's trying to balance these contradictions. It's clearly about stories – the play is held together by the fact that people are telling stories the whole time. Of course, it is possible to write an anti-narrative play such as *Waiting for Godot*, but even that is underpinned by a story; it just happens not to be told. (*Pause.*) It's easier to say what *Attempts on Her Life* isn't about. One of the things that the play is not about is the media. And when I've seen productions that push it in that direction I feel that its human qualities have somehow been missed. Because although it has the appearance of affectlessness – emotional blankness – it's actually emotionally driven. The last scene brings out the best in directors. As well as Tim's production, which presented it as a beautiful 'Last Supper', I also saw a good production at Goldsmiths College.[12] There were two directors, and an all-female cast, and they divided up the scenarios between them, with half the women having identical blonde wigs and the other half having identical brown wigs. So there was a director for the blondes and a director for the brunettes. But for the last scene they had a very good way of releasing feeling because these young women just took off their wigs, and their natural hair revealed their individuality. It was simple and beautiful.

AS: Let's move on to *The Country*, which was first a radio play.

MC: Yes, accidentally. I realised that it took me longer and longer to write plays, from the initial idea – the little scrap I hide away in the drawer – to the finished play. The original idea for *The Country* was written quite quickly, and its structure was clear. Then I accepted a commission to write a radio play and – unusually for me – I delivered a draft of this work-in-progress. So I was able to explore the text a bit before it became a stage play. The radio version was very close to the stage version, but certain important elements – which gave the final play texture – were missing. So then I struggled with it a bit more, and finished it in 1999.

AS: You wrote the play after a long period of reflection . . .

MC: For reflection, you have to put in brackets 'banging one's head against a brick wall'.

AS: (*Laughs.*) OK, but was the five-act structure there from the start?

MC: Structures are important ways of articulating ideas, or of provoking ideas. It was always clear to me that the structure was going to be one of duologues. And I was also keen that there should be five acts, like those of a classical tragedy.

AS: This was also the first time that you risked telling a retrospective story.

MC: That's true, isn't it. If you think about how you define yourself in respect of the writers you admire, I was aware that certain writers, such as Beckett or Pinter, had taken a turn at one point late in their careers, and began writing plays which were all about looking back. Pinter tried to sustain it in a couple of pieces, *Landscape* and *Silence*. And I think that's dangerous. I have always taken particular care to propel things forward, that's my preferred method. Not looking back. So this is a play that pushes forward constantly and then hits retrospective narration – if you like – in a similar way to *Old Times*.

AS: Oh yes, you directed a reading of *Old Times* for the 'Playwrights' Playwright' series at the Court in 1999. Why did you choose that play?

(*Pause.*)

MC: Good question. I think because I was simply attracted to the writing. It has some really surprising phrases in it, such as: 'I remember you dead.'[13] And there's a couple of passages which describe a decadent party at which people are sitting on a sofa, arguing about China and death. The speeches have an enormous self-contained integrity and energy, they're dense but at the same time transparent, which is difficult to pull off, this thing of being simultaneously clear and complex. (*Pause.*) But, you see, I came to

Pinter quite late. So I found this whole thing about *The Country* being influenced by Pinter a bit strange. It took me by surprise.

AS: *The Country* is full of evasions. It's a play where questions are constantly being answered with other questions.

MC: For me, the question is the ultimate in discomfort. And, in these interviews, Aleks, I'm always uncomfortable because you're asking the questions and I'm answering them. So it's not surprising that, in a play which has its share of discomfort, there should be many questions. I get irritated when people, probably influenced by European philosophy, talk about language being a barrier to communication. And they ask me whether my plays are about a failure to communicate. And I always say, 'No, I don't think so.' They are all about communicating. Obviously, some of my characters would prefer, at certain moments, not to communicate, but that doesn't mean they can't.

AS: And do you think of Richard and Corinne as having the same social background?

MC: Very much so. They're not people who've inherited their middle-class status – they've climbed up to it – which is why they're ill at ease with it, why Richard gives Sophie, who cleans their house, too much money – out of guilt. It was interesting that Luc [Bondy] wanted to be particularly clear about this point, perhaps because in some European countries there's a more recognisable bourgeoisie – to which these characters don't belong. Of course, I also belong to this socially mobile generation. But scarily, and contrary to what you might think, upward social mobility has declined since the sixties and seventies.

AS: And what about the offstage characters, such as Morris?

MC: I really like Morris. I like the way he talks Latin. I did experiment with a scene in which Morris appears but it didn't really work. He's best kept at a distance.

AS: And the way his phone calls always crash in on the conversations.

MC: I've always hated the phone. I always get someone else to answer if I can. For me, it's always an instrument of doom. I've always found writing phone calls tempting, and difficult.

AS: You once mentioned a problem with the last scene.

MC: There's a slight dramaturgical problem in some people's minds due to the discovery of Rebecca's watch. Some people think the play's a thriller, and that Richard has killed Rebecca. I'd like to point out that this is not the case because he couldn't play the last scene if he was a killer. Morris just finds the watch, that's all. You see, objects have a life of their own in plays. Each has its own little story.

AS: So what's the story behind the scissors-paper-stone game?

MC: Actually, the idea for that comes from Debussy's Preludes for piano. They are slightly programmatic, and their titles come not at the beginning, but at the end, preceded by the same little ellipse . . .

AS: Nice. Now, how did *Cruel and Tender* come about?

MC: When Luc directed *The Country* in Zurich I met him to discuss the play, went to some rehearsals, and we got on very well. He was keen to work in England and we had some meetings to decide on a project we both wanted to do. Then, out of the blue, Luc called me and said, 'I'd like you to read two Greek plays.' One was [Euripides'] *The Madness of Herakles* and the other was the *Trachiniae*. So I read both and I called him back and said, 'The one I really like is the *Trachiniae* because it's just so strange, and somehow fits my mentality.' So, we had a deal – even though at that point we had no idea where the thing was going to go.

AS: You know Greek from school. Did you read the original?

MC: In the first place, I whizzed through the Penguin translation, but it was really interesting to look at the Greek original because there are some strange things in it.[14] When Herakles is brought in, injured, the verse goes completely mad. Odd little onomatopoeic phrases express his distress. It must have been the most extraordinary thing at the time because he's using the lyric form that's usually reserved for the chorus. This is why, when he comes in, I have him sing the Billie Holiday number.[15]

AS: Yes, and you also changed the axis from West–East to North–South, and immersed yourself in the mind of the military.

MC: That's right. We started working on this piece in 2003 and the War on Terror was in full swing, but I was concerned not to reduce the play to an anti-war diatribe. So I started with the original. In the play, Herakles is quite repulsive, which is why – I assume – it is so rarely performed. So the challenge was to understand him. I went to the British Library and read books on Vietnam, and post-traumatic stress. There's a book called *Achilles in Vietnam*, which tries to show how accurate Homer was about the behaviour of soldiers in combat.[16] And, of course, the more I read about soldiers, the more I understood that killing hardly ever comes naturally to people, which is why military training is so intense – you have to train young men to behave in this way. And the testimony of returning veterans was particularly disturbing: men who'd get up regularly through the night to 'patrol' their homes, who saw their loved ones as if they were looking through 'a dirty pane of glass' (an image I never found a place for, unfortunately), and of course men with paranoid fixations about 'the government'. So I came to see the General very much as a victim of his political masters. I was also fascinated by the idea – suggested by these lyric outbursts in the Greek text – of him going mad. And this led to playing with the idea that he was pretending to be mad to escape responsibility for his actions.

AS: And Amelia?

MC: In the first half of the play I found myself in the mind of Amelia, whose instincts, unlike my own, are towards the right. And I was pleased with those passages where Amelia demolishes her left-wing student friends, who are childishly happy if a banker gets shot or an army officer gets burned alive. Amelia is strong and direct – like both of my Jennifers, come to think of it. She doesn't have any of the countercultural baggage that haunts my two Lizes. She's also in an impossible situation. And it's exactly the same position as in *The Country*. A man brings another woman right into his wife's house. And the consequences flow from that.

AS: Where did you get the idea of the chemical weapon from?

MC: Water was really important in the gestation of this project.

My meetings with Luc always seemed to be in swimming pools, or lakes – the Limmat in Zurich. Then I was on holiday in France, in the sea, and I was thinking about how to find a modern equivalent of the poisoned shirt, and my daughter had this brilliant idea of psychotropic drugs. It was only after I'd finished writing that I found this web page about recent Pentagon research into using psychotropic drugs to induce happy states to mentally disable your opponents. The dreadful thing is that you just have to dream up some kind of awful imaginary weapon – and someone is already developing it. Of course, in the play Amelia has been tricked. The chemical isn't the 'happy' drug she thinks it is, but one of the organophosphates, which were banned by the Geneva Convention, although countries are still developing them. And we're not talking about Iraq, we're talking about the UK and the USA.

AS: Also, there's all that very vivid imagery, like the 'spike' close to the heart.

MC: These images are things I really value about this piece of work. Someone just sent me the programme from a recent production and one of the passages they printed is that where the General is saying that 'every child with no shoes / wandering up to a checkpoint' is a threat and 'even the lamp on the bedside table / even the coiled filament inside the lamp / is a threat' (p. 58). And I thought, yes, that's good work, the shift I mean from war zone to domestic interior using a visual image. I'm pleased to see this in print – because you don't always feel that about your own work in print. The more I read the Greeks, and about the Greeks, the more I realised that they were people who talked of heroes and gods but the images they used were rooted in the everyday. In *Trachiniae*, Deianeira realises that the love potion is a poison when she sees that the pad of wool she used to apply the liquid has crumbled away and what's left is dust – like the sawdust in a carpenter's workshop.

AS: Could you talk about your most recent plays?

MC: You mean the short ones? Well, the funny thing about those is that they take us right back to the beginning, don't they – to *Three Attempted Acts* – making a triptych. The difference is that *Three Attempted Acts* took, what, maybe four months to write, whereas *Fewer Emergencies*, I mean the *Fewer Emergencies* sequence, was assembled over a number of years, four years, I think. It began with the writing of *Face to the Wall*, which in fact had a production before the trilogy was even completed.[17] And the funny thing was was I took part in it. I played the piano when the song begins. I hadn't been on a stage since the days when I used to put on plays at school, all those weird plays by Ionesco, and Orton – I've suddenly remembered being a big Joe Orton fan when I was sixteen. And that was a great joy thirty-odd years later, to be backstage with the actors in the first London theatre I'd ever visited, waiting in the dark for the black shutter to go up and the whole fucking scary thing to begin.

6 'HEARING THEIR VOICES'

Crimpland's Contours, Playwright's Voice, Linguistic Toolbox and Marks on the Page

When he surveyed the landscape of new writing in contemporary British theatre in 2000, director Dominic Dromgoole singled out Martin Crimp as a writer who, with his 'astonishing skills of draughtsmanship', has 'carved out his own theatrical territory, Crimpland'.[1] To find your way around this imaginary Crimpland, a set of maps might be useful, a way of looking at the verbal markers, the psychological signposts, the social geography and the dramatic territory of the plays.

Crimpland's Contours

When you unfold these maps, the first thing to strike you is the contrast between Crimpland and the more familiar scenery of British drama. Playwright David Greig, who shares with Crimp a European perspective, once compared him with French writers such as Albert Camus: 'Like contemporary British writers such as Martin Crimp or Caryl Churchill,' he wrote, '[Camus's] play is not a realistic representation of the world on the stage – mimicry – but a manipulation of the materials of the stage in order to create a world – theatre.'[2] This emphasis on the theatricality of stage representation is then contrasted with the literal-minded realism that is British theatre's standard mode. According to Greig's historical revisionism, the most popular playwrights in the West

End in the early 1950s were French wordsmiths such as Jean Anouilh rather than British Loamshire playwrights. But then, 'after 1956 and *Look Back in Anger*, a new category of "realistic" work came into being that has since become the default mode of new plays in London':

> This English realism, this 'new writing' genre which has so thrived in subsidised spaces over the past 40 years, attempts, as one of our leading playwrights put it, to 'show the nation to itself'. It seeks out and exposes issues for the public gaze. It voices 'debates' rather like columnists in the broadsheets. Its practitioners are praised for their 'ear' for dialogue as though they were tape recorders or archivists recording the funny way people talk in particular sections of society and editing it into a plausibly illustrative story. English realism prides itself on having no 'style' or 'aesthetic' that might get in the way of the truth. It works with a kind of shorthand naturalism which says, 'This is basically the way I see it.' Distrustful of metaphor, it is a theatre founded on mimicry. In English realism, the real world is brought into the theatre and plonked on the stage like a familiar old sofa.[3]

When Crimp started his career in the early 1980s, the British new-writing scene had exactly this familiar, insular feel. At its worst, English naturalism provides fertile ground for small plays with small casts about small domestic subjects. Like an episode from a soap opera, or a tiny slice of life, realism values an accurate snapshot of real life over metaphor, symbolism or imagination. At its most ambitious, English naturalism blossomed into the 1970s state-of-the-nation play, with its broad speeches about social issues and its firm moral standpoint. At its most experimental, it spawned the new female playwrights of the 1980s, who turned it on its head, creating plays with flashbacks, multiple viewpoints and simultaneously occurring scenes. But the default position of English naturalism has always been the linear, social-realist play – often set on a council estate or in a living room – which tells simple stories by direct means in a healthy, vigorous and muscular way. It is in opposition to this English naturalism that Crimp has worked. But what kind of a writer is he?

Playwright's Voice

Playwrights write dialogue; it's often all they have. But very few writers have a distinctive voice, a way of using words that is so personal and so stylised that it's instantly recognisable. Graham Whybrow, literary manager of the Royal Court, suggests a thought experiment: 'Just imagine taking a single page of a writer's work and throwing it on the floor in a mass of other pages, written by other writers. If you can identify that writer from one page then they have a distinctive voice.'[4] It's this individual feel that runs through all of Crimp's work.

Crimp's language is both natural and stylised. Journalist Robert Butler talks about how dialogue can be both distinctive and convey a multiplicity of meanings: 'Crimp sculpts apparently shapeless speech – overlapping lines, simultaneous conversations, stacked thoughts, delayed replies, hesitations, interruptions and repetitions – into something telling. He is wonderfully attentive to the status details these mannerisms reveal.'[5] The rhythms of Crimp's dialogue are meticulously judged and the absurdities of everyday speech are often pushed to the limit. This is dialogue, but it's polished dialogue; it's dialogue that has been sweated over. As Dromgoole says, 'He is an avid student of speech, its trips, stumbles, losses of way, and occasional scary definiteness.' He also 'catches the insecurities of modern speech, its need for affirmation and terror of exposure'.[6] Typically, 'Crimp thrives on those conversational out-takes that journalists routinely snip away: hesitations, repetitions, exclamations and that minute vibration of the larynx that is described in his stage directions as the "faint laugh".'[7] But while the language of some playwrights is stylised in the direction of artificial clarity, Crimp's style is a complex mix of the certain and the uncertain. Lucy Taylor, who directed a revival of *The Country* (Belgrade Theatre, Coventry, 2005), says, 'Onstage, most people expect a language that has been deliberately simplified – but Crimp's language is very like the way people speak, and so it confuses some people. They're not used to this kind of language in the theatre.'[8] As usual, he defies expectations.

It's always been obvious to Crimp that stage language is not the language of everyday speech. However, the relationship between playtext and everyday speech is supremely important. The stage is no place for abstract language. The energy of dramatic language comes from the spoken word, and every writer has their own way of projecting that into the theatrical space. For Crimp, this was the reason he began writing for theatre: 'I love listening to people talk; I love hearing their voices. I want to hear the spoken word out loud. When I write, I speak it out loud to myself, or you could say I speak out loud what I am writing for myself.'[9] Let's look, and listen, a little closer.

Repetition
Repetition is never just repetition. In stage dialogue, it's a device to convey intensity or comic effect, to describe an insecure character or to indicate unsettled emotion. From the beginning, Crimp understood the uses of repetition. In *Living Remains*, Woman's opening lines are: 'It's me! I remembered! I'm here!', followed by variations of 'Surprise surprise! It's me!' and 'surprise surprise, it's me, hello' (p. 1). Reminiscent of Meg's lines at the start of Pinter's *The Birthday Party*, their repetitive cheeriness is clearly a cover for guilt and anxiety. Crimp's Woman knows that her relationship with her husband is on the brink but she's hanging on to the illusion that things are hunky-dory. Her subsequent repeats of 'Are you sure?' are riddled with pure anxiety.

In *Dealing with Clair*, Mike and Liz's repeated desire 'to behave honourably' (pp. 13, 15) is echoed in James's 'naturally I want to behave honourably' (p. 28). That 'naturally' emphasises the sinister tone of the repetition. Repetition, especially repetition with variation, also creates a musical verbal texture, a reminder of

Crimp's musicality. As critic Irving Wardle said about *No One Sees the Video*: 'With its comic patterns of repetition and distorted response the lines are music to the ear.'[10] Sometimes, the music is a rasp of anguish: in *Play with Repeats*, when Tony realises that he will never achieve promotion at work, he repeats 'You keep saying that' (p. 228). It's the bewilderment of dawning self-knowledge.

Not every critic has been so keen on Crimp's repeats. Jeffrey Wainwright argued that *Getting Attention* 'was devoted to inarticulacy', and quoted a passage of 'inconsequential repetitions' – 'Beer Bob? You'd like a beer wouldn't you? Nick, you ask Bob if he'd like a beer. You would like a beer wouldn't you Bob?' – before sticking in the knife: 'As stage-talk denoting working-class unease and vacancy, this is superannuated.'[11] Presumably, Wainwright was making a political point – people don't talk like this except in the fantasy world of middle-class writers. In this case, however, the subtext of the dialogue is Carol's preoccupation with getting Sharon to sleep, and although she's trying to appear friendly, she really wants Bob to leave so she can be alone with Nick, and perhaps have sex. Here, the repetitive friendliness is dismissive aggression: Carol wants Bob to go. Typically, Crimp's characters are neither vacant nor inarticulate – they're just indirect in the way they choose to communicate. Sounds like real life.

Pause
Pauses or hesitations are clear signs of something else happening. Pauses show characters stopped short by their own ungoverned thoughts, or trying to conceal their real emotions, or simply silent in front of a void. Pauses can be disconcerting, or just hesitant. Most often, a pause reveals a character's awareness of a hidden motive or a subtextual meaning. About *Getting Attention*, academic Peter Kemp pointed out: 'From Pinter [Crimp] has learnt how to place pauses to menacing effect, and one of Nick's intimidatory techniques is to go ominously mute. Amid these conversational hiatuses, a query like "She eaten it yet?" has a sinister echo. Crimp has an exceptionally acute ear for the way in which people talk.'[12]

The influence of Pinter is clear in these sinister effects: in his review of *The Country*, Charles Spencer sums up: 'As in Pinter, much of the dialogue is clipped and self-consciously stichomythic. As in Pinter, single words – "solicitous", "clean" – acquire a sinister resonance. As in Pinter, an unseen character, in this case Richard's partner in the medical practice, Morris, assumes increasing significance.'[13] Of course, Crimp himself, in *The Misanthrope*, makes a joke about Pinteresque pauses (p. 122), and he's also self-critical about too much verbal stylisation: 'I'm wary of the trap of style. Sometimes in Pinter's work you feel that he's doing more Pinter. He's a brilliant, fantastic writer. Some of his late work is really impressive, like *Ashes to Ashes*. But there's just a sense sometimes that he is copying or repeating himself.'[14]

Double meaning

Double meanings either suggest a revealing slip of the tongue or are loaded with deliberate menace. In *Definitely the Bahamas*, the inconsequential chatter is full of Freudian slips, double entendres and suggestiveness: 'It's a shame Frank doesn't have a flash' (p. 45) or Marijka's 'Which meat am I to put out, Mrs Taylor?' (p. 55) or Milly's point about sex 'being rammed down your throat' (p. 57) or the pun on 'stud' (p. 58). Jeremy Kingston put it well when he said, 'Any word with a double meaning may be repeated once or twice to cast a tinge of unease across the summer landscape.'[15] When, in *Dealing with Clair*, Liz says she finds Clair 'cold and rather impenetrable' (p. 41), the sexual connotation is clear. A phrase such as 'we might begin to get on top of one another' (p. 62) refers to both overcrowding and sex. James's 'there's a certain kind of man who would exploit this situation' (pp. 28, 38) is both ambiguous and loaded with menace. His sinister comment about Clair drying herself in the shower – 'once she's thoroughly rubbed' (p. 86) – is lascivious despite its surface banality. It also carries a faint echo of someone being rubbed out, killed.

Some double meanings emphasise the density of Crimp's text. The titles of *Four Attempted Acts* and *Attempts on Her Life* are obvious puns, and so is *The Treatment*. Ditto for *A Variety of Death-Defying Acts* and *Getting Attention*. The very first line of *Dealing with Clair*, a title which also has several meanings – including the ominous sense of eliminating a problem – is about dealing with feelings of aggression (p. 7). Ironically, of course, Clair ends up as the victim of James's murderous aggression. In *The Country*, Richard says he found Rebecca on a deserted 'track' (pp. 312–13), a word which recalls the track marks of a junkie's needle. Its repetition underlines the connection. And it's then echoed in Richard's point that the shower curtain 'makes a noise on its track' (p. 33). These instances also echo James's musings about 'gravel tracks' and railway 'track' (pp. 37, 56). At another point, Corinne's 'I uncovered her' (p. 306) refers to both removing a blanket and to investigating a mystery. Finally, there are puns on the word history – Rebecca studies history (p. 322), the doctor takes a history (p. 342), and the whole play explores its characters' personal histories.

Rhetorical question

Rhetorical questions are questions that don't need an answer. Their form contradicts their content. In *Living Remains*, Crimp's individual voice can already be heard in rhetorical questions such as 'And disappointed, yes?' and 'And cheated, yes?' (p. 3). Typically, in his plays, the question 'What?' has a dozen or more uses. In *Dealing with Clair*, James's 'What? (*loud*) What?' conveys meaning by sheer volume (p. 72). In *Play with Repeats*, the reiterated exchange of 'Wouldn't what?' and 'What?' (p. 196) signals an intensification of the tension. In *No One Sees the Video*, characters are often surprised or flabbergasted by the intrusive nature of market research. At such moments, the verbal equivalent of the sound of a jaw dropping is the characteristic '(What?) Sorry' (p. 28).

Sometimes the rhetorical question is used as a tactical evasion. In *The Country*, some six hundred questions are asked.[16] As director Luc Bondy observed: 'Quite frequently someone is saying something and the other starts off with "What?". I told the actors that the characters are saying "what?" in order to gain time.' And Crimp added: 'Everyone in the play has to think on their feet because so many lies are being told. [. . .] Most of the time they are not listening to each other but calculating something quite different in their heads. And the "what?" is a way of gaining time before they answer.'[17]

Crimp, naturally, is ambiguous about evasive questions. A typically ironic moment in his short story, 'Stage Kiss', goes as follows: ' "Are you happy?" to which I reply "Are you?". In the theatre, these lines could prove unplayable, and I'd suggest a cut' (p. 141).

Echo

Echoes are a feature of Crimpland. For example, the same character names occur again and again. In *Four Attempted Acts*, there is a dizzying whirl of relationships: Mrs Cook recalls the Mr Cook of *Living Remains*. Mr De A, the dentist in the second story, is the offstage suicidal husband in the last. Another patient is Mrs Cook. Mr Petley of *A Variety of Death-Defying Acts* is Yvonne's rapist, Mrs Petley is her neighbour *and* the neighbour of her boyfriend. Mr Lebrun is the mad scientist of the first story and his wife is the victim of the dentist in the second – later, Yvonne plans to stay with them. In the final story, Dr De A must be related to Mr De A, and Mrs De A wants to buy a new white piano from Cooks. The effect of this storm of names is summed up by actor Auriol Smith: 'As an audience you think to yourself, "Oh, is that the same one?" and it sets your mind rolling. But Martin doesn't give you an answer.'[18] In *The Misanthrope*, the name of the female character in Crimp's parody of David Hare's *Skylight* is Clair, which is also the name of another character, and of yet another character in 'Stage Kiss'. A Morris appears in *The Misanthrope*, and so does a Simon. Milly, in *Getting Attention*, mentions her husband Frank, thus recalling the Milly and Frank of *Definitely the Bahamas*. There are Lizes in *Dealing with Clair* and *No One Sees the Video*. In the latter play, Paul is the name of Liz's husband and, wickedly, also the name of her young hotel pickup. Nasty Nicks and strong Johns abound. As well as the obvious Annes in *The Treatment* and *Attempts on Her Life*, the au pair in *Dealing with Clair* is Anna, which is also the name of the builder's wife. Jennifer appears in *The Treatment*, *The Misanthrope*, and is Colin's offstage wife in *No One Sees the Video*. One of Simon's friends in *The Treatment* is called Max (as in *Definitely the Bahamas*). Corinne is the name of a character in Crimp's story, 'The Hotel Stuart', part of 'Little Romance'. Sometimes these characters have an affinity; more often, the names are the same for purely playful reasons.

There are other, subtler, echoes: Amelia's statement in *Cruel and Tender* that she married the first man who remembered her eyes echoes those moments in *One More Wasted Year* in which Antoine obsesses about the colour of his eyes (pp. 10, 12), as well as Clarisse's question: 'What colour are my eyes?' (p. 29). In *The Treatment*, there are countless references to eyes and to blindness – and Anne and Simon disagree about the blueness of her eyes (p. 321).[19] Talking of *Cruel and Tender*, the General's image of being ordered 'to extract terror like a tooth from its own stinking gums' (p. 67) echoes the sadistic dentist in *Four Attempted Acts*.

Sometimes a word seems like a pre-echo: at a pinch, the line 'It's just like old times isn't it?' (p. 16) in *Living Remains* recalls both Pinter's *Old Times* and reminds us – now – that Crimp directed *Old Times* in 1999 for his 'Playwright's Playwright' reading at the Royal Court. Some echoes are images: the image of a dump on which scavenging kids search for food in *A Kind of Arden* resurfaces like a bad dream in the 'Mum and Dad' scenario of *Attempts on Her Life*. Occasionally an echo is explosive: when Clair goes missing, Mike assumes that her fate was 'rape, abduction, or whatever' (p. 80), which echoes his drunken conversation with Liz, which takes a lurch when Liz says: 'You mean you want to rape Clair' (p. 58). Such dropping of an explosive word suggests, without anyone ever saying anything explicit, that Mike has fantasised about having sex with, maybe even raping, Clair. Sometimes, the explosion occurs out of earshot: two characters from *Definitely the Bahamas* get a passing mention in *Dealing with Clair* as Liz scornfully mentions 'some friends of ours' – Max and Poppy – 'who panicked completely and ended up living on a railway' (pp. 16, 95). Typically, the faint laugh here conceals someone else's howl of rage.

Word game

Word games are usually self-reflexive, sometimes impish. One of the pleasures of Crimp's use of language is his sly references to his own art, to the use of words. Almost every play has a comment about language: in *Living Remains*, there is a quirky bit of self-reference in the line, thrice repeated, that Cook 'had a way with words' (p. 20). In *Four Attempted Acts*, Mrs Cook puns on the word language – 'Language is one thing I can't abide' (p. 11) – while in *Play with Repeats*, Tony is trying to convince whoever will listen that 'the language we speak tells us' that 'everything should be possible' (p. 192), and Heather says that 'the words we use are just the shadow of a language that we've lost' (p. 240), while Lawrence, her tutor, talks of 'what could've been, what might've been. These are the tenses of remorse and regret, but also the tenses of endless possibility' (p. 250).

One of the themes of *The Treatment* is the way we use language: Andrew, for example, says: 'words can't fail, Anne, only *we* can fail' (p. 296) and claims that 'The words, just the words, brought the emotion into being' (p. 351), while Jennifer asks the crucial question about the trustworthiness of language: 'What if Anne is lying?' (p. 361). Allied to these ideas about words is the question of the relationship between real characters and their representation. During one discussion, Andrew says, 'We don't often meet real people here.' And then: 'We started out real, but the real-ness has burned out of us' (p. 352). This is a more sophisticated version of the references to theatre in *A Variety of Death-Defying Acts*, when 1st Clown argues that if they were living in a play instead of reality, then 'we would not suffer this anguish of uncertainty. We would simply learn our parts, and then go through the motions, night after night' (p. 49). However crude, it's a Beckettian point.

In *Attempts on Her Life*, the 'Untitled (100 words)' scenario offers a festival of self-reflexive ideas: Anne the artist offers a 'scenario' (p. 255) by objectifying herself; this is theatre 'for a world in which theatre itself has died' (p. 254) and, most satirically, 'It's surely the point that a search of a point is pointless and that the whole point of the exercise – i.e. these attempts on her own life – points to that' (p. 251). The pun on Anne's suicidal 'attempts on her own life' is repeated twice (p. 253). Elsewhere in the play, the suffering Anya is 'beyond words' (p. 217), but that, of course, doesn't stop others from describing her. Then, in *The Country*, Richard says to Rebecca that there is a limit to what you can 'achieve in words', to which she replies: 'There's not a limit to what can be said, only a limit to how honest we are prepared to be' (p. 343). As Crimp comments: 'There is a lot of lying going on – because the truth is often difficult to swallow.'[20]

Linguistic Toolbox

Crimp has a whole toolbox of linguistic devices. He expertly uses evasion, miscommunication and incomprehension. In 1991, Jeremy Kingston argued that, in *Getting Attention*, 'Crimp's dialogue contains trademark sequences of "unpartnered" conversation: two people talking as if the other is listening, though the responses never mesh. It is an image of mutual alienation but, as always, gives an awkwardly contrived feel to a scene.'[21]

In *Definitely the Bahamas*, the conversation between Milly and Frank is certainly unpartnered, with their disagreement about exactly where their son went on holiday being mirrored by other cross-purposes. In *Getting Attention*, the cross-purposes either conceal a character's needs, or help them evade uncomfortable questions.

Crimpian dialogue is harsh, often based on interrogation and characterised by ellipses. In *The Country* almost every question is answered by another. A typical example being:

— Why do you say that: purse?
— Why do I say it?
— Yes. Why do I say it when it's not English?
— What is not English? (p. 297)

Rebecca's judgement on Corinne, 'the more you talk, the less you say' (p. 328), sounds almost like a manifesto. Ever since Crimp discovered the work of David Mamet in the late 1980s, he has used his own 'ear for the nuances of register, etymology and connotation' to create linguistic power plays and ambiguous exchanges of meaning.[22]

Other devices include interjections and self-corrections. One of the most characteristic is the dialogue stutter, as in Tony's nervous 'Not this. Not this life' (p. 206) in *Play with Repeats*. Another device with a Crimpian flavour is the pointed aside, as in Tony's 'and correct me if I'm wrong' (p. 208) or Colin's 'I stand corrected' (p. 26). In *No One Sees the Video*, the market researcher's prompt, 'in your own words', makes a point about manipulation. When Crimp's characters say 'obviously', it usually means the opposite, and that someone is trying to convince another. A delight in cliché and commonplace phrases, often with a sinister or darkly humorous intent, is there from the start: in *Four Attempted Acts*, the creature Billy is 'not past biting the hand that feeds' (p. 3) and the dentist puns grossly when he says, 'I'd bitten off rather more than I'd expected to chew with the abscess' (p. 23). In *No One Sees the Video*, Colin's 'Well I respect that' (p. 44) is an empty cliché, a result of his attempts to charm.

One of the keys to Crimp's tone of voice is the idea, expressed in *No One Sees the Video*, of transcribing interviews. The resulting stops and starts, hesitations and grammatical lapses create a musicality that has been characterised as 'that extraordinarily faithful hyper-realistic dialogue, that also seems strange and otherworldly and poetic, at one and the same time'.[23] As early as

Dealing with Clair, Crimp used the 'is is', a proofreader's nightmare: 'The thing is, is it's an elegant house' (p. 27). By the time Crimp writes *Attempts on Her Life*, the aside or interjection has become a trademark, with countless uses of 'exactly', 'OK' and 'that's right'. He also exploits, especially in *Attempts on Her Life*, the present tense and present continuous tense, which is ambivalent in that it could both be telling a fictional story or recalling a real-life event.

Perhaps the clearest example of Crimp's unique voice is in *Fewer Emergencies*, in which the stops and starts of the dialogue mimic the writer's own thoughts, the way his mind works. These devices all create a distinctive Crimpian flavour: a well-crafted, highly polished and edgy style – elegant, harsh, sardonic – which is both ruthless and entertaining, and which can punctuate a surface normality with sudden glimpses of abject sadness, immense loneliness and spiritual emptiness. 'I use these impersonal interactions,' Crimp once explained, 'but in a context where there are full personalities smouldering away underneath. There is a counterpoint between dialogue, which on the surface is impersonal, and the real human beings underneath.'[24]

Marks on the Page

A writer's distinctive voice is conveyed by marks on the page: one of the arcane pleasures of reading Crimp's work is his stage directions, punctuation and typography. From the start, he has been precision personified. The typed manuscript of *Living Remains* is remarkably clean – clearly the result of several drafts – and the stage directions specify exactly what Crimp had in mind for Woman's dialogue: 'gently', 'vehement', 'slightly petulant', 'with sudden unrestrained violence'; she even 'slaps thigh'. And, of course, 'pause' is differentiated from 'slight pause'. As Crimp's textual practice developed, such luxuriant directions rapidly died out.

By the time of *Dealing with Clair*, the first of Crimp's plays to be published, his unique textual voice was well formed. In a note he says, 'The much overworked indications "pause" "slight pause" etc. have been replaced throughout by a single comma on a separate line. The exact duration of any hiatus must be determined from the context.'[25] The comma on a separate line is a musical notation, and looks less intrusive than having the word 'pause' all over the place. It can be read as a letting go of the strict demands that Beckett or Pinter might make, with their explicit pauses and silences. Crimp offers his directors and actors more choice. There is, however, a hint of truculence in Crimp's note in *Play with Repeats* that a pause 'should no more be ignored than a rest in a musical score' (p. 182). Then, from Caryl Churchill, Crimp learned the usefulness of slashes and dashes as accelerators of dialogue. These create stage dialogue that quickens the dramatic action.

Sometimes stage directions speak volumes: Crimp's characteristic stage direction is the nervy, and self-conscious, *'faint laugh'*. Not an outright laugh, but an indication of complicity: the characters agree on a mutual self-irony, a mutual self-awareness, a mutual subtextual caress. Other stage directions are louder. The last line of *Play with Repeats*, as Tony's co-workers absorb the fact of his death, is *'They surrender to the relentless optimism of the music'* (p. 272). It feels like a small defeat for humanity. In *The Treatment*, the stage direction *'Andrew penetrates her* [Anne] *without any preliminaries'* (p. 334) makes it clear that the sex is about power and possession rather than eroticism.

Sometimes the marks on the page are playful. Crimp's note to *The Misanthrope* states that character names are placed centrally on the page, instead of on the left-hand margin, 'to conform to the printing practice of Molière's time' (p. 104). At other times, they are positively scholastic: in *The Maids*, Crimp distinguishes between the French *tu* and *vous* by using superscript letters – ^{t}you and ^{v}you – which increases the text's density without adding much to meaning. In *Attempts on Her Life*, Crimp had to persuade his publishers to allow him to use small caps – in defiance of house style – for the headings of the scenarios. The trademark symbol – ™ – that occurs in 'The Threat of International Terrorism' every time Barbie or God is mentioned is amusingly tongue-in-cheek, and in 'The New Anny' the small print is literally in small print (p. 239).

The Country's five acts are denoted by Roman numerals, in keeping with the play's references to Latin and Virgil, and the several mentions of scissors in the play correspond to the slashes in the text, which mean that one character cuts into another's speech. Here the lack of character names on the page (a device previously used in *Attempts on Her Life*) has two reasons: 'One: the play is made up of couples, Richard and Corinne are one couple, Richard and Rebecca another couple. For me a couple is always *one* animal.' The sounds come from one and the same animal. The other reason was practical: 'I didn't want always to be reading these names on every single page. Besides, they're not necessary, because they are real dialogues and you don't have to explain who is saying what.'[26]

Crimp's plays, in various ways, embody their writer's voice – and the verbal markers of his theatrical landscape are articulated by the marks on the page. In the context of what David Greig calls 'English realism', it is clear that the language spoken in Crimpland is a highly stylised version of spoken English. The fuel comes from listening to real people talking but the written text is the result of a transformation wrought in the crucible of the writer's imagination, where what has been heard is blended with what has been read, or remembered, and what is thought, or dreamt of. Whether it is the polish of individual lines, or the dramatic compression of feeling, the dialogue in Crimp's plays exists in a constant tension between the language of the everyday and the heightened feelings of dramatic art. He is a master of minimalist stage poetry. As Crimp said almost a decade ago, the problem with Britain's text-based theatre culture is that it often lacks 'a strong sense of theatrical events'. Such 'lightweight' theatre is 'swift to react, it's interested in illuminating different areas of society, but perhaps it's formally conservative'.[27] So although there certainly are moments of postmodern playfulness in Crimp's text-based theatre, the main tradition that he speaks to is that of the high modernism of Ionesco, Beckett, Pinter and Churchill, a tradition of heavyweights who experiment in form and explore theatricality itself. But if these marks on the page are dramatically lifeless until they are articulated by the actors onstage, how do such stage characters relate to one another?

7 'VIEWED WITH HOSTILITY AND SUSPICION'

Troubled Selves, Cruel Liaisons, Modern Marriages, Nuclear Families and Victimised Children

Crimpland is peopled with characters. But just as stage language is not the language of everyday speech, so stage characters are not everyday characters. And, just as the energy of theatrical language comes from the spoken word, so the dramatic integrity of a character comes from closely observed individuals. Like real individuals, fictional individuals are involved in relationships, and dramatic action depends on these staged interactions. What makes them come alive is, of course, the actors. 'The characters in the play invent themselves while they are speaking and through their speech,' says Crimp.[1] Typically, in Crimpland, the dialogue they speak 'appears to be just the tip of the iceberg' and 'calls for a whole world to exist beneath the text. Actors are always disappointed when they look and perhaps discover there is nothing underneath,' he adds, somewhat sardonically.[2] But if actors make characters flesh and blood, the characters created by the playwright's imagination have a different origin: they might be inspired by real people, but – during the process of writing – they are forged from ingredients including isolated memories, psychological insight and philosophical detachment. Chance plays its part. They are, in short, fictions.

Although the quintessentially Crimpian character is the unknowable Anne – a presence ambiguously conjured as an absence – most of his personages are more 'there'. Some of Crimp's characters are satirical creations, some are 'real' individuals, and some a mix of both. They all have relationships, but some common human relationships are notable by their absence. In Crimpland, there are no extended families, no sisters, no brothers, no gay couples, no flat-sharing lads, no girl gangs, and very few fathers and sons. Of all the relationships shown in Crimp's plays, the most common is the married couple, closely followed by the mismatched couple. In scene after scene, one half of each couple sees themselves mirrored in the other, and often their impulse is to smash this mirror. But before you can be one half of a couple, you have to be a self.

Troubled Selves

One is not born but, rather, becomes a self. Crimpland is 'full of hollow folk, all with offstage lives of loneliness and mystery, suddenly trapped together in a mutual obsession'.[3] Like all selves, they can only know themselves by knowing an other, but if the typical Crimpian self is a lonely hollow, what typically happens is that their mutual obsessions lock them into master and slave relationships. Hollow selves are also mysterious selves – they cannot be truly known. One clue to their hollowness lies in the idea of bad faith, their attempts to evade what one cannot evade, to evade what one *is*. The Crimpian self often seems to exist on an uneasy borderland between familiarity and estrangement. On the one hand, they enjoy material security, bodily comfort and safety; on the other, they suffer mental stress, emotional discomfort and fear: 'The appurtenances of comfort are all in place – television sets, cassette recorders, microwaves – but they are at best a distraction from, and at worst a substitute for, self-recognition.'[4] A favourite word used to describe the conversations between these various selves is 'brittle'. On the surface, the exchanges are perfectly civilised and even charming; underneath, there's constant tension and unease. You can feel a whole world of disconcerting feelings: discomforting, discreditable, dishonest . . .

In *Dealing with Clair*, James embodies a satirical idea of an English self: cool, detached, aloof. 'What you call cold,' he says to Liz, 'isn't that just a way of dealing with strangers?' He finds that letting other people know too much about him is unsettling: intimacy, he says repeatedly, is 'stifling' (pp. 41, 84). Of course, this portrait is dramatically ironic – James, after all, has a lot to hide. For him, the city is the perfect ambience. His idea of city life is one of isolated 'strangers' respecting each other at a distance (p. 69). In another scene, Mike echoes this idea of the English character as one which insists on a respectful distance when he says that his sexual interest in women is based on respect, a desire which is quite unlike that of the rapacious Arabs, or Italians (p. 59). Satirically enough, these typical Anglo-Saxon attitudes are finally revealed, in James's case, to be psychopathic. The faint laugh sticks in the throat.

No One Sees the Video shows how the individual self is turned into a 'consumer subject'. Flesh and blood characters find that 'their confessions about their behaviour and their desires as customers allow their interviewers to classify and categorise them according to certain norms and to transform them into computer statistics'.[5] But, as the character of Liz shows, the self can be fluid: Liz begins as a sceptical interviewee and turns into an expert interviewer. Despite her liberal instincts, she is drawn into the ethically suspect world of market research. 'Under the barrage of consumerist interrogation and the intimidating technology of video recording, a sense of personal identity proves fragile.'[6] Yet, despite the fact that her beliefs turn out to be shallow, she also grows closer to her daughter, so the play ends on a faint glimmer of hope. No such hope is available to Tony in *Play with Repeats* – his Faustian and hubristic attempt to relive his life, to realise his self's potential, ends in calamity.

Crimpland is peopled with unpleasant selves, characters the audience cannot easily identify with. Director Lindsay Posner says, 'Martin is one of the few playwrights who can provide an audience with an engaging, entertaining and sometimes challenging evening, without you feeling sympathy for a protagonist.'[7] When his characters share a laugh, pleasure in cruelty is rarely far away. Laughter comes not from enjoyment, but from embarrassment and uncertainty. And, always, there's an 'insistent tone of suppressed violence and hatred between the characters'.[8] In *Dealing with Clair*, for example, when James tells Mike and Liz that he wants to gazump the Harraps' previous offer, Liz remembers Mrs Harrap's disability. Mike calls it 'a crumbly spine', and suddenly *'all three let themselves go with hearty laughter'* (p. 40). Not very nice, but, as David Mamet reminds us, 'a play is not about nice things happening to nice people'.[9] Onstage, scenes such as this are fun, but cruel fun. Beneath the merriment, there's a wriggle of suppressed feelings of fear, disgust and hatred.

Cruel Liaisons

All happy couples resemble each other; each unhappy couple is unhappy in its own way. Sometimes, in these relationships, one is cruel to be kind – cruelty as the twin of care – at other times, one is cruel just for fun. In Crimp's early plays, the couples are all mired in cruel liaisons and perverse situations. Each couple is a double-self, both divided and in conflict. Pain and pleasure cohabit the lives of the Cooks, Lebruns and De As. Mr Petley's circus is crammed with twisted relationships, bringing to mind Proust's definition of love as reciprocal torture. In these early works, almost every liaison is a mismatch. Crimp, says actor Auriol Smith, 'pursues that whole area of control and cruelty really juxtaposed very closely to both a sexual pleasure and an emotional pleasure, and at moments I think the audience are really quite alarmed at their own reaction'.[10] As in Ionesco's *The Lesson*, to give but one obvious example, the relationships are characterised by the spirit of domination, and 'language is shown as an *instrument of power*'.[11] Again, this power is usually sexualised. Especially significant in Crimpland's cruel liaisons is the reciprocity of pain and pleasure, strength and submission. Michael and Irene (*Definitely the Bahamas*) and Max and Poppy (*A Kind of Arden*) clearly have relationships in which the sadistic power of the man has corroded the marriage from the inside, with the women barely able to suppress their tears in front of strangers. Michael's and Max's sadism recalls the sadism of Mr De A, the Ionesco-style dentist who enjoys inflicting pain while pontificating about 'man's manifest indifference to man' (p. 22). Nor do animals get a much better deal. In *Four Attempted Acts*, Mr Lebrun – despite his protestations – is clearly torturing the creature Billy, a vivisectionist nightmare; in *A Variety of Death-Defying Acts*, Miss Kopinski's miniature dog Oscar suffers from an eye disease: 'He's always had that discharge I'm afraid' (p. 59).

As part of a cruel liaison, every sadist needs a masochist. In *Definitely the Bahamas*, it slowly emerges that Michael is not the charming romancer of his parents' imagination, but a predatory sadist trying to force himself on the au pair, who masochistically remains with the family. The relationship between James and Clair, in which both meet in the intimate surroundings of another couple's home, is a classic mismatch: James is male, rich, independent, powerful and verbally domineering; Clair is female, dependent, detached and vulnerable. Yet although she's obviously his victim, she's not merely a loser – in the scene when he makes her play snap, you do feel that her senses have awakened, however momentarily. In *Play with Repeats*, Tony's imagination of his relationship with Heather – expressed, during his sexual assault on her, in the excruciating line: 'I want to marry you. We're going to have children' (p. 244) – is a ghastly mismatch with her sense of reality. Finally, *No One Sees the Video*'s Liz manages to keep Colin at a distance, and, despite his fantasies, he never gets close enough to her teenage daughter to do any damage. But the mismatch still feels dangerous.

In *Getting Attention*, the relationship between Carol and Nick has an autistic quality, with neither really connecting with the other, except sexually. Each is narcissistic, loving their own bodies: she sunbathes; he lifts weights. And Nick is both sadistic and vulnerable. He demands 'respect', while at the same time struggling to keep his self-esteem. Unable to understand children, he responds to Sharon with what he has picked up in his past, the iron rules about discipline that a previous generation imposed on their children. His cruelty clearly comes from his own sense of inadequacy. Carol is also vulnerable. Having been abandoned by one man, she is desperate to please another. She masochistically tolerates his treatment of Sharon. Here, the psychological weaknesses of both seem to fit together like a jigsaw. Unlike some of the couples portrayed in Crimpland, this relationship is much more realistic, a cruel liaison which doesn't feel exaggerated.

Modern Marriages

Modern marriage is a prison with two jailers. Now, after more than thirty years of feminism, you could say it's become an equal-opportunity oppressor, trapping men and women equally in a life of drudgery, emotional anaesthesia and deadening habit. As with Pinter, the typical Crimpian marriage ends up in a home which is just a room, a safe box, while outside 'is a world which is most inexplicable and frightening, curious and alarming'.[12] Crimp's marriages often result in comedies, but menacing ones. The marriage partners are typically in a master and slave relationship, in which these roles are easily swapped over. As in Genet's *The Maids*, for instance, the master–slave relationship is distinctly sado-masochistic: 'loving each other in disgust' (p. 30). Ambivalence, in Crimp's temperament, is the key.

In Crimpland, images of marriage can provoke a dry laugh. In *Four Attempted Acts*, Mrs De A ominously says, 'Adult is not a word we like to use here. It stinks of marriage and mediocrity' (p. 46). In *No One Sees the Video*, both the jargon of market research and the economic basis of marriage are, at one point, simultaneously parodied: 'A household for our purposes consists of certain elements, i.e. we're talking either husband or, failing husband, income' (p. 33). Although Crimp often writes in the great tradition of modernism, which is always sceptical about the sanctity of marriage, he also enjoys satirising this point of view. In *The Misanthrope*, for example, Marcia says, 'Marriage is just an anachronism / darling – a relic of late-twentieth-century capitalism / or didn't you know?' (p. 192).

Crimp's marriages are often based on an unhealthy symbiosis. In *The Treatment*, the typical master–slave relationship is vividly articulated by Jennifer in one of the restaurant scenes: 'Didn't somebody say that the ex-waitress is the shittiest customer and the ex-customer makes the most servile waitress' (p. 301). Near the end, when Nicky tells Jennifer, 'I'm no longer your servant' (p. 376), she's throwing off her chains. More permanent are the two unions, forty-somethings Andrew and Jennifer and twenty-somethings Simon and Anne. These are day and night versions of the same marriage: Andrew and Jennifer have an open marriage, their relationship is full of talk; Simon and Anne have a closed marriage, silence rules their lives. Andrew and Jennifer have been together for sixteen years and are locked in mutual subjugation: in one scene, Jennifer performs fellatio on Andrew – on her knees. For his part, Andrew is thinking not about Jennifer but about Anne (pp. 307–8). In Crimpland, the man's mind is often elsewhere. But Andrew's infidelities are part of his marriage – the couple discuss them; they conspire against whoever is outside the couple. Each sexual infidelity is a not a betrayal of marriage, but its reinforcement. 'Power can deprave relationships without you realising it, and it's tragic that Jennifer and Andrew's relationship exists in a world where they need a more and more extreme stimulus before they actually feel anything.'[13] Of course, Crimp questions this complicity by having Jennifer ask whether Andrew can say the words 'I love you, Anne' 'without to some degree participating in their meaning' (p. 309). In a nice twist, Andrew actually falls in love with Anne, claiming that 'the words, just the words, brought the emotion into being' (p. 351). In the best post-structuralist tradition,

Crimp's Andrew is a victim of language. And, in a neat symmetry, he ends up on his knees to Jennifer – this time psychologically. He threatens to leave, but Jennifer responds, 'The truth is Andrew is that you will never go,' and then she cruelly parodies his future with Anne: 'Have *babies*? Move into the *suburb*? Barbecue a pig on the fourth of *July*? (p. 361). In this case, language creates a reality in which Andrew will not participate.

The other marriage in *The Treatment* is a parody of the first. At first, Anne and Simon seem like a mismatched couple, with Anne determined to escape. Gradually, however, you realise that Anne and Simon are both at home in perversity. They mutually embrace the roles of master and servant, switching between him making her concede physically, and her forcing him into emotional submission. When Anne escapes and Simon finds her, he assumes that she's ashamed (p. 320). At first Anne denies this and then admits: 'I've escaped from the man who silenced and humiliated me. So why does it feel like I'm betraying him?' (p. 332). Why indeed. Both juvenile and perverse, both dependent and stifling, founded on both need and denial, this couple are a nightmare of silence. As Simon says: 'You do not reveal to strangers what goes on between *us*' (p. 357). He silences Anne because she is critical of him (p. 344), not only by putting masking tape on her mouth, but also by denying that she has any life story. You can see why Anne calls him 'emotionally dead' (p. 331). Yet Anne herself cannot bear the fear of freedom – she cannot live outside this dysfunctional couple. She asks Simon, who hates the sight of blood, to hurt Clifford, to enact her revenge. The brutality of their mutual crime not only binds them together for ever, it also means that Anne is now unable to leave their apartment. Home is where the guilt is. Finally, Crimp reveals that Simon not only ties Anne up, he also shops for her, feeds her and washes her. She is pregnant but he has already infantilised her. Simon and Anne's relationship is a dark study in perversity. Yet, in Crimpland, perversion always has a familiar face.

Nuclear Families

The modern nuclear family lives all by itself in a box. Across the social acres of Crimpland, the nuclear family looms large in the foreground, and couples with children are often the objects of parody. In *Definitely the Bahamas*, the pride of Milly and Frank in their son starts off as a cliché and ends up as a droll mockery. In *The Misanthrope*, Crimp's Alceste denounces a shamed politician's 'grinning parody / of the nuclear family' as 'complete with wife, dogs and children' (p. 110). Note that the pets come before the kids. In *The Treatment*, the family is also occasionally the butt of jokes, for example when Anne says, 'I'm pregnant. Of course I have a husband' (p. 380), and once with a racial sting: 'It's one thing to hang out with a black man, but something else again to marry him, to have his children,' says John, who is of course black (p. 325). There is a particular irony in the fact that, in *Attempts on Her Life*, the glowing image of the perfect family – "Cos family is at the heart of things, I guess' (p. 247) – is that of the American survivalists who hate Jews and gays. In another scenario, Mum and Dad, whose daughter sends them photos from the world beyond their suburban box, are reincarnations of Milly and Frank.

In *Dealing with Clair*, Crimp's view of the family is pointedly satirical. Mike and Liz are competitive yuppies, but the sardonic thrust of their dialogue only partly obscures what's happening to them as a couple. They are clearly suspicious of each other. Mike suspects Liz of not taking him seriously and Liz suspects Mike of lusting after Clair, or Anna, or any other woman. And they're both right. At one point, when they embrace, Mike's thinking of Clair, not Liz: 'Sweet, isn't she?' he says (p. 17). The saddest moment comes when, after their drunken sexual banter, Liz finally touches Mike 'gently', only to find that he's already passed out (p. 63). Suspicion's twin emotion is guilt: the cover of the first published edition of *Dealing with Clair* has a picture – R. B. Kitaj's *Study for the World's Body* – of an embracing couple, who have the guilty looks of disturbed wrongdoers.

But the most fully realised family in Crimpland is Richard and Corinne's marriage. Here is suspicion and guilt perfected. Once again, a safe domestic space has been put into question by an intimidating stranger who threatens the couple's private territory. At first, Rebecca appears to be a harmless patient; then she turns into a cancer at the heart of the marriage, 'an obscene foreign body erupting within the bourgeois domestic space'.[14] Typically, she is seen as threatening the children. The picture, however, is subtle, with, for example, the offstage Morris acting as the couple's conscience: the ring of the phone onstage signals the promptings of an external morality. But the relationship between Richard and Rebecca is itself a mismatch, the married lover and the single mistress, the doctor and the student, the dealer and the addict. Richard and Rebecca are as mired in suspicion and guilt as Richard and Corinne. Their game of question and negation results in an absurd dialogue during which he denies that his house is a house (p. 334); that his children have names (p. 340); and even her presence: 'No. You're wrong. You're not here' (p. 341). The drive to negate in *The Country* defies reason. The strategy of each character is not so much self-realisation as self-protection, and the tactics include infantilisation and interrogation, evasion and reiteration – the aim is to subdue the other. If necessary, to cancel them out. Each of the players in this adult game of triangular love – even the wronged wife – uses information as power. Each scene shows the explosive potential of withheld knowledge; each of the three individuals plays with the other, until one of the pair reveals their trump. As director Anne Tipton says, Crimp 'addresses the place of the woman in the home', but in doing so he also shows that in this game of happy families, there are no winners.[15]

Unusually for Crimp, *Cruel and Tender* has a father and son relationship at its heart. Amelia and the General have a grown-up son, James, who provokes her attendants to treat him like a child: 'Don't talk to your / mother like that,' says the Housekeeper (p. 4). This son has cost Amelia her career: 'I abandon my course at university / to become the mother of a child –' (p. 2). At first, this couple seems similar to Andrew and Jennifer in the openness of their trust, but Crimp also emphasises the pain of truth-telling: Amelia compares being told by her husband of his infidelities to 'having my face sprayed with acid' (p. 22). Of course, the General's final betrayal is really too much for even the most honest couple. Not only has he massacred a city for the sake of one young woman, he's also brought her into his home. Although the home is described in stage directions as 'temporary', all the familiar juxtapositions of Crimpland are here: home is safe, warm and familiar; the world is terrifying, catastrophic and unrecognisable. When the two can no longer be kept apart, the result is tragedy. Amelia says of her husband: 'the more he fights terror / the more he creates terror – / and even invites terror – who has no eyelids – / into his own bed' (p. 2). In this wildly metaphorical world, a chemical weapon can be nicknamed 'baby' (p. 30). Contrasting the cosy nuclear family with an alien threat, Crimp compares Amelia's definition of marriage – 'When a man marries a woman, he stays with that woman' – with Laela's: 'A man can have two wives under one blanket' (p. 27). At the end of Bondy's production, says director John Ginman, 'a hesitant-looking James and a calm Laela [are] alone at the back of a darkening stage', 'in a way that seems to signify the beginning of a new family group'.[16] The end is indeed prophetic: 'The children of the people of iron will cheat their parents' (p. 70).

Victimised Children

Childhood is no place for children. The sunny view of children is that they are little innocents; but in Crimpland a dark cloud always casts a long shadow across this idealised landscape. Gradually, children have loomed larger and larger in Crimp's work. Although they rarely appear onstage, they are often present, sometimes insistently present. And, even when they are not, their absence attracts attention. The first hint of Max's cruelty in *Definitely the*

Bahamas comes when his much younger wife, Poppy, confides: 'Max doesn't believe in children' (p. 4). Max, it emerges, has bullied Poppy into not having children because babies are just 'adding to the suffering' of an already cruel world (p. 13). Similarly, Heather's tutor in *Play with Repeats* disputes her idea that the children are the future: 'He says: look at the world, what right do we have to a future?' (p. 238). In *Getting Attention*, every character is obsessed with kids. Milly wonders why 'people like that', meaning Carol, are 'allowed to have children in the first place' (p. 168). Your attitude to children is an index of your humanity.

In Crimpland, children are often victims, often cruelly disabled: in *Living Remains*, Cook's daughter Susie is 'paralysed from the eyes down' (p. 12). Rose, Mrs De A's musical daughter in *Four Attempted Acts*, is dressed as a child, but is too old to be an infant. 'My daughter is not a freak,' insists her mother (p. 47), but actually she is. Or, as Crimp's stage directions indicate, 'just faintly bizarre' (p. 49). One of the painters, an incidental character, in *Getting Attention*, has a sister who 'had a mongol' (p. 163), and *The Treatment*'s blind cab driver says that he was born blind as a punishment for his mother's sexual 'sin' (p. 306) – having a child out of wedlock. Yes, the world of Crimp's plays is coloured by parental anxiety.

Even when children are just mentioned in passing, they are often used as images of the world's injustice. But although the poverty-stricken local kids of *A Kind of Arden* are victims of Third World inequality, the kiddie cult in *Definitely the Bahamas* is more sinister: they get high on drugs, kill large dogs and drink their blood (p. 40). Here the victims have become spectres, the vivid imaginings of Western fear. In *The Treatment*, those fears come home to roost: Anne spots some New York beggars: 'Look at that woman and her *child*. The garbage they are *eating* it' (p. 305). At another moment in the same play, a New York cop reports how an eight-year-old Chinese boy was found, shot through the back of the head (p. 294). The main exception to these images of threatened children is Jo – Liz's daughter – who comes across as both a satire on rebellious teenage attitudes and as a genuine anti-consumer.

It's difficult to work with child actors. During rehearsals for *A Variety of Death-Defying Acts*, the child character didn't survive the first draft.[17] But absent children always manage to make themselves heard: 'The offstage crying of the daughter of Liz and Mike in *Dealing with Clair* signals the self-absorption of her repulsive parents. The future of even a daughter of privilege is bleak.'[18] Richard and Corinne's children are never seen, but they are ever-present, constantly referred to, offstage objects of acute anxiety. Corinne, for example, can barely believe that Richard dares to 'bring this . . . person here while your children are asleep' (p. 314). Within a couple of pages of the start of the play, Corinne says of Rebecca: 'I'm glad she's not my child' (p. 293), an early attempt to infantilise a potential threat. Then, at a critical moment, Corinne runs off, taking the kids. They, after all, are the couple's investment, and Crimp's subtext here suggests the anxiety of privilege.

In Crimpland children can be also used as a weapon in verbal power play: James in *Dealing with Clair* pretends to have several children, then admits to having only one. At one point he asks Clair if she has any and her response of 'You're joking' is a bit of bravado that hides a secret desire: immediately after, 'she has temporarily withdrawn into a private world' (p. 30). James clocks this, and, being a sadist, at another meeting asks her the same question yet again (p. 68).

In *Attempts on Her Life*, children are both abused and abusers. For example, there's a lot of information about the terrorist's childhood: she's a bed-wetter, who's 'cured' by means of electric shocks, an echo of the sadistic parents of *Four Attempted Acts*. Likewise, the children that Anne sees on the rubbish dumps (p. 228) echo those eating garbage in New York and those scavenging in *A Kind of Arden*. In 'The New Anny' scenario, children are mentioned three times: 'our children will be safe and happy in the back seat' (p. 235), 'No child's pelvis is ever shattered by a chance collision' (p. 238), and 'Smoking can harm your unborn child' (p. 239). In *Fewer Emergencies*, children once again pay the price of their parents' careful insulation from the realities of life. As Crimp says: 'The plays are united in fact by images of childhood: in each, children are witnesses of events they can't understand, and are viewed with hostility and suspicion by the adult protagonists. The child's gaze is something that the adults find unbearable.'[19] You can see why Amelia tells her childless attendants what it's like to have kids: 'When you do have children / they'll break into your life / you'll see / like tiny terrorists / who refuse to negotiate' (p. 7). The notion of child soldiers and child terrorists spreads like a lurid stain across the play. It's an extreme image, but a resonant one.

Each self is somebody else's stranger. As well as having distinctly Crimpian characters onstage, the drive of Crimp's plays is provided by encounters between strangers. And when strangers meet, can danger be far away? It's an urban trope. As a writer, Crimp is fascinated by characters who suddenly appear from around the corner. 'I am interested when I don't know where my people come from and this is frequently to be seen in my work.'[20] His plays are full of places where strangers meet – in a dental surgery, by the pool, viewing a house, in a pub, in the street, on a housing estate balcony, at an office, even uninvited guests in the home – and the incident that kick-starts a Crimp play is typically a meeting between strangers. Woman meets a stranger in a graveyard, a dentist treats a patient, Mrs Tighe meets Poppy while on holiday, Clair introduces Mike and Liz to James, Tony has a drink with Nick and Kate, Liz is accosted by a market researcher, Milly and Bob watch Nick and Carol on their estate, Anne tells her story to Andrew and Jennifer, Richard brings Rebecca into his home, and the General sends Laela to his. The interaction of strangers is inherently interesting because rival definitions of the self come into play – and dramatic conflict thrives on this difference. At its best, the confrontation with a stranger is a path to self-knowledge. Clair learns about herself when James persuades her to play snap, Tony understands the limits of his quest for self-improvement when Heather rejects his advances, Andrew learns about his own desires when he falls for Anne, and Corinne understands her own marriage when Rebecca tells her the truth.

In an English realist play, as in traditional drama, 'the author's job is to invent a story, set characters in motion, and give the illusion of not being present: the characters "have lives of their own"'.[21] But as well as writing, and interrogating, this tradition, Crimp has also written pieces, such as *Attempts on Her Life* and *Fewer Emergencies*, in which he forsakes the role of being the invisible puppet master of his characters. 'In these plays the process of invention of story and character is made visible to the audience. The story isn't told "on stage" but in the minds of all the participants – the audience included. It's a bit like injecting the story intravenously, rather than simply swallowing it.'[22] This kind of innovative theatre, says Crimp, reflects a contemporary sensibility:

> I do think part of modern 'identity' is to live inside our heads (a bit like being shut in a car, endlessly driving). In the 19th century the theatre abandoned the street and moved into the tortured drawing-rooms of Ibsen and Feydeau; and in the 20th, Pinter and Beckett transformed it into a mental space, which some writers (the Kane of *Crave* and *4.48 Psychosis*) continued to explore.[23]

In these mental spaces, the relationships between characters are at two shifts from reality, and the actors act a representation of a representation. That's what makes *Attempts on Her Life* and *Fewer Emergencies* so fascinating. Elsewhere, Crimpland people exist in a tension between the imaginary and the actual. Crimp fields a mix of characters, but the typical character is a hollow shell, a self who is either searching desperately for something to fill the void, or is locked in a mutual embrace where one half of the couple's presence gives meaning to the other half's absence. Each marriage is a union of lonely souls; each nuclear family an embattled island. Although a Crimpian character might experience little hugs of self-loathing, or equally recognisable downward spirals of self-hate, there is nothing heroic in their stage presence. You have to struggle to care for them. Identification is hard work. But if many of them bear the marks of their origins in Crimp's satirical impulse, what are the politics of satire?

8 'MY PLAYS EMIT CRITICISM'

Satirical Stance, Ironic Distance, Power Games, Male Gaze, Consumerism and the Culture of Contentment

Crimpland has its own politics. But just as stage language is not the language of everyday speech, and stage characters are not ordinary people, so the politics of Crimp's plays are not those of the state-of-the-nation play, but the politics of the everyday. And their political energy comes from Crimp's critical point of view. As he says, 'My plays emit criticism in the same way that uranium emits radioactivity: but uranium has other properties – and so do these plays.'[1] Crimp's politics are the politics of discomfort, criticising assumptions and questioning norms. Because he is not enslaved to any political ideology, there is no rest from criticism, no comfort zone of certainty. His writing challenges not only the values of society, but also his own values. As Paul Taylor once said about *Attempts on Her Life*: 'The play would not be so disturbing if it did not honourably risk a confusion between its own values and those depicted.'[2] Although Crimp's plays are neither didactic nor preachy, they clearly have a political point of view. During his career, he has witnessed the upsurge in feminist theatre in the 1980s, the decline of political theatre in the 1990s, and its revival, in the form of verbatim theatre, after 9/11. Crimp's work has developed both as a reflection of and in opposition to these trends. But its politics can be best understood as those of a critical modernist, someone who believes that art can make a difference, someone who once summed up his position succinctly as: 'I'm a satirist, not a moralist.'[3] For although he's not a moralist in the sense of 'pronouncing a series of moral judgements', he does mercilessly expose the folly of 'a number of clearly recognisable contemporary attitudes'.[4]

But the politics of satire is tricky territory. For while satire is the key to Crimp's temperament, so is irony. As he points out, 'Irony goes hand in hand with satire.'[5] And there's surely a contradiction between a satirical outlook and an ironic tone. Satire is warmly engaged – you can't be a satirist if you don't care – while irony is a kind of detached knowingness. If satire is modernist, then irony is postmodernist. Crimp has certainly been aware of this problem: 'I remember reading one of Koltès's little notes stating that all dialogue is ironic. I'm still trying to work out exactly what that means. Perhaps what he means is that seeing anything framed in the context of the theatre implies that you have a distance from it.'[6] It's certainly true that, in the theatre, both satire and irony depend on audience complicity. But because both are indirect ways of saying what you mean, the risk is that some audiences might not get the message. Still, when they do, the result is a collective political knowing, a shared understanding.

Satirical Stance

Satire is a mirror in which you see everyone's face but your own. Satire attacks human vice, folly or stupidity by using irony, derision, ridicule, sarcasm, parody or caustic wit. It aims to expose bad faith in all its guises – hypocrisy, pretension, vanity, pedantry, idolatry, bigotry, sentimentality. And, by such exposure, to encourage change. Satire puts ideas and attitudes under the gaudy light of humour, and enjoys seeing them squirm. It articulates cultural anxieties, and is the most political of comic forms. But whereas Horatian satire is gentle, exposing the truth with a faint smile, amused but not scornful, Juvenalian satire roars with savage indignation, splashing vitriol, lacerating with bitter invective. When satire is purely playful it takes the guise of parody. When it is deadly serious, it elevates cruelty to a political art. Crimp has been influenced by both the Horatian satire of Shakespeare and Jonathan Swift's Juvenalian outpourings: 'One of my favourite pieces of writing,' he says, 'because of its mix of anger and the beauty of the writing, is Swift's *Modest Proposal*,' in which Swift argues that eating babies would be a solution to overpopulation in Ireland, and hunger in England.[7] A similar mixture of rage and elegance motivates, for example, Crimp's Alceste.

From the start, Crimp had a satirical impulse: *Living Remains* is both a satire on a marriage and a catalogue of humorous asides, one of which mildly describes Mr Cook as having 'a house in the country [. . .] he goes there at weekends and shoots animals with his gun' (p. 8). Then, in plays such as *Dealing with Clair*, Crimp's satirical glance ranges over the lifestyle of the newly rich and upwardly mobile yuppies such as Mike and Liz, showing how the path to greed is paved with good pretentions.

In *Attempts on Her Life*, the scenario 'Untitled (100 Words)', where the critics discuss the artist Anne's work, shows Crimp at his satirical best. Clearly, it's 'a satire of those mind-numbing *Late Review*-type conversations', but one which mocks not only the work of contemporary artists, but also both the commentary of critics and, even more self-critically, the way a playwright might go about staging this satire.[8] When Crimp writes lines such as 'theatre – that's right – for a world in which theatre itself has died' (p. 254), he is clearly mocking himself as well as pre-empting criticism of his own work. At its best, political satire is a restless questioning quest. In the much-quoted paragraph when Crimp riffs on the idea that 'it's *surely* the point that the point that's being made is *not* the point and never has in fact *been* the point' (p. 251), this at first feels like a manifesto for what the play is about – and many critics read it like that. But Crimp is more savvy than that, and the passage is also a parody of postmodernism and a skit on his own play. At moments like this, Crimpian satire relentlessly resembles an exhilarating and infinite hall of mirrors, where, as Royal Court literary manager Graham Whybrow says, 'Crimp displays his fascination with the slipperiness of the sign'.[9] Meaning, and knowability, come under intolerable strain. At its best, Crimp's satire is both joyfully playful and intensely critical: 'Even if there is a point, he will then suggest that there isn't, and question why there isn't.'[10] It's a high-risk strategy, but a compelling one.

Crimp's writing has a political edge, but as well as being critical of power it is also sceptical about radical politics. In *The Treatment*, there's a gentle satire on 1960s activism when John remembers how he and Jennifer used to lie down in the street to protest: 'We felt that our actions might transform the world. We felt that if our own relationships were free of the tensions of race, sex, money then the world itself would alter.' As Crimp makes clear, John *'laughs at the naivety'* of such ideas (p. 325). In *Play with Repeats*, Heather talks about her pro-feminist tutor in a spot-on parody of 'right-on' attitudes to women (p. 237), and then there's a lengthy burlesque on catastrophist views of civilisation in the guise of her tutor's book, *A World in Decay* (pp. 45–7). This is all good-natured stuff compared to Crimp's exasperated condemnation, in *The Misanthrope*, of political playwrights who ' "workshop" a revolution': 'The political complexities / of several centuries / are thoroughly investigated for about ten days' (p. 138). Explicitly political theatre, he implies, is just too easy. And, in *Cruel and Tender*, radical student politics get an even sharper tongue-lashing, especially the squatters who mouth slogans: ' "Overthrow the state" / "kill the pigs" blah blah blah / "liberate" – by which they meant fuck – / women' (p. 36). Here, Crimp gives voice to both a right-wing military wife and to a female scepticism about the political posturing of men.

In *The Misanthrope*, the joy of its verbal high jinks lies in its lampooning of vice. But although Alceste mocks, with deadly sarcasm and wit, the follies of the media scene, he is himself undermined in the end. No one escapes the taint of moral culpability, not even Crimp. He is aware of the implications of a satirical stance. So much so that, sometimes, he clearly thinks that satire is not enough. When, in *No One Sees the Video*, Nigel behaves like a sexist, his words might be a parody of traditional male attitudes to women, but Crimp underlines the point theatrically when Liz suddenly *'throws her drink in his face'* (p. 69). For a moment, one action speaks louder than words.

Ironical Distance

Irony is a language game. It means saying the opposite of what you mean. So more is meant than meets the ear. As a literary device, it loves artful double meanings. It is inherently critical because it draws attention to the gap between the act of saying and what is actually said. And, by playing with meaning, it questions what we take for granted. At times, irony implies a nostalgia for a time when everything was as true as it appears, even if such a utopian time has never existed. At its worst, irony means having it both ways, an English speciality. Allergic to literalism – its words express something different from their literal meaning – irony conveys incongruity, humour and sarcasm. The user of irony assumes that their real meaning will be understood. Dramatic irony occurs when the audience knows facts of which the characters in the play are ignorant. In fact, irony postulates a double audience, some hearing without understanding, while others understand both the meaning and the bafflement of those who don't. Crimp's irony could be described as a sceptic's irony. Having once said, 'Irony is just me,' he values scepticism because

> it's not the same as postmodernism, because postmodernism – it seems to me – is an embrace of the strange contradictions and even injustices which are so deeply part of our culture, both locally and globally, whereas scepticism is quite different because it does imply a moral position – not an ideological position, but a position of what you might think is right or wrong. That's what my irony is about.[11]

Typically, Crimp's irony is complex, referring both to the fate of his characters and to theatre as an art. A good example occurs within a couple of minutes of the start of *Play with Repeats*, when Nick's girlfriend tells Tony: 'We're actors', while Tony objects that life is not an act. He adds, 'An actor is repeating a part, but this is different' (p. 185) – the double irony here is that the exchange is spoken by actors and that Tony is about to re-enact episodes from his life. In *The Country* there is a constant sliding between the characters' ironic utterances, and those of Crimp himself. Richard's dialogue during the play's opening scene sounds ironic, but actually he's simply lying. But Corinne's 'It's your job to bring a strange woman into our house in the middle of the night?' (p. 292) is full-on irony.

In *Dealing with Clair* or *The Treatment*, Crimp portrays not only the ridiculousness of some contemporary ways of thinking but also how, under the veneer of pious good intentions, there lurk some deeply unpleasant realities. When Mike describes raising the price of the house and selling property as 'a hateful business' (p. 42), he is being both sincere and insincere at the same time. If he really meant what he said, he probably wouldn't act as he does. He aims to disarm criticism and defend himself from the truth – it *is* a hateful business. The blind taxi driver in *The Treatment* is both an entertaining 'ironical comment on the notion of the blind seer' and a statement about 'the moral bankruptcy' of the city.[12] In *Play with Repeats*, Lawrence complains that he finds his pupils have 'a calm acceptance of the past' – 'there was no outrage' (pp. 247, 248). It's both his character's point of view and a Crimpian comment on politics in the Thatcher era.

Examples of dramatic irony abound in Crimp's work. One occurs in Act III of *The Country*. By then, the audience surely knows what Corinne only barely suspects, that Rebecca is her husband's lover. Another occurs in Scene 2 of *No One Sees the Video*, when Colin meets John in a pub. Both men treat us to their opinionated views about politics: the Fall of the Berlin Wall – 'a new dawn' plus 'unrest, ethnic violence, disintegration' (p. 16); nature versus nurture – 'no one's going to tell me that I'm made of these things [genes] and that because of these *things*, these *acids*, I am in some way programmed' (p. 17); anti-Muslim and anti-gay prejudice – 'to me these things [Muslims and gays] are a mental illness' (p. 17); fear of Aids – 'the dreaded' (p. 18); and mindless vandalism – 'he sprays the letters C-U-N-T' (p. 19). The dialogue not only satirises popular attitudes to contemporary issues in the early 1990s, but is also an ironic comment on both men. Neither realises that the playwright and audience are mocking them. The humour comes from our distance from their drunken attempts to talk. Both are shown as predatory males, circling each other. Having a sniff.

Power Games

Politics are about power. And Crimp is fascinated by power games, and by the question of whether the urge to control is a sign of strength, or weakness. *Living Remains* is about the politics of power in personal relationships. Even Woman's paralysed husband can exercise control. And does so. Power is also expressed through cruelty: Cook 'had to grind friend and enemy alike with fist and heel to get where he is now' (p. 8). In *Four Attempted Acts*, the dentist is deliciously cruel. He uses his power over patients to withhold injections because he thinks his patients are already numb: 'The truth is they couldn't suffer if they tried,' he rasps (p. 22). And the play's rape story shows Crimp's satirical bite – it parodies clichés about rape victims deserving their treatment. Then, in Yvonne's monologue, her key line – 'Please don't tell me what I should do' (p. 32) – is an attempt to reassert her power. Which she does. But by lying, a tactic used by the weak.

Unlike the simple English realists, Crimp did not at first respond directly to the domestic social and political events of the 1980s. His early plays do not dwell on the problems of Thatcherism, but have a wider global agenda, starting with *Love Games* and its explicit interest in Eastern European politics. By the time of *Definitely the Bahamas*, Crimp is more concerned with how fascistic attitudes are manifest in everyday life as well as in history. Typically, women are at the receiving end of cruelty, which is perpetrated by bullies such as Max and Michael. Poppy and Irene have both had forced hysterectomies: 'She [Irene] said there's hardly any scar' (p. 63) is an echo of Poppy's 'And there's hardly any scar' (p. 13). Both phrases powerfully suggest the mental scars of disempowered women.

No One Sees the Video has a clear gender politics. And it's about power. Liz first appears as a harassed shopper who is classified as belonging to socio-economic group A on the strength of her husband's job as a writer, which is doubly ironic – her husband has left her, and a self-conscious writer is making the point. Crimp then charts Liz's increasing independence up until the time she can play the role of a travelling business executive as well as any man, picking up younger sexual partners in hotels. Her transformation from unwilling interviewee to competent interviewer illustrates the way that roles can be swapped in any system of power. The woman is the protagonist, but she's not above criticism.

The satirical bite of *Cruel and Tender* comes from Crimp's understanding of how politicians and the media maintain power by manipulating the truth. For example, in a deliberate echo of *No One Sees the Video*, Richard says, 'You know what journalists are like – probe probe probe – why do we always assume we're being / lied to?' (p. 9). The irony is immediately apparent to the audience. And when Jonathan the politician arrives, his frank admission that the government told the General 'to forget the conventional rules of engagement' (p. 13) is in stark contrast to his lie that the General has saved Laela's life 'to remind each one of us – of our common – I hope – humanity' (p. 14). And when Richard accuses Jonathan of being economical with the truth, Amelia's response is: 'Of course he's lying – it's war it's his job / to lie' (p. 17). But as well as the clash between truth and lies, Crimp also understands – perhaps as a result of Mamet's influence – how the use of language itself is a weapon, an instrument of power. He says, 'Literature and violence have had a long, perverse and extremely fruitful relationship. You might say that at the moment of "denouncing" violence, the writer uses language to re-enact it.'[13]

Male Gaze

Crimpland is pro-feminist in its politics. Time and time again, Crimp's protagonists are women, and – when they are victims – our sympathies are clearly being enlisted on their side. But this is feminism under an ironic male gaze. The plays are full of knowing jokes about the women's movement. When James calls Clair a girl instead of a woman, he corrects himself: 'It's one of those dreadful words men use to belittle women. It's funny isn't it, how you are terribly aware of everybody else's faults, and then you find you share them too' (p. 29). Instead of making Clair a conscious feminist who objects to being patronised, Crimp shows her as coolly detached. It is the verbose James who tramples his way through clichés and solicits audience sympathy for his faux-reasonable intellectual points.

In *Play with Repeats*, there is a typically Crimpian inversion when feminism is advocated by a man. Heather says that her tutor, Lawrence, believes that a woman 'shouldn't let herself – historically speaking – be defined in terms of her sexual role i.e. wife, mistress, mother. He says it's degrading', and adds, 'a woman can't turn her back on her sexuality any more than a man can. She can't become neutral. Because isn't that neutrality equally degrading? You can't ignore what you biologically are' (p. 237). Once again, the clichés of social discourse about feminism are questioned, inverted.

Crimp's narratives end up 'often revolving around violence to women'.[14] Clair remains a victim; Liz is a victim of her own success. Crimp himself has stated that 'There is a certain objectification of women in those plays; the woman is the victim and I don't really escape from that'.[15] In a more complicated way,

Carol in *Getting Attention* is both a victim and a perpetrator of violence. In *Play with Repeats*, Crimp shows how Tony, given a second chance to talk to Heather, ends up by attacking her sexually. As she resists, he says, 'I love you. I'm in control' (p. 243). He doesn't, and he isn't. Here the politics of a masculinity in crisis implicitly argue that violence is always an immanent threat.

In *The Treatment*, says Paul Taylor, 'control, rather than truth, was the name of the game'.[16] Anne might be a victim, but she's a complex one. At one script conference, Nicky asks Anne if she struggles when her husband ties her up. '*Inwardly* I struggle,' is the reply. Nicky then voices the feminist position: 'I object very strongly to the idea of woman as victim, woman as dead meat' (p. 346). But the ironic thrust of the argument soon emerges: just because you've lived through an experience, says Nicky, doesn't mean you know all about it. Nicky points at Anne and says: 'This is not my idea of Anne: passive? humiliated? victim? – She's "lived" it. Haven't we also lived?' (p. 347). Nicky imposes her feminist interpretation of Anne's experience, negating Anne herself, and thrusting herself ambitiously into a central role in a project which will inevitably obliterate Anne's real life by imposing John's fantasy of it. But, as always, the satire is even-handed: an ideology is being mocked, but so are the personalities of those who espouse it.

Likewise, *Attempts on Her Life* is more than a simple account of the objectification of women. 'The woman is still seen as an object,' says Crimp, 'but in a very different way, because the irony of it is much more extreme and it is precisely about how women are viewed within our culture.'[17] In this play, the primary target of the satire is global capitalism. At one point, Crimp turns Anne into a make of car, showing how capitalism personifies the commodity as a woman so that the male consumer is encouraged to buy. As in porn, the woman comes across as always available, always flattering the male ego. The female body and female sexuality sell goods.[18] At the same time, Crimp parodies the feminist critique which uses body art to erase the difference between art and life.

The result of this even-handed criticism, which allows the spectator no complacent certainty, is an 'anti-ideological' politics, as urgent and topical as that of any political play.[19] Of course, not everyone agrees with this: freelance writer Keith Miller once argued that Crimp's theatre 'implies a view of essential human decency corrupted only by media overkill which is sentimentally inaccurate'.[20]

If Crimp might be accused by feminists of appropriating their critical viewpoint, he is on safer ground when he examines voyeurism, a recurring theme in his work. Voyeurism is literally the male gaze. In *No One Sees the Video*, the only way that the man, Colin, can realise his fantasies about the woman, Liz, is to keep and replay his videotapes of her interview. His voyeurism is a more literal counterpart of Tony's desire to replay his encounter with Heather in real life. Tony comes unstuck, and Colin is hardly the embodiment of happiness. *Getting Attention* is also about voyeurism. Bob is a father who has lost custody of his own children, but his unhealthy obsession with Carol, and his voyeuristic attention to the sounds of her lovemaking – 'there used to be a lot of, yes, sexual noise' (p. 154) – has blinded him to the evidence of Sharon's abuse. In *The Treatment*, Crimp shows 'the interdependence of voyeurism and exhibitionism' by juxtaposing Clifford's screenplay of Brooke – a voyeuristic artist who paints a complicit couple making love – with Anne's relationship to Andrew and Jennifer.[21] Anne then says she has been more humiliated by Clifford watching her being fucked by Andrew than she's ever been by her husband. Art is a product of voyeurism and exhibitionism, but not only is Anne finally excluded from the film of her life, but so is Clifford, its writer. And, ultimately, from those productions in which he doesn't participate, so is Crimp.

Not all of Crimp's work sees women as victims. In *Cruel and Tender*, for example, the play starts with a modern cliché, just as the original begins with a Greek proverb. Amelia says: 'There are women who believe / all men are rapists. / I don't believe that / because if I did believe that / how – as a woman – could I go on living / with the label "victim"?' (p. 1). Once again the politics are the politics of radical criticism, raising a point and then undermining complacency through irony. Finally, having shown women as victims, whether complicit or complex, Crimp wrote *The Country*, which implies the opposite view. As he says: 'It's a play in which a man is punished by two very strong women (*laughter*).'[22] In the sexual politics of Crimp's plays, the male gaze has finally turned in on itself.

Consumerism and the Culture of Contentment

Crimp reserves some of his fiercest criticism for consumerism and the culture of contentment. As the word implies, consumerism can sometimes destroy both those who sell and those who buy. Writing about *Dealing with Clair*, Michael Coveney pointed out 'its sense of unchallenged materialism, smirking double-cross, and free market bargaining masked in a thin veneer of hollow social intercourse', and Jack Tinker said, 'Whether Mr Crimp is saying that the tragic disappearance of Suzy Lamplugh is a direct result of the evils of market forces, is debatable. But the evils of human nature are never far away when forces of greed are unleashed.'[23] Amid James's creepy confidences, there's a moment when the author allows him to make an unironic political point: Clair and her estate agent colleagues 'do feel soiled after a day of buying and selling, selling and buying' (p. 85). Similarly, Tony in *Play with Repeats* can surely be seen as 'a casualty of competitive values'.[24] Neoliberal market economics don't smell of roses.

In *No One Sees the Video*, the critique of consumerism is explicit. Crimp comments that 'Market Research appears neutral because it presents itself to the public as such – "We just want your views, we just want your opinions" – so that we can sell you something. Advertisers always say that people will only buy products if they are good. In fact, this is not really the case because the market researcher's job is to go out and find how you can actually sell the product, regardless of what it is.' For Crimp, this political position is rooted in personal ethics. Talking about transcribing market-research tapes at home, he said, 'I didn't like it very much. It felt a bit strange when I found myself dealing with tapes about cigarettes and things that I don't actually approve of.'[25] The play is also sprinkled with references to alienation in a machine world of video images and consumer goods, a point first made when Liz reveals that her husband deserted her by leaving a message on her answer machine. Politically, the play shows that capitalism 'cannot live up to the ideological promise of dispelling the customers' feelings of emptiness'.[26]

A political reading of *Attempts on Her Life* would see Anne less as a total enigma and more as a woman forced to assume different roles by the constraints and expectations of a consumer society. After all, in this play, 'Everywhere the language of consumerism is dextrously interwoven with images of atrocity and apocalypse.'[27] For example, in an early scenario, 'Tragedy of Love and Ideology', both consumer capitalism and its discontents are mercilessly satirised when Anne, 'in her naïve and passionate opinion', attacks the leaders who have destroyed

> everything she values in the name (a) of business and (b) of laissez-faire.
>
> — In the name (a) of rationalization and (b) / of enterprise.
>
> — In the name of (a) so-called individualism and (b) / of so-called choice. (p. 212)

Crimp's politics are about questioning and understanding, rather than preaching or explaining. He emphasises the way the culture of contentment – those social classes which enjoy the benefits of material abundance – see the poor and the marginalised. *Getting Attention*, for example, was written as a reaction to the tabloid journalism that denounces abusers as 'monsters' instead of trying to understand them. Crimp portrays Nick as a strict disciplinarian, 'firm with children and not giving children attention because they will only want more and take more'. And adds, 'I don't suppose I've offered any explanations except perhaps in the isolation of the characters.' Since Nick and Carol are not in abject poverty, the play is 'a matter of character rather than a matter of social forces and environment'.[28] The play reflects mounting social anxieties and moral panic about child abuse, but by seeking to understand what John in another play calls 'mindlessness', whether vandalism or violence, Crimp was making an implicit political point. Two years later, when the Jamie Bulger case hit the news, John Major took exactly the opposite stance when he said, 'We must condemn a little more, and understand a little less.'[29]

Of course, the greatest disturbance of contentment is terrorism. Just as *Attempts on Her Life* gives a fragmented view of identity that reflects the violence of the post-Cold War world, so it also shows how contemporary global power politics mean that the girl next door has an equal chance of becoming a terrorist – or a victim of terror. Only slightly less disturbing is the moment, in *The Country*, when Rebecca mentions her 'crazy' friends who live in the city and are too 'terrified to leave' (p. 325). Here their terror is a result not of bombers but simply of living a highly stressful life; it's the terrorism of the system itself. Both *Cruel and Tender* and *Fewer Emergencies* also articulate, while simultaneously criticising, the politics of the War on Terror. The irony of *Cruel and Tender* is that the General, whose actions can only appal a liberal audience, turns out – because of his honesty as much as his physical ruin – to be oddly sympathetic: a victim of both politicians and of his son. The play explores not only political manipulation, but also the gender politics of war, implicitly arguing that men's warlike nature is socially constructed and that women are complicit in this because they create the domestic environment that men imagine they are protecting. In *Fewer Emergencies*, the fears engendered in the wake of 9/11 are prophetically shown to impact on every aspect of domestic life. In both plays, the anxieties of an age of global terrorism are always refracted through the dark glass of a writer's imagination, and thus cast darker shadows than those thrown by the weak candles of verbatim theatre. Crimp is more a visionary than an ideologue.

Crimp's plays all carry a political charge, but they are meant to provoke rather than console. Instead of offering an easy political slogan or a clear right-on message, as so much English realism does, they constantly suggest a receding corridor of never-ending criticism, in which the playwright is as sceptical of himself, and of the authority of his work, as of the people he is criticising. In this, Crimp is a modernist, something of an ironic utopian, exposing the miseries of everyday life while taking a gamble on the possibility of better times, a better world. There remains a constant tension between his satirical conception of his characters and their basic humanity, between his tendency to ridicule everything and his own deeply held beliefs. Typically, you can expect Crimp to say: 'I would stress that these are theatre-works, not political tracts, even if they have been deliberately constructed on cultural fault-lines.'[30] Of course, the paradox of satire is that you have to love as well as hate the object of your gaze. And, in the English tradition, satire is both an unmasking of power and an admission of the inability to do anything except laugh at it. But if this means it's a form of passivity, there is also evidence that this ever-restless writer wants to move on, and that means subverting his role as a satirist – an identity which has served him well for a quarter of a century: 'I want to avoid the trap of being just a satirist. I think that my work is characterised by diversity of output.'[31] Or maybe this is just another strategy of evasion.

Finally, it's worth remarking that there is something inherently political in the difficulty that characterises Crimp's work. Easy texts, including playtexts, tend to support the status quo. The difficult text, because it forces audiences to re-examine their beliefs, whether political or aesthetic, always embodies a critical point of view.

CONCLUSION: 'LOOKING FOR CONSTRAINTS'

When British suburbia dreams collectively, it dreams house prices, the costs of living, the schools for its kids, and what to buy when shopping. When the dream turns into a nightmare, it sucks in images of violence, the smell of burning, flashes of porn, and a choking sense of fear. Crimpland is British suburbia seen through the eyes of a satirist and a sceptical modernist. Suburban subjects are Crimp's dramatic universe. In a handful of masterworks, such as *Dealing with Clair*, *Attempts on Her Life* and *The Country*, Crimp stages an idea of suburban life as a place of vivid contrasts: the contradiction between home as a place of safety and the outside world as a place of fear; between the family as a haven and as a hell; between children as innocents and as terrors. These contrasts run through his work. For example, in *Dealing with Clair*, there is a brief moment when Liz and Mike instruct Clair: 'Just make sure no one sees the stain' (pp. 16–17). At first, Clair doesn't know what they're talking about, but then she realises she's standing on a carpet stain. In the end, the worry is in vain – James spots it anyway. But, as well as being a humorous moment, the stain on the carpet is typical, a symbol of the hidden shame, the secret desires and the spoilt promise of a suburbia that is constantly put into question. Sometimes Crimp articulates this theme explicitly. In 'Four Imaginary Characters', an 'immaculate' Austrian suburb faces 'a disused concentration camp' (p. x). In *No One Sees the Video*, the teenage Jo reacts with horror to her parents' split: 'This is so *embarrassing*. This is so *suburban*' (p. 41). Later, she defines suburbia: 'It means all the television aerials are pointing in the same direction' (p. 55). From *Definitely the Bahamas* through to *Fewer Emergencies*, Crimp's prime targets have been social conformity and the culture of contentment, those twin angels that hover over the suburbs.

Let's take a walk down the typical suburban street. The pavements are clean and level, and the trees are lovely to look at, nice and green. The houses are neat and tidy, and the families that live in them look comfortable and contented. Mummy and Daddy have good jobs; they are happy and satisfied. They have lovely children who are well looked after by nannies, and have everything they could possibly need. Every morning, they take their children to good schools, where they learn to be as clever and happy as Mummy and Daddy. But, wait a minute, something's wrong. The clean pavements could be treacherous, so mind your step. The trees look threatening at night. The houses have the air of mausoleums. Mummy and Daddy are shouting; strangers are eyeing up the kids; and the news on the telly is full of ugly pictures and vile events. Welcome to Crimpland.

In this dystopic suburbia, the emotional temperature depends on the contrast between the idea of security and the fear of disruption. Private safety is constantly compromised by public danger. And domesticity is never as secure as it looks: betrayal is the worm in the bud. Like a voyeur, the suburbanite peers out of their place of safety at the foreign lands beyond. However snug, they just can't help their minds wandering, can't help imagining the horrors beyond. Everywhere, there's evidence of treachery, abuse and terror. And these external threats are internalised. Certainty is undermined by the uncertain, culture by the uncultured, comfort by the uncomfortable truth. All those troubled selves, cruel liaisons and unhappy couples are both suburban subjectivities and the product of a critical attitude to suburbia. The writer in suburbia loves to walk, to observe, to listen, while remaining distant, semi-detached, a stranger among strangers. Inviolable. And just as the actor cannot experience an emotion without imagining how it can be shown onstage, so the writer cannot experience daily life without rewriting it.

The best guide to Crimp's life as a writer – the word is usually spat out, like a rasp – is Crimp himself. His work tells us that he is precise, hard-working and a perfectionist. His writing is polished and well disciplined. Typically, during rehearsals for *A Variety of Death-Defying Acts*, only one line was cut, and three words altered.[1] When Crimp prepared his *Plays One* and *Plays Two* for publication he changed very little, with the exception of *Dealing with Clair*, where he altered the position and content of the monologues. In 'Four Imaginary Characters', Crimp portrays the writer as a parasite who takes over the body of an ordinary man, 'the way a hermit crab moves into an empty shell' (p. viii). Typically ironic, this prose piece reveals who Crimp is as well as who he isn't, a strategy of evasion that suits his temperament well.

In 2005, Crimp summed up his aim: 'As a writer, you're aiming at complexity but the kind of complexity that will dance. Rather than the intractable kind of complexity that's hidden in a fist you can't get at.' And then he added, 'The role of the writer is to imagine as strongly as possible [. . .] That's how to discover things. You have to be like one of these vicious dogs that, once it grabs hold of something, won't let go. Take an image, get hold of it with your teeth and worry away at it until you're satisfied you've got everything you can out of it.'[2] As a writer, Crimp is aware of current affairs, but political issues are not what get him out of bed in the morning. His priority is 'to write a play – first and foremost that is what I'm trying to do. I think at the same time it's impossible to avoid the radiation – if you like – of current affairs.'[3] He's an intellectual writer in the sense that relentless self-criticism is his chosen path, although it might be more accurate to say that his path chose him. Vocation is sometimes profoundly involuntary.

Two recent incidents illustrate how the writer responds to everyday events, how suburban safety is confronted by a dangerous world. One morning, Crimp noticed that the mud scrapers outside a local playschool, in a Victorian church, had rubber covers to protect the children, and he was struck 'by the gulf between how we protect our children and how futile it would be to protect a child if you were being bombed by a military super-power'. Later that day, he wrote *Advice to Iraqi Women*. On another occasion, in Zurich, in 'squeaky clean' Switzerland, he walked into an anti-globalisation demonstration, and was caught between protesters throwing rocks and police firing tear gas. Choking on the tear gas 'made me think of something [film-maker Luis] Buñuel said: he had spent half his life championing revolutionary acts and when they were actually happening outside his window he felt ashamed because he realised that what he really wanted was order, not chaos and bloodshed'.[4] Soon after, Crimp wrote *Fewer Emergencies*.

Crimp doesn't fit neatly into the theatre studies mould where you can list which playwright influenced which of his plays. With him, influence takes the form of osmosis. In *Dealing with Clair*, for instance, the scene in which James talks about Clair taking a shower – 'rubbing herself dry', 'clean', 'dry', 'radiant' (pp. 86–7) – has a scent of Pinter's *Old Times*, where Kate takes a bath – 'an equally good rub', 'clean as a new pin', 'shiny as a balloon'.[5] In other plays, you can occasionally detect the inflection of another playwright here or there, but otherwise his tone is original and personal. Often, he has been inspired by modern art rather than by naturalistic theatre, Marcel Duchamp rather than George Bernard Shaw. The plastic arts tend to be 'more experimental' than mainstream theatre.[6] But Crimp also inhabits the world of books. He might mention how the banter between Don Quixote and Sancho Panza in Cervantes' novel must have influenced the rapport between Vladimir and Estragon in Beckett's *Waiting for Godot*, or he might discuss Proust's sense of time. He's as likely to talk about Paul Auster or Patrick White as about Tolstoy or Flaubert. He's read Baudrillard, but he'll talk about him as a poet rather than as a philosopher. When, in *Attempts on Her Life*, a

'Chinese proverb' is quoted – 'the darkest place is always under the lamp' (p. 251) – you're reminded that Roland Barthes is one of his favourite writers: in *A Lover's Discourse*, the same proverb occurs.[7] He tends to like writers who are distant from what he does. He's read French minimalists; he admires Peter Handke. Other writers have percolated slowly through his consciousness. All have gone into Crimp's theatre toolbox, which includes devices on loan from Ionesco, Beckett, Pinter, Mamet and Churchill, and these have served him well for the past two decades and more.

Because he's a musician, it's not surprising that Crimp occasionally makes explicit reference to classical music, from Mozart's piano sonata in A (K331) in *Four Attempted Acts* through 'music on the old instruments' in *Play with Repeats* (p. 241) to playing Schubert 'on authentic pianos' and singing Bach in *The Treatment* (p. 295). But the real influence of music can be heard in Crimp's fascination with the musicality of certain words – for example, 'turmeric' in *Dealing with Clair*, the 'void' in *No One Sees the Video* and 'solicitous' in *The Country*. Like live music, these words resonate onstage.

But writing is a place of discomfort for Crimp. The epigraph of *The Misanthrope* quotes Barthes: '*Il n'y a aucune bienveillance dans l'écriture, plutôt une terreur*' (In writing there is absolutely no benevolence; rather, a terror) (p. 96). And both men mean it. When Crimp read Handke's *The Afternoon of a Writer*, he immediately recognised himself in what he calls 'this wonderful description of how he did not feel he was a writer until the time came when he couldn't write'.[8] On another occasion, Crimp said: 'I do know that *le bien écrire* and *le mal écrire* are like Scylla and Charybdis, and I must steer perpetually between them.' Or, 'To put this a different way: writing for the theatre means making a steel wire strong enough and tense enough for actors to balance on. They must be afraid but at the same time free (like the writer).'[9]

If what makes Crimp unpopular is his difficulty, where does that come from? From the start, he has avoided easy naturalism, the default position of most British new plays, and used a method more familiar to European avant-garde modernists than to British playwrights. Perhaps he was born into the wrong culture. Anyway, he chose forms that called into question the usual conventions of storytelling and representation. His brand of modernism tells stories but in an indirect way, in a way that calls attention to their telling. And his constant theme is the unknowability of the other. He practises the drama of denial, denying audiences the usual easy identification with characters, easy plot resolutions or conventional situations. His studied satire, irony and ambiguity are deliberately aimed at upsetting expectations.

Crimp has always set himself creative constraints. As he says, 'I'm just always looking for new rules, I'm looking for constraints, looking for constraints all the time, and it's the constraints which will let the material be created by me. It's the constraints that I need.'[10] He's referring to the paradox that too much freedom leads to creative impotence. Gilbert Adair, who translated Georges Perec's *La Disparition*, says that Perec believed that 'contemporary literature was *trammelled by its own freedom*', hampered by the lack of those formal constraints typical of past ages.[11] Today, when anything goes, there is an absence of the prohibitions, inhibitions and constraints that once gave writers something to kick against. Crimp says, 'It would be lovely if there were established forms such as there were at the end of the nineteenth century. With each piece of work you have to find your own structure.'[12] So the struggle with theatrical form has led Crimp to relentlessly experiment in structuring his work. The attack on old forms is a modernist project and this attack is also an enquiry, with the method often being as meaningful as the finished result. In some cases, such as *The Treatment*, *Attempts on Her Life* and *The Country*, this has been a triumph; in others, such as *Dealing with Clair* and *Getting Attention*, it's been less successful. In each case, the attempt – to use a Crimpian formulation – has been an experiment. If Crimp's plays tend to avoid engaging the emotions, one of the reasons for this might well be what one young director called 'his obsession with form'.[13] The shape of Crimp's career has been determined by his desire to synchronise both form and content, without repeating himself, and his restless experiments in form have perhaps made his work seem more difficult than it really is.

One of his favourite forms is the monologue: *Living Remains* is clearly experimental, and the constraint that Crimp set himself was to write a play in which the dialogue consists of one character asking questions and the other only answering Yes or No. Within this rule, Crimp was free to playfully explore a theatrical landscape that's recognisably modernistic, a long way from English realism. In *Definitely the Bahamas*, he uses a monologue as the dramatic revelation when the victim, drowned out by suburban banalities, finally finds her voice. Monologues reappear throughout his work, often – as in *No One Sees the Video* – in the guise of a one-sided phone call, or as excerpts from a book or as testimony. A variant of the pure monologue is the prompted monologue, a recognisably Beckettian device. In *Living Remains*, Woman's monologue is prompted by her husband's answers. Crimp returned to the prompted monologue in *Attempts on Her Life*'s 'Strangely!' scenario, where, despite the debt to Beckett, the style of the writing is completely Crimpian. Other scenarios in the play include heightened monologues.

The stage is a merciless place. Under its lights, everything is revealed with acute clarity. But this well-lit revelation can sometimes banalise the extreme or the extraordinary. So some things are more powerful if they remain unshown: a missing scene can be stronger than an explicit revelation. A couple of Crimp's plays are crime stories, written with the firm rule that no police investigation will be shown. In *Dealing with Clair*, there is no explanation of Clair's disappearance, so her vanishing is spooky. In *Getting Attention*, Nick and Carol are arrested, but their crime is not explained – it's a play, not a newspaper story. The result is that each member of the audience has to create their own image of horror. This requires an effort. The lazy reaction would be simple dissatisfaction with the plot. The missing scene is also an implicitly critical device; by withholding explanation, Crimp challenges the comfort of clichéd accounts of extreme human behaviour.

In *The Treatment*, which stages a mythical urbanism where a blind taxi driver is completely believable, Crimp's experiment in form is to use simultaneous conversations, creating an explosion of onstage activity, an emotional, informational and theatrical barrage whose effect is joyful in its exuberance. The two simultaneous conversations that end Act One juxtapose Jennifer and Nicky's master-and-slave argument about shredding a script with Andrew and Clifford's facilitator-and-client dialogue in which Clifford's script is enthusiastically praised as 'a *mindfuck*' (p. 317). By contrast, the three simultaneous conversations that open Act Three blend vivid images of sickness, old age, death and cryogenics (pp. 339–43). By taking this form, Crimp's three conversations manage to indirectly, even subliminally, imply that Anne has aged prematurely, has had something inside her die and that her essence will be preserved for ever.[14] Out of indistinct words come blurred, but powerful, stage images.

Attempts on Her Life is clearly experimental in form, and – in an echo of Beckett's project – is an example of playwright stripping away the inessentials to arrive at a dramatic core. But Crimp also had another agenda. He made it a 'completely open' text partly in reaction against the 'closed' stage directions of Beckett's plays, and partly as a response to the rigid control habitually exercised by the Beckett Estate. So he chose a form which liberates directors and actors.[15] But although it seems that the play permits them to do anything they like – a parody of postmodernism's 'anything goes' – in practice this total freedom is usually curtailed, because the text still directs, as it were, its own production: directors and actors find that Crimp's words push them in certain directions. Finally, this play's form also flirts with numerology: Crimp says, about the number of scenarios, 'Seventeen is a prime number and with a prime number you never quite fathom things out.'[16]

With *The Country*, Crimp returns to a mythical world, except that this time it's domestic, and to a new set of rules. It 'was a deliberate attempt to escape from my position as a satirist, because, if you want to develop as an artist, you have to break with your own habits'.[17] So the creative constraint was to write a five-act play where each act would consist of a duologue. Thus the play, which is about a love triangle, looks in turn at the different couples of that triangle. The form intensifies the couple dynamic in the story and releases its energy. And the scissors-stone-paper game is there, says Crimp, 'to remind me that a play is a game. It helped me to hang on to the model of the play: there are dialogues and at the end of each dialogue there is always a winner and a loser.'[18] Unsurprisingly, there was 'a new set of rules for *Cruel and Tender*, which was that I would be obedient to Sophocles's original structure'.[19] Finally, Crimp is perfectly aware of creative constraints of another kind, those of live performance itself: 'I like to make things floating and ambiguous, but in performance you can't leave it at that.'[20]

Despite this evidence of a modernistic desire to experiment with form, Crimp's output is full of unresolved tensions, which not only give it its distinctive flavour, but also often make it difficult to appreciate. One such tension is between the high seriousness of his modernist influences, and the sheer playfulness of post-modernism. When reviewing *The Treatment*, Michael Billington praised the way that

> Crimp combines a vivid portrait of the labyrinthine strangeness of New York with a self-referential postmodernism. At one point, for instance, the writer [Clifford] announces that he'd like to introduce a Shakespearean element into Anne's story. This has its payoff a few scenes later when the writer, now discarded, is blinded. [. . .] And the echo of *King Lear* comes full circle when a sightless cab driver – having just returned from New York I don't find this at all improbable – gives the Gloucester-like writer a lift.[21]

More explicitly, in *The Misanthrope*, Crimp satirises the uses of a postmodern world view: 'And the human animal looks far less fearsome / through the prism / of postmodernism. / The world's a mess. Absolutely. We've fucked it. / So why not just sit back and deconstruct it?' (p. 112). Then his masterpiece, *Attempts on Her Life*, boasts an epigraph from arch-postmodernist Baudrillard: 'No one will have directly experienced the actual cause of such happenings, but everyone will have received an image of them' (p. 198). This summarises one of postmodernism's core beliefs: that reality cannot be truly represented. Neither words nor images nor theatre can show us the real. You can only represent your version of reality, and every version is of equal value: the Anne of *Attempts on Her Life* is, in one sense, a creation of postmodern philosophy. Or, in Crimp's own words, 'I realised I had unconsciously created a "postmodern" artefact, since it was a received idea, now fading a little, that identity was "culturally constructed". But I must say, this wasn't my intention.'[22] Instead, Crimp insists that

> The big criticism of the postmodernists is that they have no moral position therefore they have no position full stop. They embrace the world in a way that is implicitly uncritical. That's not a position I could endorse because otherwise I couldn't write a piece that is satirical because satire can't exist unless it's from an identifiable position. Your position is implicit in satire. I would describe my position as universally critical. Critical of the world around me but mainly critical of myself.[23]

So if there's a tension in his work between the severity of a modernist and the pranksterism of a postmodernist, Crimp fits much more comfortably in the modernist camp. That's the thrust of his project.

His work also shows a steady development from a modernistic absurdism to a much less abstract theatricality. From *Living Remains* to *Definitely the Bahamas*, Crimp clearly inhabits an absurd universe, one with its own logical illogic. The most absurd is *Living Remains*, especially its central image of a person so disabled that they can only press a buzzer to communicate, an image of loneliness and isolation that gradually, and paradoxically, becomes a figure of power. The play also recalls Ionesco with its stage business in which Woman produces a gift, 'a shapeless package wrapped in newspaper' (p. 7) which, when unravelled, is an empty revelation: 'There is nothing inside the parcel – It is made entirely of newspaper' (p. 15). Most of the characters in the early plays specialise in absurd logic. In *A Variety of Death-Defying Acts*, the 1st Clown says: 'We reached the inevitable conclusion that everything is a crime. Because when you start to think about it you soon realise that we're all of us guilty in some way' (p. 21). Later on, he says the opposite: 'We reached the inevitable conclusion that nothing is a crime' (p. 65). Even in Crimp's later work traces of this absurd sensibility can be found in, for example, the blind taxi driver and in the dazzling contents of Bobby's bedroom in *Fewer Emergencies*. The surface normality of Crimpland always conceals a world of weird and wacky wonders. This tension reminds us that Crimp is a playful and enjoyable writer, as well as a serious and austere one.

As a modernist, Crimp writes plays that are both experiments in form, and have a political agenda, even if their politics lie buried beneath the surface. One of the reasons for his being appreciated more in Continental Europe than in his home country is due to the greater respect that his artistic agenda inspires abroad. His satire, says Lindsay Posner, is 'often quite cruel and merciless and I think that's why he's hit a chord in Europe'.[24] Crimp is also one of the few British playwrights who is unafraid of creating characters, such as the Italian Anna in *Dealing with Clair*, who speak a foreign language onstage. On the whole, however, the British theatre tradition is indifferent, if not downright hostile, to plays that are experimental, so Crimp has occasionally had a rough ride. Asking a traditionalist critic to review an avant-garde play is like commissioning a bull to review a red rag. British public opinion is also much more sceptical about the idealistic and utopian value of culture. Utilitarian pragmatism trumps any abstract schemes for human betterment; entertainers are preferred to intellectuals. Despite this, Crimp is as much a British as a European playwright. His concern with the text as a written artefact makes him part of the great British tradition of text-based theatre, which examines language reflexively, so that the language of the plays is part of what the plays are about. As a satirist, Crimp also asserts his Britishness. For Britain prefers cultural satire to political revolution.

If Crimp is European in setting himself creative constraints for each of his plays, this sometimes leads to him being co-opted by the latest academic fad. Some European academics have identified *Attempts on Her Life* as an example of post-dramatic theatre, which is defined as the invention of new forms of performance no longer simply based on mimetic naturalism or social realism. Instead of a time and place, you have blanks. Instead of traditional characters, you have lines which can be assigned to any actor, or to anonymous speakers. Instead of dialogue, you have prose poetry. Instead of a plot, you have scenarios, a montage of fragmentary knowledge.[25] But while in *Attempts on Her Life* Crimp satirises 'outmoded conventions of dialogue and so-called characters lumbering towards the embarrassing dénouements of the *theatre*' (pp. 254–5), this is not really post-dramatic because Crimp's language remains based on the spoken word and is not an artificial literary language drawn from writerly fantasy. The words remain rooted in everyday speech. A very British instinct.

Although Crimp comes from the British tradition of new writing, he has never been part of any new wave. He's the odd man out in recent theatre history. Before the in-yer-face 1990s playwrights emerged, Crimp anticipated this contemporary sensibility: the scenes in *The Treatment*, when Jennifer performs oral sex on Andrew and then spits the contents of her mouth into an ashtray, or when Anne and Clifford tear out Clifford's eyes, anticipate the shocking stage images of Sarah Kane and Mark Ravenhill. Yet, despite this, Crimp belongs more to what the Royal Court politely calls the 'lost generation': those playwrights, born in the mid-1950s, who started to develop work in the 1980s, and then just vanished from view. He is one of the few survivors.

Despite being often underrated by the public, Crimp has been an influence on some key writers. When, in 1998, Kane was asked to name her favourite playwright, she chose Crimp as 'one of a small number of living playwrights whose plays inspire me to push my own work in new directions'.[26] Clearly, Kane's *Crave* (1998) and *4.48 Psychosis* (2000) were influenced by *Attempts on Her Life*. Similarly, Ravenhill's *Handbag* (1998) 'features sly allusions' to *Dealing with Clair* and *Getting Attention*, and his *Product* (2005), in which a producer uses a monologue to pitch the idea of a violent film to a star actress, is overtly Crimpian.[27] *The Treatment*'s gross yet hilarious story of the voyeuristic artist Brooke, itself influenced by Patrick White's *The Vivisector*, is almost a template for Martin McDonagh's stories in *The Pillowman* (2003).[28] More recently, you can also detect Crimp's influence on other European writers. An obvious example would be Roland Schimmelpfennig's *The Woman Before* (2005), which echoes *The Country* with its image of a man bringing another woman into the haven of his home, and *Cruel and Tender* in its vividly tragic ending. Crimp, with his distinctive voice, his experiments in form, his superb control and his capacity to surprise, is one of the central influences on contemporary British playwrights. This influence, however, usually takes the form of him being an exemplar of a committed attitude to new writing, rather than as a style to be imitated. Most new writing in Britain remains devoted to precisely that English realism that Crimp has spent a career avoiding and questioning.

What's fascinating about Crimp's work is both the writing surface and its depths. The polished precision of his writing – in its texture, syntax and imagery – is pleasurable to read for its own sake, and it's a constant tease to see how Crimp's writing at one and the same time is highly individual and consciously removes the person of the playwright from the process. The characteristic stop, start, stop-start hesitations and reiterations of his hyper-realistic dialogue are a perfect expression of one of his central themes: the question of identity – who are we, and can anyone ever really know. Likewise, who can hear his suburban social satire without a faint flush of embarrassment? For example, Clair's story about how Toby showed her up when after a restaurant meal he insisted that, instead of just splitting the bill, each of their friends should pay only for what they had eaten (p. 8). Excruciating. Often, the deeper you dig, the blacker the soil. From what dark psychological place does Anne's fury at being watched during sex, an anger that propels her to gouge out the eyes of the voyeur, come from? How do we really understand Carol's tolerance of Nick's abuse of her child? Can anyone follow the sadistic twists and turns of the love triangle in *The Country*? Here, cruelty is the willing desire to hurt, and how knowable is the motivation behind that? Few British playwrights are simultaneously so puzzling and so fascinating.

At the same time, Crimp is an uncomfortable writer. He's an outsider. He doesn't hang around the new-writing scene. His independence from much of mainstream British theatre can feel like aloofness. There's also something difficult to understand in his obsession with evading the autobiographical fallacy. For what is satire if not a way of keeping the world at bay? At the same time, the enigmatic suburban misanthropist is also an idealist, albeit a lonely one. Behind the façade of harshness is real desire to change things for the better. Crimp's drama is the drama of moral scruple; he doesn't denounce anybody, but he's sceptical of everyone. His kind of challenging work isn't popular because it doesn't solicit an audience's easy admiration. As Sarah Kane once remarked: 'All good art is subversive, either in form or content. And the best art is subversive in form *and* content' – and 'the element that most outrages' is form.[29] By using a difficult theatrical form, Crimp turns the classic recipe for success – 'Make 'em laugh, make 'em cry, make 'em wait' – into a modernistic 'Make 'em work, make 'em suffer'.

After Thatcher, British theatre has run on a commercial imperative – those playwrights that pull in the crowds thrive, others fall by the wayside. Even among the avant-garde playwrights, those self-conscious exponents of new writing, there's a hegemony of English realism, a mix of naturalistic dialogue and social realism always wrapped inside a comprehensible well-made play. Yet theatre directors are attracted by Crimp's work, however unfashionable, precisely because it can be staged across the spectrum from psychological realism to symbolic expressionism. The density and intelligence of the writing challenges them to come up with stage pictures that give body to its ideas. More is required than for the generic theatre of the soap opera or the bog-standard 'me and my mates' play. Crimp might be a difficult writer to love, but loving him is a way of taking a stand against cultural orthodoxy. Writers like him are a necessary antidote to the prevailing nothing-very-much-thank-you. They are Britain's own Europeans.

Much conventional theatre, even of the so-called cutting-edge variety, simply reaffirms power. The young student, or middle-aged suburbanite – neither of whom ever talks to a chav or a junkie – visits the theatre to see a naturalistic and social-realist play set on a council estate. Later, they leave convinced that the urban poor are vicious, sexually rampant and amoral. And then they sleep thankfully in their beds. Crimp's project has been to disturb that rest, to pull off that blanket of easy complacency. That's why his work, although often enjoyable, is also uncomfortable, difficult. His aim, like that of John Osborne, Dennis Potter and Caryl Churchill, has always been, in the words of David Hare, 'to hang on, to insist on what is dark, what is peculiar, what is disturbing', and in the face of the banalisation of everyday life, 'to hang on to what is *true*'.[30] When, in 2006, the National Theatre announced that it would stage a revival of *Attempts on Her Life*, directed by Katie Mitchell, it seemed that the recognition that Crimp had been denied for so long had finally been granted. After a writing career which included some fourteen plays and seven major translations, he was at last being honoured with a revival of his best play in his own country.

Crimp's sheer craftsmanship, his originality in language, his innovative attitude to theatrical form, the emotional intensity of his vision, his unblinking accounts of the dark void beneath the veneer of the humdrum, and his refusal to compromise his standards or his individuality, are reasons enough for his greatness. Whether as a passionate satirist of suburban life or as an enigmatic ironist, whether as an explorer of human relationships or as an engaged political playwright, he takes his deserved place in the great tradition of British new writing for the theatre.

THE INTERVIEWS

Sam Walters

Sam Walters is artistic director of the Orange Tree Theatre in Richmond, which staged Crimp's first six plays. He directed the original productions of *A Variety of Death-Defying Acts*, *Dealing with Clair* and *Play with Repeats*.[1]

We set up the Orange Tree Theatre – originally known as the Richmond Fringe Theatre – on the last day of 1971. Auriol [Smith] and I had a small child, so the idea of starting something local was very appealing. We wanted to look for a theatre in Richmond, located where people lived rather than in the middle of town. We were inspired by the alternative theatre movement, which had taken off, and the King's Head pub theatre in Islington had just started. We found the Orange Tree pub, five minutes from Richmond station, and the landlord let us use the upstairs room. At first, we only did lunchtime shows, then the pub was refurbished in 1974, and we started doing evening shows too. We did a mix of old and new plays, especially by local writers, and we staged [the late] James Saunders' work. David Cregan, Fay Weldon and Olwen Wymark were involved early on, and I remember the playwright Michael Richmond saying, 'We need to discover a world-class writer.' And I suppose, some ten years later, Martin Crimp was that writer.

Tony [Clark] was our first assistant director under an Arts Council scheme. At one point, he came to me and said, 'Sam, a number of the writers who have sent in plays are local – can I do Sunday-afternoon workshops?' Martin was part of that group, which also included Peter Bennett, John Norman, Rosemary Norman and Kevin Mandry. Tony would set them tasks: 'Let's have a play about two people sitting on a park bench.' And then we read plays. Martin was not very keen on having his work read out. Quite wisely, because sometimes when a reading is poorly rehearsed the work can come across badly. Martin was a writer who understood theatre from the start. He knew how to use dialogue to reveal character. His work, which was originally quite absurdist and enigmatic, has always been good to act.

A lunchtime season came out of that group, and that included Martin's *Living Remains*. It was nerve-racking because it's about a woman, played by Auriol, who has come to see her husband – who's on a life-support machine – and all he can do is move his finger enough to be able to press a buzzer. He can only answer Yes or No to her questions, so she was totally dependent on the stage manager – because if they gave her a Yes instead of a No, the whole play would collapse. They never did make a mistake, but there was always the risk.

A Variety of Death-Defying Acts had – among others – a bearded lady, a giant and a little girl. We did a reading and the little girl's part was read by a nine-year-old who was at school with my daughter – Kate Beckinsale. But that character was cut from the final draft. We had to get the advice of a professional magician to use this box which allowed swords to be pushed through a human body. One of the two policemen was played by Barry Killerby, who later became Mr Blobby. He used to leap into the audience with a plastic truncheon, hitting people over the head. Barry was an extraordinary clown, but he broke a chair almost every night, and we'd borrowed these from the pub's garden. So every other night I used to substitute another chair for the broken one. The landlord must have been mystified about these broken chairs that kept appearing. I remember Peggy Ramsay [the agent] liked *A Variety of Death-Defying Acts* very much. She rang me: 'This is an extraordinary and exciting young writer you've got.' But she didn't do much for Martin, and he soon moved to Judy Daish.

Auriol was very keen on Martin's writing. She was in a radio play with Alec McCowen, and it was her idea – while talking with him about Martin – to ask him to direct *Definitely the Bahamas*. Alec had only directed once before but he accepted after I persuaded him that there would not be any sophisticated technology involved. At that point, Alec was very big and we got a lot of attention. Critics, who hadn't seen Martin's previous work, came down because they thought: 'Who is this new writer that Alec McCowen is bothering to direct?' It was a big success and then we got the Thames Television resident-writer scheme that year, after failing the previous year. That's the power of the star. That did Martin a lot of good.

Then Michael Codron commissioned *Dealing with Clair*. He was very good at finding up-and-coming writers. When he read *Dealing with Clair*, he thought, 'Well, this isn't really West End fare,' and he rang me and asked if I'd do it. Well, of course I said yes. Michael got Tom Courtenay. Martin is a very particular writer to direct because, right from the beginning, he was very clear about what he wanted. And the fact that he's a musician means he hears things musically, and is precise about his phrasing. He's not the kind of writer who says, 'Well, here it is, take it and off you go.' Martin hears it and wants it done very specifically. As a director, I didn't bring anything particular to the plays that made them better than they already were. Tom really relished the writing, and was extremely keen on the play. He's an obsessive, meticulous actor. I'd be getting up in the morning, and the phone would ring and it would be Tom, who'd been looking very carefully at one line. If you're directing a star in a fringe theatre the situation is slightly unusual. With Martin being there in rehearsal, Tom would often turn to him. It's a common problem; there's a temptation for the actor to turn to the writer, and you, as a director, can feel redundant.

Dealing with Clair came about because Martin was selling a house, and someone offered him cash. He didn't realise that he'd written a play that would relate so strongly to the Suzy Lamplugh case. For him, it was more a play about middle-class greed. The Lamplughs were local, so the press latched on to the play. Representatives of the Lamplugh Trust came to see it. Martin must have read about the case but his play was no documentary. It's a very clever play, with subtle emotions, and, from the first page, the dialogue is such good actors' material. There's a lot of subtext, which is why actors like it. It's also hilariously funny. And the uneasy relationships are very well observed. James is a wonderful character, and Tom certainly made him quite exotic. Although Tom comes from a tradition of working-class realism, he does not come across as that. He is a very particular actor. He was also very good for the box office.

When Martin was our writer-in-residence in 1988–9, we did some readings, and I staged a play called *The Way to Keep Him* [1760] by Arthur Murphy. Then I got other plays by him out of the London Library and said to Martin: 'Could you glance at these?' He looked at them and said, 'I think this is the most interesting; it's got a tinge of Stoppard and Ayckbourn in a couple of scenes,' and that was *All in the Wrong* [1761]. I read it and decided to open the new theatre with it, so Martin was thus also indirectly involved in the move, in 1991, to the new building. By the way, *Dealing with Clair* followed *The Way to Keep Him*. Both *Dealing with Clair* and *Play with Repeats* were staged in the round. My most vivid memory of the latter is of someone smashing a bottle against a wall.[2] Thomas Wheatley was really good as the rather meticulous middle-aged man. Without stars, it got less attention than Martin had expected. In those days, critics didn't always come to see every show.

Anthony Clark

Anthony Clark directed the original production of Crimp's *Living Remains*.[3]

When I finished my degree, I was an aspiring playwright living in Manchester, and directing everything I wrote. I saw an advert for an assistant director to Sam [Walters] in *The Stage*, and I applied. In those days, to get an Arts Council bursary to train as a director you had to find a theatre to sponsor you. I was interviewed twice, got the job, and moved to London. The bursary was for one year, 1981–2, but I stayed for three because Sam kindly kept me on. With all the Charter 77 stuff going on, the Orange Tree was an exciting place to be. Part of my brief was to do something for local writers, and one of my first jobs was to clear the shelves, which were bending under the weight of scripts. I worked my way through them quite quickly, and I found a play by Martin, who was living in East Sheen at the time, and all I can remember about it now was that there was an incident which took place at a checkout point in a supermarket. The voice of the writer shone through, and it had clearly been through the sieve of a very articulate brain. So I invited Martin to join the writers' workshop. From this shelf of plays I managed to find a number of other writers and we used to hold the workshop meetings on a Sunday, maybe once every two weeks. There were about ten to fifteen writers, and these workshops continued for about two years.

During the workshops we did a number of exercises to get people to write and they read out examples of their work and talked about it. As a result, Martin wrote *Living Remains*. At the time, the Orange Tree was a room above a pub, with magnolia walls, a lot of windows and minimal blackout. *Living Remains* was part of the first new-writing season, at the end of my first year. This was in the summer and it was a profit-share. I also directed the first London production of Kroetz's *The Nest*, and Przezdziecki's *Love Games*, which Martin helped translate.

Then Martin came up with this one-woman show, which was performed by Auriol [Smith]. It was quite extraordinary. It was one of those pieces that we didn't tamper with much in rehearsal. And all I can remember now was that Martin was coming from the perspective of French literature of the 1950s: for example, we talked about Robbe-Grillet – I even remember going out and buying his novel, *In the Labyrinth*.[4] It was a different approach, and very unfashionable at that time. I warmed to it because I hadn't been brought up in this country – I'd lived in Algeria, Argentina and Austria – so I had great difficulty with naturalism and social realism, the vein of theatre so popular in British culture. I'd only started living here at the age of eighteen, so my love of theatre was not created by the kitchen-sink tradition; I felt more sympathy with a more subjective, more individual style of playwriting, which Martin certainly embodied. His play was more imaginatively challenging than work that was popular then.

Living Remains was set in a hospital, and we did it very abstractly. The musicality of the play was its strength. It was a sound poem as well as a narrative. I used to design my own work: Martin also did photography and played music, and he had very strong ideas, and I had very strong ideas, and we met somewhere in between. Certainly, in those days, there was no budget for design. For costumes, the deal was, 'Here's a few quid,' and you went to the Oxfam shop. It was a shoestring production. Auriol's performance was extraordinary, and the thrill was in the way she respected all the punctuation, and the nuance of the language, and how much humour she could elicit from that. There was a note of menace in the play and the staging was pretty still. Auriol wore an old-fashioned suit and a mask of heightened make-up, with lots of lipstick spread over her lips giving her an other-worldly look. It wasn't naturalism. When she mentioned meeting a man in a cemetery, you didn't think, 'Was that Kensal Green cemetery?' The show ran successfully for about ten days, playing to about thirty to fifty people a time.

Martin has had the terms Beckettian and Pinteresque thrown at him. I'm sure that they influenced him, but there were other influences too, especially novelists. He might be in the same modernist landscape but I think he has his own voice. He comes from a Continental tradition that Sam was sympathetic to. But it's lazy to call him Beckettian; he's Crimpian. His style is philosophical, and he's always exploring ideas.

At the time, Martin won a *Time Out* competition for a short story ['The Statement'] which he had entered using a female Middle-European name. He thought that a Cambridge-educated, middle-class man would have less chance than a foreign woman, which is possibly true. Anyway, he won. It was printed and he has continued to write short pieces. He's a writer who's explored various different forms.

Auriol Smith

Auriol Smith acted in the original productions of Crimp's *Living Remains*, *Four Attempted Acts* and *A Variety of Death-Defying Acts*.[5]

I've still got the original script of *Living Remains*, Martin's first play. It's signed by him and dated 1981. At that time, Tony Clark was running workshops for local writers. Then he organised a reading of extracts from their work, using Orange Tree actors. So my first experience of Martin's work was reading about two and a half pages of *Living Remains*. From that first encounter, I thought that this was an extraordinary, individual voice. This extract had a musicality, a precision and an originality that were totally engaging. So Martin was encouraged to finish the play and eventually Sam put it on and Tony asked me if I would like to do it.

It was challenging. The part of the stage manager, who has to press the buzzer, is hugely important and we had a very good stage manager, Sarah Whalley, at the Orange Tree. Her timing was excellent. With Martin, it all comes down to the difference between 'slight pause' and 'pause'. So even the rhythm of the unseen husband's responses has an effect on the show. It was a demanding piece – you had to have a sense of musicality in order to do it justice. And so did the stage manager. It was very well received by our audiences.

I then performed it for ten days in Manchester at a lunchtime venue. I had a new stage manager who just came in to do that job and didn't have time to discuss the play. I learned very quickly how someone who didn't know the play could destroy the rhythm of the piece. It is a play that has two characters, even if the man is invisible. When Woman asks some very difficult questions, he has to sense how long to wait before answering Yes or No. As in much of Martin's work, there's a slightly taunting quality about their relationship. At one point, she describes the fine clothes she's wearing, when of course she's actually badly dressed. She's titillating him sexually. She knows he has no way of responding except by pressing the buzzer. It has quite a cruel edge.

From the start, Martin had a very individual way of writing. There's a lot under the surface: when Woman asks her husband for permission to visit Mr Cook, you can't help but feel that she's asking for permission to go further. You sense that this woman is a very sexual being, who's also overtly feminine, and loves her clothes, but now finds herself in reduced circumstances and longs for physical love. She has a vision of herself as an extraordinarily attractive woman, but actually she's a bit tarty. I remember I wore exaggerated make-up and, because she's living out of plastic bags, shoes that didn't match: one was a high-heeled red number and the other a kind of sandal.

In the play, you're diverted by Mr Cook's story about his handicapped daughter, and him having to mop up her tears. In Martin's early plays, there always seemed to be some cruelly handicapped person. You can't quite decide whether the story about Mr Cook is fantasy or reality. Either it's a real event and she sees it as a way of having a new relationship, or it's a fantasy and she's trying to stimulate her husband. But because he can't do anything about it, that is very cruel. Martin never said which of the two options was right. It was intentionally ambiguous. The other thing that he was interested in was control. In the end, the husband has control over Woman because he withdraws his response. And I don't think that Woman had ever anticipated that. The ultimate power is not to respond.

I have recently reread *Four Attempted Acts*. Here Martin goes a lot further into the idea of juxtaposing pleasure and pain. And again control. As well as music: the Mozart is both torture and delight. Martin was obviously very interested in the proximity of pain and pleasure, and in the first attempted act, the control of Billy – whatever Billy is – is a central image. When we did it, Liz Crowther played Billy – she was in this container, this cage, covered in straw, so she looked like a large animal. And she made Billy's noises. The dentist scene was played behind hospital screens, and the staging was minimalist. The dentist had this wonderfully sadistic notion that he could now dispense with anaesthetics because he was now more accurate, while in the past he might have done untold harm when using anaesthetics because of his inaccuracy. Martin loves exploring this kind of logic. And, finally, Mrs De A claims that her husband's suicide resulted from an enjoyment of suffering, although we don't really know why he killed himself. And we don't know quite why their daughter is behaving so oddly. She's biting her fingernails until they bleed, and getting blood on the keys. So she's committing musical suicide. There's also cross-torture as one half of each couple tortures the other.

In *A Variety of Death-Defying Acts*, I played Miss Kopinski. Although this was a Christmas play, and had some slapstick humour, it also centred on control and cruelty. I remember several images of awful things, such as the escape artist in the sack who is tied up with wire, which is cutting into him. He's declared his love for Alison and she wants him to suffer. He also has a phobia about confined spaces and so Petley has coerced him into being an escape artist. Petley's idea that Alison should be a singer results in this funny but awful thing about his taking away the safety net because, if she injures herself, he will be able to control her more easily. At another point, the 2nd Clown describes the crucifixion very beautifully, and Alison calls for the box, and knives are put through her: the stage direction is 'using great force'. This makes the audience witness great pain for their own pleasure. Through all this, you begin to think that Miss Kopinski is a gentle observer, but in the end she's whacking her tiny dog with a strap to make him behave. So she's not exempt from cruelty. And the clowns finally butcher Petley.

One of the things that sticks in my mind are the lines: 'What would life, such as it is, be, without guilt, pain, anxiety and distress. It would be tedious in the extreme for all concerned. Without pain and humiliation, people would cease to feel real.' This is what the play centres on. *A Variety of Death-Defying Acts* seems to pull the themes of Martin's previous plays together, exploring the idea of how far you can push pain in the interests of pleasure. At what point, he asks, would the audience be repulsed? Finally, when the set is taken down at the end of the play, the audience get a double sense that what they've watched was a kind of act, as indeed theatre always is. So the whole event was a performance. Or a fantasy.

Joe Penhall

Playwright Joe Penhall directed a reading of Crimp's *Dealing with Clair* at the Royal Court as part of its 'Playwrights' Playwright' series.[6]

I chose *Dealing with Clair* for 'Playwrights' Playwright', when writers were asked to direct one of their favourite plays, because although it dates back to 1988, it could have been written a couple of months ago. It's completely contemporary, telling us with chilly, brutal eloquence who we are now and what we disastrously hold dear. Martin is virtually alone among contemporary playwrights in his ability to write utterly real, hilariously unlikeable characters – who remind us of our colleagues, our neigh-bours, our friends, ourselves – while still engaging our emotions and keeping us riveted. The characters in *Dealing with Clair* are not particularly sympathetic. Mike and Liz are greedy yuppies, and James is a misogynist. I'm fascinated by the way Martin takes a penetrating look at ordinary people. What he exposes, with a ruthless efficiency and a glimmer of fondness, is the notion that the man in the street is a real disappointment, usually turning out to be small-minded and egotistical. *Play with Repeats*, for example, is about an unenlightened man clumsily groping towards enlighten-ment – and looking for it in all sorts of ridiculous places.

Like Martin, I live in a suburb. I've been through the buying and selling of property myself, and it's a vicious racket. And I was intrigued to see whether this feeling would translate on to the stage. One of the ludicrous ironies of theatre is that, despite its middle-class audience, it has an enduring fascination with the seamier side of life, an age-old liberal romance with the working class. What I like about Martin is that he has the courage to address middle-class subjects. *Dealing with Clair* is a wickedly incisive study of middle-class England, and its aspirational, materialistic ethic. Martin charts the awful disinterest of Mike and Liz as they titter dumbly about the young estate agent who let them down by not turning up one day. It's a masterpiece of indifference in a greedy world, and a masterclass for all playwrights in writing the unpalatable truth.

Martin says that Clair is just the normal office girl. When you're selling your house, she's the one that's sent round, with her inexperience and her lack of real passion, and she's your representative in this traumatic transaction. I like the way Martin makes her so ordinary. He could easily have made her into a David Hare heroine: she could have been from an ethnic minority, fighting the nasty Establishment types. But Martin ruthlessly creates a social contract whereby all the characters treat Clair as a kind of punchbag. And Clair doesn't rise to the bait. If she notices it, it doesn't bother her. And that's how it is in real life. She shrugs it off, and later, over a gin and tonic, she'll talk about how she met these 'wankers'. She wouldn't make a breast-beating speech. Many playwrights make the mistake of giving their characters their own arguments. But not Martin.

With James, Martin creates this creepy anti-hero who deliciously corrupts your expectations: lone wolves are often charismatic. At the same time, Martin taps into our collective insecurities: the insecurity that Mike and Liz won't be able make as much money as their neighbours; the insecurity that Mike is going to have an affair with the au pair. Mike does show interest in other women – he's got a subtle naughtiness to him.

Martin says that *Dealing with Clair* is about decadence: 'These people are dripping in excess.' They have plenty of cash, an au pair and sex on the brain. There's that scene when Mike and Liz are hopelessly drunk and flirting with each other, and it's awful in its banal decadence. So once I'd grasped that, I directed it with as much psycho-sexual subtext as possible and that gave it life. The idea of sex is there from the start, yet when Liz asks Mike if he wants to rape Clair, it seems to come out of nowhere. Psychologically, the play is about a very subtle urban guerrilla warfare.

The clincher is the fact that Clair obviously meets a horrific end – young women disappear all the time in London – but all that anybody cares about is house prices. What's so brilliantly creepy is that Martin makes it look as if she might have been seduced by James, when in fact the unavoidable evidence is that she's been dragged, kicking and screaming, against her will. There isn't a whiff of violence onstage, yet Martin slips in this implication – which just grows and grows like radiation – that this woman has met a horrible fate. With the actors, we discussed where Clair is during the scene when James talks to her mum on the phone. Lifeless in the cupboard? In the bathtub? Or buried in the garden? The real engine of this play is the sense of menace, and what generated the least heat onstage was the subtle chicanery of the vendor–buyer transactions.

For this reading, Martin wrote a list of what the new house prices would be, about three times as much as in the text, but in the end we didn't use them. It was clear that this wouldn't matter to an audience. In a way, changing the prices would also spoil the metaphorical power of the play – the piece is really about people's callousness.

Jude Kelly

Jude Kelly directed the original production of Crimp's *Getting Attention*.[7]

Before I arrived in 1988, the West Yorkshire Playhouse didn't really have a new-writing policy so I was jump-starting a new-writing programme for a theatre which had two large spaces, the Quarry (750 seats) and the Courtyard (350 seats). My aim was to convince our Yorkshire audience that contemporary playwriting was about them – not so much a theatre-going choice as an active debate about identity. It was all in the context of a broad education and community policy. In the early 1990s, we were debating the issues thrown up by recent regeneration policies – the relationships between art, violence, urbanism and the environment – within a new-writing and citizenship framework.

I first heard about Martin when I read *Dealing with Clair*. It was rare to come across a really distinctive voice, and even rarer to come across an ethical voice. I knew as soon as I'd read *Dealing with Clair* that I wanted to direct one of his plays. In 1991, I put together a season called 'Lifelines', in which I was trying to prove that theatre mustn't have any taboos, because although child abuse was gradually being talked about in the media, theatre was silent about it. There was a real risk that child abusers would be demonised, so I wanted to stress that we were not talking about some strange people that we never come across. We were talking about people who hadn't fully grasped what respect, dignity and humanity are all about because they'd had too little experience of those things themselves. But you can only tackle a subject like that if you have good writing.

Getting Attention was staged in the Courtyard, which is quite a large space. At the time, the miniature play, often put on in studio spaces with a hundred seats, was becoming the norm, and I didn't think that was very healthy because it meant that too many new plays were playing to small coterie audiences. *Getting Attention* was based on a real case, and it played on the fact that many neighbours have a gut instinct that something is wrong yet they fail to cross the threshold into action.

Sharon was invisible, but *Getting Attention* showed how Nick and Carol were the two other children in the story. As Sharon's mother and stepfather, they were also trying desperately to get attention. Neither of them had any core identity and they could only get an identity if it was reflected back from somebody else. They were so needy themselves that adding a child to their relationship just seemed to be too much to deal with: a child has more illogical needs and can offer no sexual gratification. Martin's aim was for the audience to discover a compassionate empathy, not a sentimental one, for the characters. The play was saying that so many people are so neglected themselves that their need for attention makes them inadequate, sometimes violent, parents.

Nick treats Sharon in a very authoritarian manner. If you ask kids in care or youth custody to act out a figure of authority they will invariably act out the most horrifically authoritarian version of authority. If they have to choose between acting as a victim or as an authority figure, they usually choose the authority figure. With Nick, you feel that what he is meting out was meted out to him in the first place.

What the cast loved about the play was that although the characters were a bit inarticulate they could communicate by using powerful gestures. A lot of the meaning of the play's world was in the actions of the characters and not in the words. And they found this very challenging to act. Nick and Carol constantly gravitate towards sexual contact because that's the only way they know how to communicate. Nigel [Cooke] is not normally cast as a manipulative brutish character, but he played those animal qualities really well.

I played Sharon in the sound recording of the scratching, which we made in a studio. And that was a horrific experience. Just acting out the sounds, the scratching and the scrabbling, necessary to convey her state, meant that you began to experience just how horrible that must have felt like. A child of Sharon's age can't digest what's happening to them when they're trapped. They simply don't know. And I found that really upsetting and disturbing.

When the production transferred to the Royal Court, it was a challenge to compress the play into a much smaller space. Actually, I think it was better in the Leeds space because the audience was larger and therefore more mixed: the bigger stage made the play clearer. Distance from the action gave the audience a sense of perspective. One of the problems of staging plays about difficult subjects in studio theatres is that it gives the impression that we are looking at people in a zoo. They are not us. In a studio, both the play and its audience seem marginalised. I didn't want the play to be sensationalist so I was worried that a coterie audience would just watch it and remain unaffected.

Martin takes big risks, and he deserves better than a voyeuristic audience. He doesn't judge his characters, and he doesn't judge society either. Other writers feel compelled to explain everything, but Martin doesn't. That's not because he doesn't care; his is a different quality of enquiry. What Martin does is to bear witness. He asks us to look and trusts us to make up our own minds.

Lindsay Posner

Lindsay Posner directed the original productions of Crimp's *No One Sees the Video*, *The Treatment* and *The Misanthrope*.[8]

I first became aware of Martin's work when I read *Dealing with Clair*. Then, just after I had taken over the Theatre Upstairs at the Royal Court, *No One Sees the Video* came in. What appealed to me was the same thing that appeals to me about Pinter and Mamet. Martin's plays are completely unsentimental, tough and bleak, but at the same time funny and entertaining. He hits a contemporary nerve with his tone, and although he isn't cynical, he understands the nature of the moral shifts in our culture in a way very few other writers do. Whether he's writing about the advertising business or the film industry, he documents the moral relativism that at times betrays a lack of real values. I love the way that his plays engage you, but do not draw you sympathetically into the life of the characters. So there's no catharsis. The experience is a bit like watching people in a goldfish bowl, and he shines a harsh spotlight on them. In some ways, the writing is cruel, but brilliantly modern for that reason. He's such a careful writer, and he clearly conceives of his plays, and develops them, as intellectual jigsaw puzzles, with cross-references both to his own plays and to situations within each play. With Pinter, you could say that his plays write him; Martin isn't that kind of instinctive writer. That's why his plays have an idiosyncratic coolness, which is a strength.

I wanted to direct *No One Sees the Video* because I connected with the dialogue. I remember immediately thinking that Celia Imrie would be ideal for Liz and Neil Dudgeon for Colin. I have a minimal aesthetic and Martin's plays suit that. We went for a stark look, using a white cyclorama that felt abstract and yet enabled the play to live. We also used a sound score of electronic music, linking the scenes and corresponding to the abstract nature of the set.

No One Sees the Video never felt like an unfinished play, although a knee-jerk response from the critics was to call it under-dramatised. Martin is clearly influenced by Mamet, with the elliptical nature of the dialogue, and also the use of interruptions. The rhythm of his writing is very musical. In *No One Sees the Video*, he was interested in the way language can be used to intrude into people's lives. The more you classify someone, the more you demean them. Here the language becomes almost male and phallic: it's penetrative and intimidating. In the scene between Colin and Jo there is a definite sexual frisson, and Martin is quite unflinching about showing characters who are not quite facing up to the darker side of sexuality. Obviously, the challenge is always to present this kind of moment with subtlety onstage, without being either too overt, or too titillating. You really need to convey a sense of danger without lapsing into cliché.

As a result of the success of *No One Sees the Video*, we commissioned *The Treatment*. I remember everyone being very excited when it was received. It is a very big, dense city play, a bit reminiscent of Kafka's *Amerika*. We had a very strong cast. Sheila Gish felt just right for the part of Jennifer. She was brilliant at acute one-liners, at irony, and she had an enormous range, being particularly good at playing repressed hysteria. Mark Strong was excellent as Simon. And it was practically Jacqueline Defferary's first job. I remember seeing a lot of people for the role of Anne but only she had the right sort of quirky, slightly offbeat quality. Given that the play is set in New York, it was a good idea to have at least one American in the cast, and Larry Pine was clearly the best for the part.

Martin didn't rewrite anything. I think barely a line was changed. The only area where the writing became a bit self-conscious, and perhaps not as fully realised as in the other scenes, was in some of the encounters between Simon and Anne. Retrospectively, I felt that Martin hadn't quite written that through properly, but, as a director, you always have to make a decision about whether, if you ask for a rewrite, it might be counterproductive. So, in this case, we left it as it was.

★

With *The Treatment*, Martin developed his feeling for theatrical imagery. And there were some wonderful moments: for example, all the scenes with the blind taxi driver had a vivid theatricality. And the ending, with the New York boogie-woogie playing, was exhilarating. I remember that we had cascades of paper flying around for that final scene. And the fact that Clifford is blind is so apt – he can't read the script he's hanging on to. In that image, Martin managed to capture something about New York that's both ironic and liberating. We also had a city soundtrack, full of urban noise. And when we used music, we made a deliberate cacophony of pop, rock and street sounds. I tried to get that sense of frenzy in the set as well. *The Treatment* is all about the place of art in society, and asks questions such as: When does art become immoral? And: To what extent can one exploit people legitimately? As a rule, I don't talk much about themes with actors: you can't play the symbol and you can't play the theme. But the psychology in *The Treatment* is challenging, so we spent some time unravelling it. Sometimes Martin deliberately withholds a character's biographical detail. But however ambiguous a line is on the page, an actor needs to know whether they are telling the truth or not, or what they are concealing, otherwise they can't act it.

Martin managed to create an artificial version of America – and to get away with it. Which is quite unusual, because normally a dramaturg will say, 'Don't be ridiculous, you can't write that – I mean, when were you last in New York?' But all this literalism was irrelevant to Martin because he set his own agenda and tapped into something he understood about the city. He created a coherent world. *The Treatment* had thirteen rave reviews but it played to disappointingly small houses, about 50 to 60 per cent full. Everyone was expecting it to transfer, but it didn't hit a popular nerve.

The Misanthrope had a contemporary edge and needed a perspective that could rediscover it. I couldn't see a justification for doing it in a traditional way. It wasn't commissioned so me and Martin touted it to theatres and Tim Supple [artistic director] at the Young

Vic went for it. I'd worked with Ken Stott a few times at the Court and he immediately struck me as someone who is a brilliant comedy actor with a dark side. And he was dead right to play Alceste. And if Célimène is a Hollywood starlet, as in this version she was, that obviously was our first port of call. Originally, we wanted Rachel Weisz to do it, but her agent got her a Hollywood film and she broke her contract. But Elizabeth McGovern was a splendid replacement. I remember that, in rehearsals, she couldn't – as a film actor – at first understand why the speeches were so long. The whole notion of Molière elaborating on a theme was odd to her. She'd say things like, 'This is a crock of shit. I've already said this in the first two lines, couldn't we lose the next ten?' But she came around eventually.

Martin's free verse doesn't follow Molière's verse form, but it works, and feels classical. It was easy to act as well. And we kept the speed up. What I enjoyed about directing it was that, true to the original play, Martin managed to hit a few living targets, including satirical bites at David Hare and at theatre critics. Quite predictably, most of the critics spent a large part of their reviews writing about the Covington character. There's nothing more adorable than seeing yourself onstage. And Martin had given it a frisson of contemporary provocation. I don't buy the argument that we lost the danger or the darkness of the play. In our production, the danger lay in being sued, which can ruin your life completely.

Martin's Alceste is a complicated mixture. He's a playwright who's not fashionable. Playwrights who aren't fashionable are often not fashionable because they make a stand, sometimes an affected stand, of integrity that puts them outside the mainstream. Alceste feels contempt for the system. Unfortunately, this is mixed with a feeling of inadequacy and a secret jealousy of those playwrights who know how to play the game, and are upwardly mobile, and successful because of their networking. That's why he's angry. On the one hand, he knows he's talented; on the other hand, he's not prepared to play the game. But there's also a part of

him that's frightened. By contrast, Jennifer's feelings are superficial. Perhaps in the original play they are not, but it felt much
more appropriate to have something more cynical in our version.
For a moment, Jennifer is happy to give her love for Alceste a
chance, but he soon gets on her nerves.

In order to create a salon set, we built a maple floor up over the
auditorium, and there was a glass stairwell through which the
actors entered this penthouse area. It was meant to look a bit like
the Louvre, to give it that French resonance. In the tradition of
Molière, who would have had his band of musicians onstage, we
had a musician, Ben Davis, sunk into the stage, and the actors
walked around him. He played variations on Lully by Paddy
Cunneen.

Audiences loved the play and we nearly transferred it, but Ken
Stott wasn't available so that idea petered out.

Tim Albery

Tim Albery directed the first production of Crimp's *Attempts on Her
Life*.[9]

Stephen Daldry asked me to direct *Attempts on Her Life* because he
thought that my previous experience of devised work, and the use
of a mix of actors, dancers and music, would be suited to a piece
that was clearly not a traditional well-made play. So I had several
exploratory meetings with Martin about a year before the show
opened. We had time to build up trust and to consider changes to
the script. Martin's original had quite a few stage directions
because he felt that, given the lack of character and the simple dash
before each new speaker, he ought at least to suggest a setting for
each section. For example, he originally specified that the
'Strangely!' scenario should take place at a military roadblock in a
Third World country. I suggested that being so specific would stop
us from thinking laterally, that it might be better to have nothing

in the way of indications, apart from 'Silence' or 'Pause' to indicate the rhythmic shape of a scene. If you are going to tear theatrical form apart, you might as well give the director and cast total freedom. Since then, Martin says that one of the joys for him is seeing productions of *Attempts* all over the world which have exactly the same words spoken by a completely variable number, age, sex and race of actors playing totally different people with completely different stage designs.

Attempts is a template for the purest kind of play: it's just dialogue. There's nothing else: no character, no plot, no setting. The only character is Anne, who – as we know – has several different personalities, most of which are mutually exclusive. Starting with the title, which has multiple meanings, the play, in its fragmentation and irresolution, is a quintessentially modernist play. So it's no surprise that it's been done so often in Europe. It's a gift to any director, designer or actor. It's so self-aware and yet, as you discover in performance, the reality of actors playing flesh-and-blood people tends to create an unsettling counterbalance to the inherent wit of the script. So, for example, the 'Mum and Dad' scenario is upsetting and moving in performance, even though it is also a comedic parody of a typical petit-bourgeois, middle-aged, narrow-minded married couple. The task is to find the balance between emotional involvement and ironic distance.

When casting the play, I told the actors that I couldn't say exactly what part they would be playing and that they had to sign up to the whole process – all I could promise was to share out the lines as fairly as possible so that the workload was more or less equal. This was difficult for some actors to accept, but we ended up with a team which instinctively felt that the play was extraordinary even if they weren't clear how it would work. The budget allowed for eight actors, and Martin asked in the text for as great a cross-section of the world as possible: different races, languages and accents. Four men and four women of varying ages made obvious sense, and then it was a matter of finding available performers who spoke other languages: Etela Pardo is Bosnian,

Hakeem Kae-Kazim is Nigerian, and Danny Cerqueira is a Portuguese Londoner. We also had a variety of British accents: Ashley Jensen a Scot, Kacey Ainsworth with an authentic 'Essex' sound, David Fielder from the North.

My favourite scenario in terms of the work process was the last, 'Previously Frozen'. Gideon Davey, the designer, and I had decided that it should feel as if the performers were at a meal together after the show. So we had food every night provided by the Ivy restaurant, over the road from the theatre, real wine and so on, the actors by then in a version of their own clothes. On the first day's rehearsal we had read the whole play in a circle with a different actor taking over at each dash. Then before 'Previously Frozen' we broke to get lunch. Over our sandwiches, we read the scene with the actors simply taking a line when they felt like it. I had asked the stage manger to note down who spoke which line. David Fielder, for example, chose not to speak at all until three-quarters of the way through. We never looked at the scene again for about four and a half weeks. (We had a total of five weeks' rehearsal because the Court had offered a week's workshop six months before and agreed to convert it instead into an extra rehearsal week.) When we finally came to it, I asked the actors to take the same lines that they had chosen randomly on the first day. Reading it again, inconsistencies seemed to appear, with 'characters' contradicting themselves within a few lines and some of the performers wanted to swap lines in order to iron out these bumps. I asked them to invent a reason, any reason, that would allow them to say such apparently contradictory things at our notional 'dinner party'. Gradually the actors discovered various attractions and animosities towards the other 'characters', all of which came from making sense of their original random choices of line. This arbitrary division of the text seemed to me to be entirely in the spirit of Martin's writing and it undoubtedly created a scene rich in underlying tensions between the 'characters'.

The most frequent stumbling block during the process came from this notion of 'character'. Actors are trained to create character from text and from all the other indicators given by the narrative situation and backstory. In *Attempts* all those traditional aids are withheld; as with Anne herself, the notion of character is very slippery and elusive. 'Strangely!' is a case in point. It was a solo (with unseen outside interrogators) for Ashley Jensen, who has the capacity to put iron in her voice. The bit about 'Why can't she be more attractive' and 'Why can't she bend over and let us see her ass?' was vicious. It suggested an intelligent woman, the supposed victim, who could perceive what the media needs, but also that she could not fulfil those needs. Or maybe she was a media hack who's describing how another woman can't be used for the story because she's not up to scratch media-wise – the media don't want the truth, they want a sentimentalised or sexy version of the truth. As the scene progressed, who she was seemed to elide between these two possibilities. So whenever there were 'I don't know who I am supposed to be playing' and 'Am I just being myself and saying these lines?' moments, going back to the text was always the way through the problem.

Martin is the kind of writer who when he writes a comma, he means a comma, and not a full stop, and if he writes 'I mean', he means 'I mean', not 'you know'. We may not have character but we do have language, and we have to rely on that. Every single word is intended and the rhythm of the language is completely clear. The hardest thing was to get the actors to stick to the exact words on the page. On the David Mamet principle, I kept saying that the first step was to say every word in the right order. Only one scene (p. 13) didn't work. It was called 'Jungfrau (Word Association)' and, about three and a half weeks into rehearsal, Martin and I decided it should be changed. It seemed to have the wrong tone for its position in the play, and it seemed to imply that you needed to know more than was written. When read, it gave you a whole set of feelings which we couldn't realise onstage. Martin solved the problem immediately with a new scene, 'Communicating with Aliens'.

Martin was very concerned that the freedom he gave us should be enjoyed to the full. At the same time, I wanted to make sure that the piece had an overall musical shape, so that if, for example, you had one scene which was an aria, it would be followed by an ensemble, then a duet, and then a quartet. My task was to orchestrate that variety. I also wanted each cast member to have a similar workload. After a few days' rehearsal we made a definitive distribution of text which only changed a little during later rehearsals. Martin stayed away from rehearsals except when we asked him in for help during the middle weeks, and he returned for the last week. By then, we were mostly refining decisions we had already made.

In the opening scene of the staging, the cast seemed to be in the cabin of a plane that is about to crash, with emergency lighting, smoke and yellow masks on their faces. There were small microphones in the masks so they spoke their answer-machine messages through these. It made for an unnerving start. In 'The Threat of International Terrorism™', we used the full extent of the stage, which at the New Ambassadors extended a long way back. We had holes in the floor, through which half the actors' bodies emerged as if broken and wounded by an explosion, and there were open laptops facing the audience and showing pictures of buildings burning. Then two other actors went from person to person with microphones as if they were reporters. All evening we tried to create a disorientating journey, exploiting the special possibilities of theatre. As 'wings' we had the flapping, heavy-duty plastic that trucks drive through to get into depots. We aimed to create that uneasy, unsettling, J. G. Ballardesque feeling about the world which Martin's text implies. Video, hidden miking, hand-held microphones were all used as necessary; sometimes we acknowledged the audience, other times not.

Despite or maybe because of its constant playfulness, *Attempts* becomes a very serious play about the distortion of reality that we live with every day. It's about how there is nothing in our lives that is not mediated. It predicts the rise of reality TV, and *Big Brother*, and is a meditation on the idea that there is nothing so private that you cannot sell it. Being a celebrity – even if only momentarily – means being prepared to sell versions of your private life for public consumption. In this fragmented portrait of a woman who doesn't exist you get a sense of something that touches everyone: because community has collapsed, the sense of self is under threat. The play encapsulates the feeling that your own life is as vulnerable to interpretation by you and by others as everybody else's. Anne, whoever she is, is just as confused as the rest of us. Knowing too much can make you feel you know nothing – and today, there's simply too much to know.

Katie Mitchell

Katie Mitchell directed the original productions of Crimp's *The Maids*, *The Country*, *Face to the Wall* and *The Seagull*, as well as *Attempts on Her Life* in Milan.[10]

At The Other Place in Stratford, part of my remit was looking for new writers, and I read *Attempts on Her Life*. The language was very finely wrought and the subject matter, with all its images of abused women, was extremely powerful. I also found the form very exciting. I met Martin in London, then time passed, and I eventually directed *Attempts on Her Life* (as *Tracce di Anne*) at the Piccolo Theatre in Milan in 1999. I'd been to the Piccolo years before when Giorgio Strehler was heading the Union of Theatres of Europe, which involved workshops with young directors. Then the Piccolo offered these directors the chance to direct a play in the studio, although by this time Strehler had died [in 1997]. I took this opportunity to direct *Attempts on Her Life* because I didn't think I'd ever get the chance to do the play in Britain, where second productions of new plays are very rare. So I met Martin, who was very keen on the idea, although he wasn't involved in rehearsals because he was writing something else at the time.

For this Italian version, we had to perform some surgery on the text. For example, culturally specific references such as 'take-out pizzas' had to be removed, and it was too difficult to find Italian equivalents for 'The Occupier' scenario so that was dropped. Also, I had a problem with the first scenario, 'All Messages Deleted', because I thought it implied that Anne was a single composite figure, and, coming so early in the play, it planted this erroneous idea into the minds of the audience, although the rest of the piece went against it. This scenario can have the effect of implying that there is one person with one answer machine who is getting these messages. Martin had no objection to removing it, and the latest published text of the play says that the first scenario can be cut.

Before I went to Italy, I made a list of the motifs in the text: trees, ashtrays, airplanes, and so on. And the idea that occurs most often is that of children. So, on one level, the play is a vision of global capitalism and the way it menaces children. The horrors that pervade the play, from terrorist acts to sexual exploitation, from media manipulation to artistic pretension, are constantly seen as touching children. And Anne is often characterised as a child. So there's this anxiety running right through the play in which global events are felt in a very intimate, family setting. At one level, this is a play about children: how do you bring a child into a world that's as bad as this? At the end, one character says: 'He brought his own child – that's right – to watch him murder this other child's mother.'

We cast eight performers, four men and four women, but we didn't look for any of the play's characters, such as Mum or Dad figures. After a lot of discussion, I decided that the most fruitful way of directing the play was to imagine the cast as a group of young writers who had to improvise all the play's scenarios under pressure from an unseen force. So I encouraged the actors to work on the characters of these fictional writers rather than on the various characters who appear in the play. So they played these writers who were stuck in a building and under immense pressure to come up with the definitive improvisation about the play's central theme, which is global capitalism, and who kept failing, and then trying again, a bit like Beckett's phrase: 'Fail again, fail better.' So, in between the scenarios, there were scenes of absolute panic as these writers asked themselves, 'What are we going to do next?' and then someone came up with an idea, and everyone else followed. For coherence, we invented these secondary characters who could improvise all the scenarios. For my taste, *Attempts on Her Life* needs this kind of coherent ruling idea. Otherwise, it can fall apart into a series of fragments that confuse the audience.

The design, by Jeremy Herbert, was an empty theatre. The stage had a lot of depth and we used a row of chairs and the odd prop, maybe a video camera or a microphone. But, beyond the fact that you were in this stripped-back theatre, there was no other visual information apart from video images projected live on to one of the walls. In the 'Mum and Dad' scenario, for example, we had two actors, while the others filmed them. So it gave the impression of an improvised conversation, people trying out an idea. We played both the foreign-language scenarios, 'The New Anny' and 'Pornó', in Russian because one actress, Tatiana Olear, spoke Russian and she translated them. For the rhyming scenarios, we had a composer, Ludovico Einaudi, who scored these as an ensemble rap ('The Camera Loves You') and a solo jazz number ('Girl Next Door'), and he also wrote the 'passionate gypsy music' for 'Pornó'.

The 'Untitled (100 Words)' scenario draws, in part, on Jung's list of one hundred words. He would say a word, ask his patients to free-associate, timing their responses with a stopwatch, and he would then note any disturbed associations, or those which took a longer time. This word game revealed the patient's unconscious. In our production, the list of words was said very quietly by one of the cast. The effect was that this innocent list, when juxtaposed to the noise generated by the critics, had a significant emotional force.

Three scenarios – 'Tragedy of Love and Ideology', 'Faith in Ourselves' and 'Previously Frozen' – were 'free scenes', which meant that all the actors learned every line, and we improvised who said what, so the actors didn't know beforehand who'd say which line. And then there were scenes in which the lines were very strictly allocated, but where we still gave the impression that they were being improvised. A lot of the writing gives the impression that it should be spoken as if improvised, but some of it is – by contrast – very formal, for example, the music scenarios.

Attempts on Her Life, a British text that is quite subtle in its use of satire and irony, did give the Italian actors some problems. They tended to hit the line flat instead of creating the curved ball that the irony demands. They tended to think that what each character said was what they meant, when sometimes the character is clearly being ironic. And even more often the writer is using irony. For example, in 'Faith in Ourselves' they at first thought that this was a genuine scene about a victim of war rather than a discussion between media types about how to use war imagery for their own commercial purposes. Because the play's language is very powerful it's possible to get lost in the pictures it generates, and forget that it is a critique of society.

Obviously, the form that Martin has chosen is the most efficient way to communicate the play's content. For example, a normal narrative set in a cosy middle-class home with a linear story would never be able to catch the play's ideas so forcefully. The play's scenarios both create images of horror and – at the same time – comment on the way these images are created by capitalism in general and by the media in particular. Using this form, you can move from specific events to general ideas really efficiently, showing how the same pattern is repeated at every level of society, and all over the globe.

After *Attempts on Her Life*, I asked Martin to write a version of *The Maids* because I wanted to direct a piece about women and power. Although Genet wrote it to be performed by men, I was more interested in articulating his ideas by casting women. I pitched the idea to Tim Supple at the Young Vic, and he agreed. While Martin did the translation, I read everything I could by Genet, and in

particular *Funeral Rites*.[11] His *Reflections on Theatre* was also very important, and, of course, his note: 'How to Perform *The Maids*'. After Martin completed a section, we would meet and go through it line by line. It was a collaborative process and I suggested several trims that were necessary because of the difference between Genet on the page and Genet on the stage.

For both of us, the hardest thing was to understand the exact psychological steps that the characters were taking. We spent a lot of time discussing their psychology. We had to decide, at every point, what each character was really thinking, and then what they were playing. In other translations, the characters appear to take a series of incredible psychological jumps – jumps which would not be credible in life. We wanted to produce a drama that had much more organic steps in the relationship between Claire and Solange. One of the main problems was reconciling the two editions of playtexts, one published by Pavert and a later one by Gallimard.

Martin is very precise about text, and so am I, and in the published version he specified every use of the word 'you' (whether singular or plural) and so on. We also examined the way Genet repeats the same words, such as 'beauty' or 'seduce' or 'darkness'. A first-draft phrase such as 'smothered in the fog of your stagnant waters' might end up as 'steeped in your stagnant waters'. Martin also had to translate those specific cultural references, such as 'being fucked by the milkman's boy'. In the end, we had two versions, one with stage directions, and another with just the dialogue. With the cast, we went on a research trip to Paris, and met an academic called Albert Dichy, who helped us a lot.

Instead of doing Genet in a camp way, I was interested in doing him as fourth-wall realism. At the start, it's early evening and Claire and Solange are in the flat on their own, playing the game they normally play, putting on their mistress's clothing. So they don't put on all the lights because the woman across the street might see what they are doing. For that reason, we had subdued lighting. Much of the work with Martin had been diagnostic work on the text, and, once this was done, it was a matter of making the results clear for an audience. And also, because someone gets killed, it's essential to show how, in what appears to be a very safe game, something very dangerous begins to occur.

After *The Maids*, Ian Rickson [artistic director of the Royal Court] sent me a copy of *The Country*. I thought that there were a few things in the play that, on initial reading, were opaque, and so Martin and I worked on the text. One of the threads of the play is the Roman element, Virgil and so on, and we discussed how Virgil had omitted the presence of slaves in the *Georgics*. Sometimes we talked about banal things, such as whether the floor of the room should be stone, and he said that he thought stone was too cold. Wood, therefore, but certainly not carpet. And the less furniture, the more it would say. His instinct was to avoid signalling the presence of children with objects relating to them because that would be too explicit. I also asked him what Act V should look like and he said that one of the essential things was that, by now, nothing was hidden any more. So I had this image of a new dawn breaking, with lots of light. One of the changes made as a result of our conversations was the introduction of Richard's gift of shoes to Corinne, which related back to *The Maids*. Also, he cut the drinking of wine in Act V and made it a glass of water.

Martin is also interested in the choice of names. Rebecca's name is very evocative. It suggests a dark woman, with Jewish associations, part of the American Jewish intelligentsia. And, of course, it also brings to mind Pinter's *Ashes to Ashes*, which has a character called Rebecca. By contrast, a name like Sophie suggests someone who is very accommodating and generous. Corinne is a bit posher than Richard, but he has more of a social conscience than she does, although maybe his conscience is just a way of lacerating himself.

Like many writers, Martin is worried by too much scrutiny. And I'm a very scrutinising director. But I've also learned to respect his anxiety. Of course, the great thing about working with a living writer is that you can discuss the text. For example, for all the phone calls in *The Country*, Martin wrote out the unheard side of the conversation, and the actors learned the unheard parts too. He really likes the actors to be very precise and things like that helped immensely. Then, in the rehearsal room, Martin tunes in to how you are directing, and he will only give notes using the language you are using with the actors. Often, writers can confuse the work of the director. Martin doesn't.

I don't agree with those critics who see *The Country* as lacking warmth. It's clearly a play about people in trouble, which means it's full of feeling. For example, when Corinne is sitting there, having just found a needle, and thinking that Richard is shooting up again, she is tense, and therefore her language is very compressed, and you could call it cool, but that wouldn't be a helpful way of reading what is actually a passage of precise psychological writing. If anything, the play is immensely hot, particularly the explosive scene when Richard is on the telephone to Morris while his wife is confronting him with another woman's handbag. Or when Rebecca attacks Corinne, with her scalding speech about how the wife knows nothing about her husband. These are high-octane moments.

On one level, *The Country* is about what people do with their bodies: sticking syringes full of heroin into them or fucking each other, with all the mental effects of betrayal and confusion that that involves. Although the children never appear onstage, the minute that Corinne feels a real threat, she ships them bodily off to a safe place. Bodies: whether you put pure water into your body or have an alcoholic drink. It's a very visceral play. If you go through it carefully, there are countless moments when touch, or taste, or smell is mentioned. All the senses are engaged.

We had four weeks' rehearsal, which is very short, but with a living writer you can do a lot of the preparation about the backstory of the characters, which then helps the actors. As well as clarifying the psychology of the play, we also had to do the technical running of the lines so that the timing of the text was spot on, particularly the overlapping dialogue. And that took hours. Martin is so precise musically that it's very painful to him to have his lines overlapping inaccurately. His leg will twitch every time it is wrong. But getting those cues absolutely right is extremely hard work. Personally, I felt that *The Country* was perfect as a piece of writing.

We used trees suspended above the stage because we wanted to make the countryside present in the stage picture, although perhaps our solution was a bit heavy-handed. On the positive side, they did give a sense of menace and sterility. Because the Royal Court has quite a shallow stage, you can't really get a sense of the countryside beyond the room – you can only indicate countryside through lighting. But we did want to stress the idea of the country because it is central to the play: the situation of Richard bringing Rebecca home only occurs because they are not in a city. He can't leave her on the road because she might die. The small stage space also meant that we lost some of the sense of disorientation that the opening scenes should have – ideally, the room should melt into the background and there should be, according to Martin, no sense of where the walls are. In our production, you were always conscious of the walls.

When Martin sent me *Face to the Wall*, the question arose about how to put on such a short play. Directing *nightsongs*, by Jon Fosse, provided me with an opportunity to stage *Face to the Wall*. So after we opened *nightsongs*, some members of the cast also worked on *Face to the Wall*. Once again, the main thing was to find something concrete for the actors to play. The conceit we came up with was that 1, 2 and 3 were actors playing media characters and 4 was a prompter, who sat in the front row of the audience. One of the characters, 1, keeps forgetting his lines because the subject matter is so disturbing. The play has the same general style as *Attempts on Her Life*, but its content is very different, and it's aiming for a very different kind of effect. It's a much more compressed bullet of a play. It's meant to instantly disturb and unsettle you, then stop. The subject matter is very brutal, and the form is unfamiliar and disconcerting.

Edward Kemp

Dramaturg Edward Kemp worked on the original production of Crimp's *Cruel and Tender*.[12]

I saw the first production of *Dealing with Clair* at the Orange Tree in 1988 but, to be perfectly honest, it didn't particularly excite me. So I more or less ignored Martin's work until I saw *Attempts on Her Life*, which was so amazing in terms of dramatic form, and then, of course, I went back and caught up with his writing and studied it thoroughly. It's interesting that the content of his work has changed much less than its form.

Martin is one of the foremost playwrights of his generation. He sets himself rules for each of his plays, and that kind of questioning approach to theatre is very exciting. The English are deeply suspicious of theory – we value eccentricity and tradition, but not formal constraints. On the Continent, by contrast, formal rules are much more commonly used in artistic experiment. For example, Georges Perec would set himself the task of writing a novel without using the letter e.[13] Such prescriptive rules can be liberating and challenge your creativity, which then gives you the spur to finish a piece of writing.

Martin is perfectly aware of, and sensitive to, developments in playwriting in Continental Europe, especially France and Germany, and his work bridges the gap between the English and Continental traditions. In Europe, and especially in Germany, new writing has moved further and further away from traditional concerns with character, dialogue and narrative. Martin has made a journey from *Dealing with Clair*, which is in some ways a very conventional English play, to his recent work, which is much more European. But if you look at a play such as *The Country*, and strip away some of the fanciful elements – such as the linguistic mannerisms – you're left with Terence Rattigan. One of the places that Martin is writing from is that kind of core British theatre. Of course, he doesn't write about it in the same way as Rattigan, but he's recognisably in that English tradition. Martin's work also has many literary influences. When I saw *The Country*, for example, I had been reading a lot about Gertrude Stein. I have no idea whether Martin has ever read any Stein but he often hits what are Steinian cadences, permutations of a set of words, turning them around and repeating them. It's too easy to call this Pinteresque – I think he has other influences.

As a playwright myself, I'm especially fascinated by the question of how you put the words on the page. In the world of music, you have the score, which has about three hundred years' worth of agreed conventions. In theatre, there's much more flexibility, and different ways of arranging the words on the page stretch from George Bernard Shaw, who wrote novelistic stage directions, to new work, which often has no stage directions at all, and some-times no punctuation. In *Cruel and Tender*, for example, Martin uses dashes to indicate rhythms and patterns of speech. Sometimes his choices are obscure: in *Attempts*, there was a reason for not having any character names, but in *The Country* he removed the characters' names even though it's immediately obvious who is speaking. Anyway, I sense that Martin's notion is that any mark you make on the page is a communication.

Cruel and Tender was a complex co-production involving several theatres. Luc [Bondy] was about to direct Handel's opera *Hercules*, and in preparation he read the *Trachiniae*. Luc and Martin dis-cussed how you'd do a contemporary version of Sophocles' play, and this co-production gradually took shape. A lot of the problems posed by adapting Greek tragedy were solved early on. For example, Martin and Luc spent a lot of time discussing what it means to have a chorus in a contemporary setting. There was also a lot of discussion about the plot – how, for example, could you do the poisoning? Then Martin set himself the rule of mapping, as closely as possible, the form of the tragedy.

It was both liberating and nerve-racking for Martin to be given a very tight timetable. He ended up writing to order: Luc would tell him that he would be in London on a certain date, and expected to see a scene by then. So *Cruel and Tender* came to us in instalments. It was a great way to get a play because you were left breathless at the end of each instalment, waiting for the next. And each scene has a strong curtain line. So it was a bit like Dickens churning out his novels by instalments. I talked to Lindsay Posner about *The Misanthrope*: at one point Martin had got a bit stuck. So I think that the external constraint of tight deadlines inspired his creativity.

Cruel and Tender has a particular combination of head and heart, and it skates on very thin ice between being too clever for its own good and being fabulously impassioned. I remember a conversation about Alban Berg's music: Berg lived this fantastically passionate life, but he could only express this musically by having strict rules. So you get this extraordinary tension between the formality of the rules and the yearning of the music. Martin certainly felt the passion of the Greek original and when he hits the balance between formality and feeling it really works.

When we were putting the programme together, Martin, Geoffrey Layton [Bondy's dramaturg] and I had many discussions about how explicit the connection between the play and the War on Terror should be. For example, Martin was quite keen to include some passages from Baudrillard's *The Spirit of Terrorism*, particularly the material about how the tools of the West were turned against the West, which echoes the original myth's idea that the Centaur gets his revenge when his blood-soaked cloak is used against Hercules.[14] In the end, we didn't use Baudrillard because if you quote him in a programme for a European tour, especially one that includes Paris, you risk being seen as passé by French audiences. But that material was very much in our minds.

What Martin struggled most with was getting into the mind of a combat soldier. He did a lot of research, reading accounts of contemporary combat experience, and the experience of returning from war. Other reading included *Violence and the Sacred*, which examines the Hercules story in the context of ideas about ritual sacrifice, and the *Trachiniae* in the context of Freud's use of the myth of Oedipus.[15] This was also one of Luc's ways into the work. At the same time, we also considered putting into the programme a piece by Virginia Woolf about men going to war, which we found in Sontag's *Regarding the Pain of Others*, her last book.[16] It's about men and violence, and how women aren't violent. But Martin pointed out that this is exactly what the play isn't about. The play is about the same kind of violent impulse being in a woman.

What the production found, in a very satisfying way, was a visual and acting language that inhabited all three time zones of the theatre event: the period when the play was written; the world today; and the world of the archetype. For example, designer Richard Peduzzi created a set that was a completely anonymous hotel room on the edge of an international airport but its colours alluded to the classical age: the ash-grey and vermilion suggested Pompeii. On the wall was a relief of an archetypal classical image, and this was both an allusion to archetypal myths and a comment on what our civilisation does with them: we frame them and put them on the wall as replicas.

In terms of acting language, Kerry Fox as Amelia, for example, had the qualities of earth and fire, passion and intensity. During the scene change between Parts Two and Three, Amelia – to the music of Handel's *Hercules* – plays out her trauma by smearing blood over the set as the stagehands clear up and put plastic covers on the furniture. Then she picks up this exercise ball and carries it like Atlas, an age-old image. At the same time, it's a modern woman with an exercise ball. And while Kerry Fox is acting, the stagehands are moving through the set in their own world, which has nothing to do with acting. So you watched both the tragedy and its aftermath simultaneously. It was an extraordinary double image, and a stroke of genius on Luc's part.

I saw the production a lot, both at the Young Vic and Chichester, and it's not one of those easy shows that is exactly the same every night. For me, there were nights when it was a rather dry experience, much more in the head than in the heart. Then some nights it was absolutely thrilling, and exhausting emotionally. On those nights, I felt purged, stripped of those emotions of pity and terror, which is what Aristotle asks of a tragedy. In my experience, this is a rare feeling with modern productions of Greek plays. It was the play's extraordinary achievement.

David Bradby

David Bradby is a French theatre specialist, and has edited collections of plays which include Crimp's translations of *One More Wasted Year* and *Roberto Zucco*.[17]

I first came across Martin's work when I saw *Play with Repeats*, in a rather drab production at the Orange Tree, although I failed to see *Dealing with Clair*. (It's odd how you remember the plays that you've missed.) In the early 1990s, when I was head of department at Royal Holloway, I asked Max Stafford-Clark to be our visiting professor. He said that he didn't want to do that, but he suggested that the whole Royal Court could take that role, the theatre would be a collective visiting professor. We agreed a formula for this, and each year a new Court production would be studied by the whole of our first year. The students would visit the theatre to see it and then members of the production team – author, director, designer, actors – would come to Royal Holloway and talk to the students. For several years, we had this arrangement, and one of the plays was *The Treatment*. Martin came and spoke to the students.

I've seen most of Martin's work since then, and the one that really stands out for me is *Attempts on Her Life*, which is so impressive in its innovative use of form. I missed his version of *The Misanthrope*, which was booked out when I tried to get a ticket. But when I read the play, I was most impressed by its radical approach to translation. Broadly, translators have two choices: either they try and preserve a work's 'foreignness', or they try and create something which will be familiar to their audience, which is what Martin did here. His version went the whole hog, which was really good, although I wouldn't want every translation to be like this. It was as near as you can get to a truly contemporary version of a late-seventeenth-century play. It feels as if Martin worked very hard to insert this translation into the theatre culture. It has a verbal facility that is extraordinary, and these linguistic pyrotechnics are far more unrestrained than the language he uses in his own plays.

I've also seen Martin's versions of Ionesco's *The Chairs* and Genet's *The Maids*. *The Chairs* had a wonderful production, and Simon McBurney's direction managed to find the life in an old, and much-performed, play. But while Martin is extremely good at transforming classic plays into modern theatrical idioms – and this is true of both *The Misanthrope* and *Cruel and Tender* – he is less impressive in his translation of Ionesco or Genet. Martin's gift fails him a bit when he tackles the big modernist classics. Somehow, he doesn't do that much with them. I didn't feel that same surge of recognition and delight in the verbal texture of his Ionesco or Genet as I did when I read his Molière. All in all, I prefer Donald Watson's original translation of *The Chairs*.[18] Martin's version has less linguistic daring. As regards *The Maids*, I think he was a bit frightened of the more transcendental flights of fancy that Genet goes in for. For example, the moment when Madame imagines following her man off to the penal colony is conveyed in an amazing, long tirade – that kind of self-indulgent word-spinning seems to be anathema to Martin.

But Martin has an extraordinary gift for more recent plays. He has the ability to suggest what the original might have been like had the writer been working in the British theatrical culture of the late-twentieth century. So his best translations are not in his own style, but instead are wonderfully sympathetic. In *Roberto Zucco*, for example, he scripted the two comic policemen as if they were something out of Joe Orton. It's not exactly what Koltès wrote, but it's a very empathetic version that's true to the spirit of the original. If Koltès had been writing *Roberto Zucco* in English, you feel he might have done the same thing – that's a sign of a successful version.

The Royal Court had commissioned Martin to do a translation of *Roberto Zucco*, and I remember talking to him and James Macdonald about the play while the translation was being worked on.[19] Ultimately James was not able to put the play on at the Court so the Royal Shakespeare Company staged it. It was perfectly clear that *Roberto Zucco* would be the most appealing of his plays in terms of finding a readership in Britain, so I included it in the first volume of the Methuen edition of Koltès plays. Translating Koltès is extremely difficult, but in some ways *Roberto Zucco* is the easiest because, as the author himself said, he was finally shaking off the shackles of the French classical heritage. All of his earlier plays observed the neoclassical unities of time, place and action (though time is already being stretched in *Return to the Desert*). Then Koltès did a translation of *The Winter's Tale* for Patrice Chéreau [then director of the Théâtre des Amandiers, Nanterre], although it was actually put on by Luc Bondy. He said that translating Shakespeare had been the most exciting and liberating experience of his writing life. He felt he had discovered a way of structuring dramatic action in a much freer way. And *Roberto Zucco* benefited from that, being somewhere between Shakespeare and Brecht – a freewheeling epic play with its scenes linked thematically rather than by the unities. Martin succeeded in conveying this brilliantly: it's a very clever translation.

The production was very good, but I think the RSC was somewhat surprised at the excellent reception it got. In fact, they kept it in their repertoire for a year: it began at The Other Place, then toured, and finished at the Barbican Pit in London. The lead, Zubin Varla, gave the title role something that people responded to. Audiences really liked it, despite the many reviewers who complained about the play not being naturalistic, which completely missed the point. Typically, Koltès is writing in a way that contests the naturalistic form. His play shows the impossibility of understanding what it is that makes a man commit murder, especially casual killing, and it urgently asks the question: What separates that man from us? In some ways, James's production didn't go as far as it might have done. I liked the design and the rapid pacing, but Koltès needs a more imaginative use of actors. In the Chéreau and [Pascal] Gregory production of [Koltès's] *In the Solitude of Cotton Fields*, for example, at the Edinburgh Festival, the two actors performed an extraordinary kind of ballet, circling around each other, and at some moments they fell silent and did little dances to music by Massive Attack. The whole production used space, and bodily proximity, to create this sensation of desire and of the deal, not simply relying on the words. Koltès is a very physical writer.

Although Christophe Pellet's *One More Wasted Year* was part of the collection of new French work which I edited, it wasn't my favourite play. I wasn't involved in choosing it, but since it was the only play in that Royal Court season which had a full production, it had to be part of the book. To be frank, I do not consider Pellet to be an important voice in contemporary French theatre, and I don't know why the Court chose to stage this play. It's a disappointing piece, choosing to limit itself to the naturalism that most new writers in France have moved away from. It corresponds more closely to the style of play favoured by the Court than to the dominant style of verbal violence common in much French playwriting, a style that suits Martin's expressive talents better.

Gerhard Willert

Gerhard Willert has directed German-language productions of Crimp's *The Treatment*, *Attempts on Her Life* and *The Country*.[20]

I first heard about Martin in the late 1980s. A friend of mine, Corinna Brocher, who runs Rowohlt publishing company, discovered Martin's work, and introduced me to *Dealing with Clair*,

Play with Repeats and *No One Sees the Video*. When Corinna received *The Treatment*, she asked me to translate it (as *Der Dreh*), but I was unable to direct it. In 1996, Martin was in Darmstadt, where they were doing *Getting Attention* (*Das Stille Kind*), and we met and talked about my translation. After our meeting, I gave him a lift to Frankfurt airport, and asked what he was up to. He opened his black leather bag, whipped out the manuscript of *Attempts on Her Life* and dumped it on the back seat of my car saying, 'Don't touch it before I leave. Once I've gone, you can read it and let me know what you think.' That was the first draft of *Attempts on Her Life*, and I was dazzled by it, partly because, for a long time, I had wanted to find a contemporary play that challenged conventional theatre with such style. Then we had a meeting with Martin, the set designer and the composer, which lasted for two days, and after that he wrote another draft.

I saw *Attempts on Her Life* in London, and, in March 1998, I directed its German premiere (as *Angriffe auf Anne*) in Munich at the Bayerisches Staatsschauspiel, which was run by Elisabeth Schweeger. She offered us the royal stables (Marstall) as a venue; this was where the Bavarian king kept his horses, and it's a huge open space inside this beautiful baroque building. We built two stands of seating, about ten or twelve metres high, diagonally opposite each other. One was for the audience and the other for the actors. So the crowded stand for the audience was mirrored by the empty stand for the actors.

I used five actors – three men and two women. One of the men was originally from Dresden in East Germany, I had a Russian for the 'Pornó' scenario, and used Hindi for the 'New Anny' scenario (an Indian speaker taught the German actor the words). For the musical scenarios, I worked with the composer Christoph Coburger. During rehearsal, we had a lot of ideas – to use music, video and other things. But when we dug deeper, we found that we could forget all the clever ideas and concentrate on the simplest possible staging, plus some exquisite lighting. We divided the lines between the actors during rehearsal, although the really surprising thing was that there was some sort of magnet beneath the text that drew the actors to certain lines. In the manuscript, at the end of each scenario, Martin printed a sequence of small airplanes: while discussing this, we came up with this pop song, 'I Believe I Can Fly' by R. Kelly, and at the end of each scenario, the actors sang a snatch of this song, always in a different style – for example, as an old Russian hymn – which suggested that they had flown on to a new location.

Each evening, the foyer was full of the sound of 'All Messages Deleted', with the answerphone bleeping. Then, when the audience walked into the auditorium, the first thing they saw was the five actors on one of the stands. The actors were sitting, dressed like the Munich *chiceria* (literati), just like the audience. But they were completely still, like Duane Hanson's figures. This tended to throw the audience, who thought that these were also audience members, and so they sat with the actors, until they realised that something was wrong: the actors weren't moving and were part of the performance. This created a feeling of unease before the show even started. Then the lights went down, and the play began with the last line of 'All Messages Deleted'.

For me, *The Treatment* and *Attempts on Her Life* are really Part One and Part Two, a bit like Goethe's *Faust*. *The Treatment* was one of my first productions at Linz. As regards the set, it's a mistake to illustrate a play naturalistically – that tends to stifle the writing. It's childish to just paint a scene. You have to find a more evocative and a more resonant system of signs which can act as a catalyst for ideas and be abstract enough not to invade the imagination of the spectator. Florian Parbs, our set designer, had spent some time with artist Anselm Kiefer, and he created this furry carpet floor, which was very sensitive to light, and which suggested different sensations depending on different lighting. We used huge glass panels, and by using real glass we were able to give the lit panels an extreme intensity. Fake glass never has the same impact. We used projections of flickering images on the panels and, at one point, we dropped forty tiny monitors, eight by four centimetres in size, from above and these shone like the night sky, playing with the idea of nature and artifice.

What shocked our Linz audience most was the fact that Martin doesn't have a neat message. During one post-show discussion, there was a guy who had a big problem with what the play meant. So I said, 'What happens is concrete, and I can't imagine that you've been untouched by it – Martin's gift is that he gives you the freedom to think for yourself. So what did you feel?' He paused for a minute and then said, 'The longer the play lasted, the more I thought that it was like Plato's parable of the shadows on the wall of the cave' – a really marvellous interpretation.

A few people argue that, after *Attempts on Her Life*, *The Country* was a step back. I don't agree. *The Country* is not just a domestic drama. Tackling the idea of truth, it has a highly philosophical dimension. Throughout the play you can sense, between the lines, Martin's affinity to contemporary French philosophy – it's more than a joke that he calls Baudrillard a great poet of our age. (As one of the few Germans that are equally Anglo- and Francophile, do I enjoy Martin's work as much as I do because it somehow incorporates the best of both worlds?) I directed the play (as *Auf dem Land*) in Linz in 2001. For the set, we used massive loose wooden planks, a surface that was both solid and unstable, just like the marriage. On top, we put a huge wooden work table, and just two chairs. In part one, there was a large rectangular cube made of wood in the darkness at the back, where the telephone and props were. You saw the precise dimension of this object, radiating like a supernova, only in part two, when it was suspended and lit from behind. Martin said he was pleased that I'd managed to open out the play by not having walls. It was interesting that the audience left the play talking intensely about their own relationships and their own problems.

What intrigues me about Martin's work is his musicality. When I first met him, I was not surprised to find that he knows the music of Bach inside out. His work is condensed and full of counterpoint. It's a great mistake to see Martin's language as realistic: it's not. Its surface resembles everyday speech because that is the material he examines, but it is just a resemblance. He boils his material down to the bone until it reveals its structure. Hence, Martin's work is merciless in its unspectacular cruelty – he has an extremely lucid way of looking at modern life, deeply steeped in irony. There's a book by Freud, *Das Unbehagen in der Kultur* [*Civilization and its Discontents*], which addresses the unease in contemporary culture – Martin's work deals with that basic feeling of unease.[21] With the exception of Michel Vinaver in France and perhaps Roland Schimmelpfennig in Germany, I can't see many playwrights that follow this path. Crimp's essence is spiky and powerful and difficult, and that's also the fun of it.

James Macdonald

James Macdonald directed the original production of Crimp's *Fewer Emergencies*, as well as his translations of *Roberto Zucco* and *The Triumph of Love*.[22]

I'd seen and read Martin's plays before I came to the Royal Court, and a year after I became an associate we did *The Treatment*. Then we invited Martin to be our writer-in-residence, and I remember going on a trip to Paris with him and Graham [Whybrow, literary manager] to find out more about contemporary French writers. So *Roberto Zucco* came partly out of that shared enthusiasm. A translation of the play had been sent to me by Giles Croft, [then] literary manager at the National, because they'd decided not to do it. I put it forward at a script meeting, and Martin's line was that it was a marvellous play and that the Court should do it, but only if he could translate it. And so he wrote a beautiful version, which we never got around to programming – it needs a huge cast and at that point we couldn't justify putting those kind of resources into a dead French playwright's work. Then Katie [Mitchell], who was running The Other Place, asked me to direct something, and

Roberto Zucco's scale and its echoing of Shakespeare made it an ideal thing to do at the RSC.

I suspect this is the easiest of Koltès's plays for a British audience to relate to. Although Zucco is a chameleon, there is more than enough psychological continuity to sustain a British audience. Koltès writes in this extraordinary heightened language – the characters have wonderful riffs, or arcs of thought, like speeches in classical drama. But in this play the poetry is laced with demotic language, grounded in the street, and Martin found a beautiful way of doing this in English. So all one's Anglo-Saxon anxiety about the abstractness of French rhetoric was blown away. And once the actors had worked out both how demanding and how much fun this language was to play with, it became electric. Young audiences in particular were hypnotised by it.

Roberto Zucco was designed by Jeremy [Herbert], who I'd already worked with on *Thyestes* and *Cleansed*. On and off, I think we had ten weeks' rehearsal at the RSC and the set model didn't arrive until maybe the sixth week: Jeremy had this idea of using luminous paint on the floor of the set, so we ushered the actors into a windowless rehearsal room, he turned out the lights – and there was the model glowing in the dark. By that time, of course, the actors knew the play well so it was easier for them to see why we'd made certain choices. We used traverse staging, partly to shake up the way The Other Place had normally been used. And the paint was there to show ghostly traces of Zucco's journey through life. He's described in the play as a rhinoceros charging through the city, and the play is full of that energy, so we had the idea that he would always cross the stage in the same direction, passing down the space and disappearing. We wanted the feeling that he was charging down this tunnel again and again, towards death, and the luminous paint kicked in when we cut the lights at the end of each scene, outlining the shadow of a body which had already gone.

Part of what is fascinating about this play is that Koltès knew he was dying when he wrote it, and it's about a boy with a death wish.

Koltès picked the story up from the media, and he didn't do a lot of research – but his understanding of the boy was intuitive and uncannily accurate. He uses him to articulate his own anger at the bourgeois world that Zucco crashes through, but somehow always does so with great wit and playfulness. And absolutely without sentiment or moral comment. What was fun about doing this at the RSC was the fact that Koltès clearly loved Shakespeare – *Hamlet* and *Twelfth Night* especially – and set out to write a classical play on a contemporary theme, complete with plot, subplot and sly references to Shakespeare. It's something I can't imagine a British writer daring to do – we're much too reverential about our Bard.

With *Fewer Emergencies*, I did a week-long workshop with a group of actors, and later another two-day workshop with designer Tom [Pye] and the actual cast. It's such an open piece of writing that we needed to experiment with what an audience might be looking at before we could decide on the design. At one point in this process Martin described the play as just the voices in his head. The gesture he was making was to cut out all the other stuff – character, psychology, plot, setting, real time – that normally gets in between what the writer hears or sees in his head and what the audience ends up seeing or hearing. We were looking for some kind of key to help the actors locate what or who they were playing. We quickly discovered that whenever they tried to relate to each other in a naturalistic or psychological way it didn't work, because the text hadn't been written like that and it simply couldn't be reduced to a conventional scene or consistent characters. And finally the penny dropped that the best way to give the actors a reason to speak was to just say: we're all inside Martin's head.

As Martin had jettisoned all conventional theatrical procedure in this text, it felt important to do the same thing with the production. We wanted to throw up in the air what an audience might expect from a production – just as the writing challenges what one might expect from a play. And the tone of Martin's writing is often provocative in a playful and ironic way, which one needs to honour. So we started by turning the Theatre Upstairs black box into a white box, including the seating, and brought the lights up when the play started instead of dimming them. There was no set, no situation: just three or four voices discussing a possible situation, chewing away at it. The actors kept relatively still so that the audience could listen carefully and not be distracted by any action. No visible theatre lights, just an atmosphere that acts as a germ or a mood for each story. And by wrapping the set around the audience, the intention was to make them complicit: we're all inside Martin's head.

At one point in a workshop, looking for how to convey mental process, we tried doing the text with the actors sitting behind the audience so you weren't focused on them, but this taught us that you had to actually see the thinking. What worked was having several people sitting on the same eyeline, so that an audience could easily watch them thinking the same thing at the same time. This became the central image of the production – all of the actors inhabiting one imagination, regardless of whether they were speaking or not. There's always a bit of your brain that's choosing not to speak! And when it came to the [four-week] rehearsal period, we did a lot of work on what people do when they're thinking. Because the task for the actors was to embody a play-wright's mind, they met several, and they gave us classes in playwriting. And we spent a fascinating morning simply watching each other think. The process was to get good at looking like you're making it up in the moment – in one sense, this is what acting is – and to do this we had to practise really making it up. So initially it took hours to tell each story, but gradually the actors became like a single mind jumping fluently from one idea to another.

Martin is a very fastidious writer, and in *Fewer Emergencies* he musically and instinctively captures exactly how his own mind works. One of the pleasures of working on this text was to see how often an idea arrives from completely leftfield, and to celebrate these – a writer's Dionysian moments. The boldness of the play is that there is nothing there except the voice. Which makes the listener wonder: who does the voice belong to, and what is that person's relationship to their stories? In provoking this question, Martin makes you ask how emotionally connected he himself is to his material – the voice seems sometimes sympathetic, and sometimes chillingly detached. How compromised is this author in relation to the world he is describing?

Martin is a brilliant political playwright precisely because he is prepared to put himself and his own world publicly into question. The writing is both self-critical and a clever sleight of hand which turns the tables on a liberal audience. It's centred on the experience of being a 'have', and in this play Martin uses extraordinary imagery to describe the gap between the 'haves' and the 'have-nots', which in the Western world is increasing all the time. This is acute, and absolutely on the nose: he's saying it's all about us. There are more emergencies in the world because we have the goods and other people don't. And that's all you need to know – so what are you going to do about it? Which makes an audience uncomfortable. In a useful way.

APPENDIX: ATTEMPTS ON HIS LIFE

This book has concentrated on Martin Crimp's work. Biographical details, anecdotes about his life and clues to his character have been few. For good reason. In *The Misanthrope*, for example, Crimp parodies the biographical approach to playwriting when Covington says: 'it's directly based / on my own personal experience.' To which Alceste replies: 'Well that's often the case' (p. 120). To suggest some of the problems of relating the life to the work, especially when the life is relatively uneventful, I will now risk adopting a Crimpian strategy to describe his life as a writer. Since in *Attempts on Her Life*, each of the seventeen scenarios about Anne obscures as much as it reveals, it seems perfectly apt to create seventeen mini-scenarios about a character called the Writer, and a would-be biographer called the Critic.

1. The Project
For his next book, the Critic decides to focus on an individual playwright, the Writer. But he is perturbed by the popular post-modern theory that proclaims the Death of the Author. What if the Writer hasn't written his plays? What if language has merely spoken through him? The next day, the Critic catches a glimpse of the Writer at the opening of a show in London. Phew, at least he's still alive. But what is he like as a person?

2. The School

The first thing that the Critic establishes about the Writer is that he went to the same school as another famous writer. So he then scans the Writer's work for clues to his upbringing, his family, his school. With conspicuously little success.

3. The Background

For background, the Critic approaches the Writer's Agent. Does she have any background information on him? Like what? Oh, you know, feature articles, or profiles, or even revealing interviews. After a couple of days, the Agent gets back to the Critic. No, there's no background material on file. In the past, muses the Critic, writers could appear as the Underground Man, the Superfluous Man or The Man without Qualities. Today, the Writer appears as the Man without a Background.

4. The Academic

The Critic contacts the Academic. He's heard that the Writer, who is fast becoming *his* playwright, has visited the Academic's university and given a talk to his students. Surely, he must have spoken frankly about his life. So the Critic asks the Academic for a recording of his talk. The Academic tells him that the Writer refused to be recorded, and that all he remembers is that he repeatedly insisted that he is a 'satirist'.

5. The Translation

The Critic finds out that the Writer has given his most candid interview to a Foreign Critic. Seeing that the Foreign Critic has published the interview in a language the Critic cannot read, he contacts him and asks him for the original transcript. But the Foreign Critic tells him that the original transcript vanished when his computer was stolen. And he didn't keep the tapes. But he offers to send the Critic the translated version. Now the Critic has to find a translator to translate the translated interview back into English. In the process of retranslation, much is lost. The Writer remains elusive.

6. *The Programme Note*

The Critic is asked to write a programme note for a revival of one of the Writer's plays. This forces him to look in detail at his work. He is struck anew with a sense of its passion, its fierceness and its cruelty. He struggles to reconcile this with his personal knowledge of the Writer, who always appears detached, gentle and kind. It is time to stay up all night tussling with ideas about the workings of the human imagination.

7. *The Newspaper Article*

As the Writer's new play is about to be staged, the Critic tries to place an article about him in a Sunday broadsheet. But he's asked to interview the Director instead. He does so, and writes an appreciative piece about the Director's skills. In it, he includes some quotations from the Writer. The article comes back from the editors. What's all this stuff about theatre? What we want to know about is the Director's private life. What does he drink? How badly does he dress? Who is he sleeping with? To accommodate this extra material, the Critic has to cut the quotations from the Writer.

8. *The Festival*

On a trip abroad, the Critic and the Writer are both guests of the same theatre festival. They appear on the same public panels, are interviewed by the same journalists and drink the same kind of wine. For a short while they are treated as heroes – then it's time to come home. On their return, the Critic struggles to create a picture of the Writer's character. He gives up when he realises that, in the highly artificial atmosphere of a foreign theatre festival, they were both playing a role.

9. *The Research*

On a research visit to the Theatre Museum, the Critic discovers a rare newspaper article written by the Writer. It is an ironic account of his imaginary meeting with a long-dead, now classic, Foreign Playwright, whose work he has translated. In it, the Foreign

Playwright is made to say: 'No personal questions! Is this taste for sleaze / really essential to British journalese? / This nation must be utterly mind-fucked / to salivate over people's private sexual conduct.' The Critic abandons his plan to ask the Writer about how his private life has influenced his work.

10. The Music

Aware that the Writer is an accomplished musician, the Critic scans his work for evidence of a musical ear. Everywhere, references to classical music jump out at him. Suddenly his work seems to be all about music and nothing else. Even the dialogues seem like songs; while reading, the Critic finds himself humming them like tunes.

11. The Opening Night

The Critic attends the first night of a play by a young German Playwright. He finds himself sitting directly behind the Writer, the English Writer – *his* Writer. As the German play unfolds, the Critic not only watches the new play over the head of the Writer, but also sees it exclusively through the prism of the Writer's work. He leaves the theatre with a distinct feeling that he hasn't really appreciated the German Playwright's work for its own sake.

12. The Supermarket

As word of the Critic's book spreads, he hears many reports of sightings of the Writer. Oddly enough, they all seem to occur in a supermarket. Is this Writer a particularly fanatical shopper? Or more than usually hungry? Or are supermarkets simply one of the few public places left where chance encounters actually happen?

13. The Family

The Writer is a family man. The critic meets the Writer's Family on more than one occasion. And nothing he sees or hears when meeting the Writer's Family has the slightest relationship to the Writer's work. Is it possible – has the Writer really purged himself of the autobiographical fallacy?

14. The Postcard

The Writer sends the Critic a picture postcard. The Critic examines this for clues. Is there a subtext beneath the cheerful greeting? What does the image on the postcard mean? What clues does the handwriting give to the Writer's character? The idea of analysing the Writer's handwriting only shows the Critic the absurdity of his obsession with the life. Better stick to the work.

15. The Obit

The Critic learns that two Spanish Academics have interviewed the Writer. So how was he? Oh, 'He was most helpful and generous with his time, specially considering that he had arrived only the day before and had the journalists waiting for him,' they reply. When the Critic tells the Writer about this, he summarises their response as: 'Tired but helpful.' The Writer laughs: 'He was tired but helpful – sounds like a good obituary.'

16. The Interview

The Critic interviews the Writer for a magazine article. During the course of the interview, he struggles to find a way of describing the Writer's gestures, his taste in mineral water and his dress sense. At one point, in what seems like an unthinking gesture of generous revelation, the Writer says: 'It's a question of my temperament – I always want to take the devious route.' As a psychological key, it's not much, but it's the nearest the Critic gets.

17. The End

The Critic can't think of a good way of finishing his book. So he decides to write an entertainment based on the Writer's own work. But much as he flatters himself on his own satirical skills, he slowly realises that his attempt to get under the skin of the Writer is, alas, only partially successful. In the end, any resemblance between these characters and any person living or dead is purely . . .

TIMELINE

1978   Crimp graduates from Cambridge University.

1981   Joins the writers group at the Orange Tree.

1982   9 April–1 May: *Love Games* at the Orange Tree.

        9–25 July: *Living Remains* at the Orange Tree.

1984   15 October–17 November: *Four Attempted Acts* at the Orange Tree.

1985   15 May: *Three Attempted Acts* broadcast on BBC Radio 3.

        13 December–19 January 1986: *A Variety of Death-Defying Acts* at the Orange Tree.

1986   2 December: *Six Figures at the Base of a Crucifixion* broadcast on BBC Radio 3.

1987   21 April: *Definitely the Bahamas* broadcast on BBC Radio 3.

        25 September–17 October: *Definitely the Bahamas* at the Orange Tree.

1988   14 October–12 November: *Dealing with Clair* at the Orange Tree.

        Thames TV Writer-in-Residence, 1988–9.

1989   12 October–11 November: *Play with Repeats* at the Orange Tree.

1990   22 November–15 December: *No One Sees the Video* at the Royal Court.

        Receives Arts Council Theatre Writing bursary.

1991   6–9, 18–23 March: *Getting Attention* at the West Yorkshire Playhouse.

15 May–8 June: *Getting Attention* at the Royal Court.

26 May: *Dealing with Clair* broadcast on BBC World Service.

Writer-in-residence at New Dramatists, New York.

1992   24 September: *Dealing with Clair* broadcast on BBC Radio 4.

1993   15 April–15 May: *The Treatment* at the Royal Court.

1996   8 February–23 March: *The Misanthrope* at the Young Vic.

1997   7 March–5 April: *Attempts on Her Life* at the Royal Court (New Ambassadors).

22–25 October: *The Chairs* at Theatre Royal, Bath.

28 October–1 November: *The Chairs* at Gardner Arts Centre, Brighton.

5–8 November: *The Chairs* at Lawrence Batley Theatre, Huddersfield.

11–15 November: *The Chairs* at Oxford Playhouse.

16 November: *The Country* broadcast on BBC Radio 3.

18 November–18 December: *One More Wasted Year* at the Royal Court (New Ambassadors).

19 November–1 January 1998: *The Chairs* at the Royal Court (Duke of York's).

20 November–11 February 1998: *Roberto Zucco* at the RSC's Other Place, Stratford-upon-Avon.

Writer-in-residence at the Royal Court.

1998   21–24 October: *Roberto Zucco* at the Gulbenkian Studio, Newcastle-upon-Tyne.

25–28 November: *Roberto Zucco* at the Drum, Plymouth.

1999   31 March–1 May: *Roberto Zucco* at the Pit, Barbican.

1 July–7 August: *The Maids* at the Young Vic.

26 August–25 September: *The Triumph of Love* at the Almeida.

2000   17 February–17 January 2004: *The Merry Widow* in rep at the Met, New York.

11 May–10 June: *The Country* at the Royal Court.

2002   12–23 March: *Face to the Wall* at the Royal Court.

2003 7 April: *Advice to Iraqi Women* at the Royal Court.

2004 5–15 May, 17 June–10 July: *Cruel and Tender* at the Young Vic.

23 May–4 June: *Cruel and Tender* at the Wiener Festwochen, Vienna.

26 May–15 September: *The False Servant* at the National Theatre.

9–13 June: *Cruel and Tender* at the Ruhrfestspiele, Recklinghausen.

4 August–4 September: *Cruel and Tender* at the Chichester Festival Theatre.

21 September–3 October: *Cruel and Tender* at the Bouffes du Nord, Paris.

12–16 October: *Cruel and Tender* at the Théâtre National Populaire, Villeurbaune.

2005 8 September–1 October: *Fewer Emergencies* at the Royal Court.

2006 17 June–23 September: *The Seagull* at the National Theatre.

NOTES

References to *Dealing with Clair, Play with Repeats, Getting Attention* and *The Treatment* are to *Martin Crimp: Plays One* (2000). References to *No One Sees the Video, The Misanthrope, Attempts on Her Life* and *The Country* are to *Martin Crimp: Plays Two* (2005). All theatre programmes, and other documents related to specific stagings, can be found in production files held at the Theatre Museum Study Room, Blythe House, 23 Blythe Road, London W14 0QX. Website: http://www.theatremuseum.org.uk.

Introduction

1. John Whitley, 'The Enigma That Is Mr Crimp'.
2. Dominic Dromgoole, *The Full Room*, p. 62.
3. Crimp quoted in Stephen Gallagher, 'Crimp and Crave', p. 12.
4. Pilar Zozaya and Mireia Aragay, 'Interview with Martin Crimp'.
5. Crimp quoted in Gallagher, op. cit.
6. John Thaxter, 'Sex and Suffering'.
7. Ibid.
8. Caroline Donald, 'Frozen Pizza and the Search for Happiness'.
9. Rick Jones, 'Scriptwriters from Hell'.
10. Whitley, op. cit., and Paul Taylor, 'The World According to Crimp'.
11. John O'Mahony, 'Writers' Crimp'.
12. Nils Tabert, 'Gespräch mit Martin Crimp', p. 251.

13. Crimp, *Getting Attention & No One Sees the Video*, p. vii.

14. Crimp, *Plays One*, p. vii.

15. Crimp, *Plays Two*, p. xiv.

16. *Plays One*, p. xi. The director is Gerhard Willert (see interview on pp. 212–16).

17. Richard Eyre and Nicholas Wright, *Changing Stages*, p. 374.

18. Vera Gottlieb, '1979 and After: A View', in Baz Kershaw (ed.), *The Cambridge History of British Theatre: Volume 3 – Since 1895*, p. 421.

19. Dominic Shellard, *British Theatre Since the War*.

20. David Ian Rabey, *English Drama Since 1940*, pp. 192–3. See also note on p. 209: 'Crimp experiments with various forms: *The Treatment* is a memorable fable of commercial and personal rapaciousness in New York, reminiscent of Mamet; *Attempts on Her Life* (R[oyal] C[ourt], 1997) is an open text for ensemble choreography, anticipating [Sarah] Kane's *4:48 Psychosis* (2001): *The Country* (2000) is strongly reminiscent of mid-period Pinter.' Here Crimp appears not as an original writer, but as an imitator of Mamet and Pinter and an anticipator of, rather than inspiration for, Kane.

21. See Dan Rebellato, 'Crimp, Martin [Andrew]', in Colin Chambers (ed.), *The Continuum Companion to Twentieth Century Theatre*, pp. 182–3.

22. See Peter Thomson, 'Crimp, Martin (Andrew)', in Thomas Riggs (ed.), *Contemporary Dramatists*, pp. 123–4. Although this book was published in 1999, the entry only includes *Dealing with Clair*, *Play with Repeats*, *No One Sees the Video* and *Getting Attention*. Crimp's best work, such as *The Treatment* and *Attempts on Her Life*, is listed but not discussed.

23. Keith D. Peacock, *Thatcher's Theatre*, p. 16.

24. Quoted in Stephen Lacey, 'British Theatre and Commerce, 1979–2000', in Kershaw, op. cit., p. 426.

25. Robert Hewison, *Culture and Consensus*, p. 285.

26. Peacock, op. cit., p. 215.

27. See John Fletcher and James McFarlane, 'Modernist Drama:

Origins and Patterns', in Malcolm Bradbury and James McFarlane (eds), *Modernism* (Harmondsworth: Penguin, 1976), pp. 497–513.

28. See Martin Esslin, *The Theatre of the Absurd.*

29. Quoted in Paul Allen, *Alan Ayckbourn: Grinning at the Edge*, (London: Methuen, 2001), pp. 274–5.

1: 'A Knock at the Door'

1. The theatre was an upstairs room in the Orange Tree pub, on the corner of Kew Road and Clarence Street. Its office was in Hill Street. In 1991, the theatre moved across Clarence Street to a new building, formerly a Victorian school, and was the first purpose-built theatre-in-the-round in London.

2. The other venues were Soho Poly and Ambiance (Rosalind Asquith, 'Subversion at Lunchtime or Business as Usual?', in Sandy Craig (ed.), *Dreams and Deconstructions*, p. 150).

3. Sierz, interview with Walters, 25 February 2005. In 2005, Crimp said: 'It never really occurred to me that I would actually become a writer of plays. This happened quite by chance. I had written a play, and I got involved through it with the theatre on my doorstep, the Orange Tree Theatre. That again was also by chance, because it was geographical' (Pilar Zozaya and Mireia Aragay, 'Interview with Martin Crimp'). See also interview with Anthony Clark, pp. 177–9.

4. The *Love Games* programme note says that 'the play was written in 1981 and produced in Warsaw prior to martial law being declared in Poland'. At the time, Poland was the subject of much discussion in left-wing circles. In August 1980, an independent trade union, Solidarność (Solidarity), led by electrician Lech Wałęsa, emerged during strikes in Gdansk. An early example of People Power, Solidarność soon won a reduction in working hours and the relaxation of censorship. Then, after a return of tensions due to food shortages in autumn 1981, the Soviet Union pressurised Polish leader General Jaruzelski into declaring martial law on 14 December

1981. Wałęsa was arrested and was still in prison when *Love Games* premiered, and Solidarność featured in post-show discussions on 23 and 24 April 1982. In November, Wałęsa was released and in 1983 martial law was lifted. Solidarność played a central role in the overthrow of the Communist state in 1989. See Neal Ascherson, *The Struggles for Poland* (London: Pan, 1988), and Misha Glenny, *The Rebirth of History: Eastern Europe in the Age of Democracy* (Harmondsworth: Penguin, 1993).

5. *Guardian*, 10 April 1982; *London Theatre Record*, Vol. II, Issue 8 (1982), p. 181. No review mentioned the writers.

6. *Living Remains* programme. The other play was Peter Bennett's *Ultraviolet*. The programme note states: 'Both Peter Bennett and Martin Crimp are members of the Orange Tree Writers Workshop which has been meeting regularly since September [1981].'

7. Reminiscent, surely, of Molloy's 'One knock meant yes, two no' in Samuel Beckett, *Trilogy: Molloy, Malone Dies, The Unnamable* (London: John Calder, 1959), p. 18. All references are to *Living Remains*. See also interview with Auriol Smith, pp. 179–82.

8. Mary Luckhurst's comment that *Living Remains* is 'about a woman trapped in a cubicle' is wrong. The woman is outside the cubicle; her husband is in the cubicle. The play was written in 1981 and first performed in 1982, not 1983–4 as stated by Luckhurst (Luckhurst, 'Political Point-Scoring: Martin Crimp's *Attempts on Her Life*', p. 53). As a lunchtime show, *Living Remains* was not reviewed by the major critics. During its run, the Orange Tree also held a rehearsed reading on 11 July 1982, organised by Amnesty International, of *The Trial of Vladimir Bukovsky*, about the Soviet dissident (*Living Remains* flyer).

9. See Peter Clark, *Hope and Glory* and Arthur Marwick, *British Society Since 1945*.

10. W. B. Yeats, 'The Second Coming', 1921.

11. Edward Bond, *Plays 4: The Worlds, The Activists Papers, Restoration, Summer* (London: Methuen, 1992), p. 75; Caryl

Churchill, *Plays 2: Softcops, Top Girls, Fen, Serious Money* (London: Methuen, 1990), pp. 137–8.

12. Jim Cartwright, *Plays 1: Road, Bed, Two, The Rise and Fall of Little Voice* (London: Methuen, 1996), p. 82.

13. A flyer advertising the theatre's 'Play a Day' series shows that Clark directed a reading of *Four Attempted Acts* on 18 May 1984. All references are to *Four Attempted Acts*.

14. Christine Eccles, *City Limits*, 19 October 1984; *London Theatre Record*, Vol. IV, Issue 21 (1984), p. 920.

15. Dominic Shellard, *British Theatre Since the War*, p. 193.

16. All references are to *A Variety of Death-Defying Acts*. See also *A Variety of Death-Defying Acts* programme, and interview with Auriol Smith, pp. 179–82.

17. Lyn Gardner, *City Limits*, 20 December 1985, and Christine Eccles, *Time Out*, 19 December 1985; *London Theatre Record*, Vol. V, Issue 25/26 (1986), p. 1222.

18. *A Variety of Death-Defying Acts* programme.

19. Heiner Zimmermann, 'Images of Woman in Martin Crimp's *Attempts on Her Life*', p. 70.

20. Jeremy Kingston, picture caption, *The Times*, 24 September 1987. Auriol Smith discussed Crimp with McCowen, and she suggested his name to Walters when the latter realised that he couldn't direct Crimp's next play because he was busy with two other plays. Walters, email to Sierz, 19 April 2005.

21. All references are to *Definitely the Bahamas*.

22. *Sunday Times*, 4 October 1987; *Daily Telegraph*, 28 September 1987; *Guardian*, 28 September 1987; *Punch*, 14 October 1987; *London Theatre Record*, Vol. VII, Issue 20 (1987), pp. 1253–5.

23. 'A cheap holiday in other people's misery! / I don't wanna holiday in the sun / I wanna go to new Belsen' (Sex Pistols, 'Holidays in the Sun', 1977).

24. No byline, 'Coat in the Act', *Evening Standard*, 7 September 1988. Unsurprisingly, Courtenay is quoted as saying, 'When I read it [the playtext] I thought it was very interesting and full of good writing.'

25. All references to *Dealing with Clair* are to *Plays One*. See also interview with Joe Penhall, pp. 182–5.

26. Luckhurst's idea that Clair 'simply decides to "vanish" into another life and identity' (op. cit., pp. 52, 54) is unlikely. She has been abducted and murdered.

27. *Daily Mail*, 3 October 1988; *Independent*, 18 October 1988; *Daily Telegraph*, 18 October 1988; *London Theatre Record*, Vol. VIII, Issue 21 (1988), pp. 1443–5.

28. Reminiscent, perhaps, of the 'Miss Barclay can't have vanished into thin air' episode in Joe Orton, *What the Butler Saw* (London: Methuen, 1976), p. 25.

29. Sierz, interview with Walters, 25 February 2005.

30. All references to *Play with Repeats* are to *Plays One*.

31. There's also a touch of Ionesco's Old Man from *The Chairs* in Tony's idea that he has accumulated a lifetime of worthwhile wisdom. See Chapter 4.

32. *Guardian*, 16 October 1989; *City Limits*, 19 October 1989; *Daily Telegraph*, 16 October 1989; *London Theatre Record*, Vol. IX, Issue 21 (1989), pp. 1384–5, and Vol. IX, Issue 22, p. 1506.

33. Peter Thomson, 'Crimp, Martin (Andrew)', in Thomas Riggs (ed.), *Contemporary Dramatists*, p. 124.

34. *Play with Repeats* programme.

2: 'Denial, Brutality and Sheer Human Confusion'

1. Colin Chambers, *Inside the Royal Shakespeare Company*, p. 132.

2. See Richard Eyre and Nicholas Wright, *Changing Stages*, p. 247, and Irving Wardle, *The Theatres of George Devine*, pp. 170, 199–200, 212.

3. Michael Billington, *One Night Stands*, p. 308.

4. Philip Roberts, *The Royal Court Theatre and the Modern Stage*, p. 206.

5. Ibid., p. 210.

6. David Edgar, *State of Play*, p. 19.

7. *Guardian* advert, 22 November 1990.

8. Caroline Donald, 'Frozen Pizza and the Search for Happiness'.

9. Billington, op. cit., pp. 328, 347–9.

10. Donald, op. cit. The focus on the language of work is a reminder of the influence of David Mamet on Crimp. See also interview with Lindsay Posner, pp. 188–92.

11. All references to *No One Sees the Video* are to *Plays Two*.

12. *Guardian*, 29 November 1990; *Daily Telegraph*, 29 November 1990; *Time Out*, 5 December 1990; *Herald Tribune*, 5 December 1990; *Observer*, 2 December 1990; *London Theatre Record*, Vol. X, Issue 24 (1990), pp. 1593–4, 1599.

13. Quoted in Donald, op. cit.

14. Ibid. Compare Crimp's 'a post-consumer play, i.e. it describes a world in which the equation of consumption with happiness is no longer debated, but is simply as axiomatic to daily life as Newtonian mechanics' (Crimp, *Getting Attention & No One Sees the Video*, p. vii). Here he also describes one of the play's themes: 'I was fascinated by the idea of a person who finds herself forced by circumstances to defend everything she most despises.'

15. Ibid.

16. All references to *Getting Attention* are to *Plays One*. See also interview with Jude Kelly, pp. 185–7.

17. *Guardian*, 8 March 1991; *Independent*, 11 March 1991; *The Times*, 11 March 1991; *Independent*, 18 May 1991; *Guardian*, 18 May 1991; *Theatre Record*, Vol. XI, Issue 5 (1991), p. 294, and Vol. XI, Issue 10, pp. 603–4. The previous play in the season was Kay Mellor's *In All Innocence*.

18. Crimp quoted in Jane Edwardes, 'Kid Gloves'.

19. See Wendy Lesser, *A Director Calls*, pp. 89–118.

20. Author's own copy.

21. Sheila Johnston, 'Tales from Hollywood', cutting in Theatre Museum, no newspaper, no date.

22. Crimp quoted in John O'Mahony, 'Writers' Crimp'.

23. Crimp quoted in Rick Jones, 'Scriptwriters from Hell'.

24. All references to *The Treatment* are to *Plays One*. See also interview with Lindsay Posner, pp. 188–92.

25. *Guardian*, 22 April 1993; *Sunday Times*, 25 April 1993; *The*

Times, 22 April 1993; *Evening Standard*, 21 April 1993; *Theatre Record*, Vol. XIII, Issue 8 (1993), pp. 403, 431–4.

26. No byline, 'A Return to Court', *Evening Standard*, 7 April 1993.

27. Johnston, op. cit.

28. David Ian Rabey, *English Drama Since 1940*, p. 192. Reminiscent, perhaps, of the blind guide in the Isle of Mull episode in R. L. Stevenson, *Kidnapped* (Harmondsworth: Penguin, 2005).

29. Antony Thorncroft, 'Award for Young Dramatist', *Financial Times*, 8 September 1993.

30. See Aleks Sierz, *In-Yer-Face Theatre*, pp. 90–100, and Graham Saunders, *'Love Me or Kill Me'*, pp. 8–12, 37–8.

31. Crimp, Paul Godfrey, Meredith Oakes and Gregory Motton, 'Blasted: A Savage Play Looks Beyond Indifference to a Savage World', *Guardian*, 23 January 1995.

32. *Guardian*, 13 March 1996; *The Times*, 1 May 1996; *The Times*, 14 May 1997. See also Benedict Nightingale, *The Future of Theatre*, pp. 17–22.

33. Dominic Cavendish, 'Martin Crimp Talks about *Cruel and Tender*'. Note: Crimp's *The Misanthrope* is in this chapter because, unlike his other translations, he sees it more as an original play than as a straight translation. All references to *The Misanthrope* are to *Plays Two*. See also interviews with Lindsay Posner, pp. 188–92, and David Bradby, pp. 209–12.

34. Quoted in Matt Wolf, 'Thoroughly Modern Molière', *The Times*, 6 February 1996.

35. *Daily Telegraph*, 15 February 1996; *Spectator*, 24 February 1996; *Guardian*, 15 February 1996; *Observer*, 18 February 1996; *Theatre Record*, Vol. XVI, Issue 4 (1996), pp. 205–7. Tom Stoppard's *Arcadia* also has two characters with names which refer to critics: Bernard Nightingale and Valentine Coverly.

36. Crimp, 'Mol Flounders'. The helicopter is a reference to Alain Boublil and Claude-Michel Schönberg's musical *Miss Saigon* (1989).

3: 'Privileged Distance from Death and Dismemberment'

1. See 'Why London rules', *Newsweek*, 4 November 1996; *Sunday Times*, 5 April 1998; Chris Smith, *Creative Britain*.
2. David Edgar, *State of Play*, p. 23.
3. There's a brief parody of Major's ill-fated Back to Basics moral campaign in *The Misanthrope*, p. 110.
4. All references to *Attempts on Her Life* are to *Plays Two*. See also interviews with Tim Albery, pp. 192–7, Katie Mitchell, pp. 197–204, and Gerhard Willert, pp. 212–16.
5. Note in *Attempts on Her Life* (1997), no page number.
6. *Evening Standard*, 13 March 1997; *Independent*, 14 March 1997; *Sunday Times*, 23 March 1997; *New Statesman*, 21 March 1997, p. 48; *Financial Times*, 15 March 1997; *Guardian*, 13 March 1997; *Theatre Record*, Vol. XVII, Issue 6 (1997), pp. 311–12.
7. 'I asked Martin, "How would you answer the question of who Anne is?" and he said, "She's a theatrical device."' Anne Tipton, interview with Sierz (4 May 2005).
8. Nils Tabert, 'Gespräch mit Martin Crimp', p. 253.
9. Ibid., p. 259.
10. *Daily Telegraph*, 21 May 1996; *Theatre Record*, Vol. XVI, Issue 11 (1996), p. 653.
11. Edgar, op. cit., p. 31.
12. Mary Luckhurst, 'Political Point-Scoring: Martin Crimp's *Attempts on Her Life*', pp. 49, 59, 52, 55, 59–60.
13. Heiner Zimmermann, 'Images of Woman in Martin Crimp's *Attempts on Her Life*', pp. 81, 79, 84.
14. Ken Urban, 'Review of *Attempts on Her Life* by Martin Crimp at Soho Rep, New York'.
15. Merle Tönnies, 'The "Sensationalist Theatre of Cruelty" in 1990s Britain', p. 66.
16. Caroline Egan, 'The Playwright's Playwright'.
17. Ibid.
18. See Graham Saunders, *'Love Me or Kill Me'*, Aleks Sierz, *In-Yer-Face Theatre*, Dan Rebellato, 'Sarah Kane: An Appreciation', in *New Theatre Quarterly* 59 (August 1999), pp. 280–1 and David

Greig, 'Introduction', to Kane, *Complete Works* (London: Methuen, 2001).

19. Quoted in John Whitley, 'The Enigma That Is Mr Crimp'.

20. John Bull, *Stage Right*, p. 93.

21. Paul Taylor, 'The World According to Crimp'.

22. All references to *The Country* are to *Plays Two*. See interviews with Katie Mitchell, pp. 197–204, and Gerhard Willert, pp. 212–16.

23. *Guardian*, 17 May 2000, *Country Life*, 25 May 2000; *Independent*, 18 May 2000; *Daily Telegraph*, 18 May 2000; *Mail on Sunday*, 21 May 2000; *What's On*, 24 May 2000; *Evening Standard*, 17 May 2000; *Theatre Record*, Vol. XX, Issue 10 (2000), pp. 616–20.

24. The use of the word 'craved' here and in Rebecca's 'Why do we immediately crave what will most do us harm?' (p. 321) is an echo of the title of Kane's 1998 play, *Crave*.

25. Constantine P. Cavafy, 'The Town', 1910.

26. Eleanor Margolies, 'Elements in Contention', *Times Literary Supplement*, 9 June 2000, p. 21.

27. Crimp, interview with Sierz, 16 August 2005. All references to *Face to the Wall* are to *Fewer Emergencies*.

28. *Guardian*, 16 March 2002; *The Times*, 25 March 2002; *Theatre Record*, Vol. XXII, Issue 6 (2002), p. 330.

29. Michael Billington, 'Drama Out of a Crisis', *Guardian*, 10 April 2003.

30. John Ginman, '*Cruel and Tender*: Metaphysics and Performance in a Time of Terror', p. 113.

31. Back-cover blurb. All references are to *Cruel and Tender*.

32. Crimp, 'Sophocles and the War Against Terror'.

33. *Cruel and Tender*, note in playtext, no page number.

34. Luc Bondy, interview with Sierz, 31 March 2004.

35. *Evening Standard*, 14 May 2004; *Daily Telegraph*, 15 May 2004; *Guardian*, 14 May 2004; *Sunday Telegraph*, 16 May 2004; *Theatre Record*, Vol. XXIV, Issue 10 (2004), pp. 632–5.

36. Sierz, interview with David Farr, 26 November 2004. See also interview with Edward Kemp, pp. 205–9.

37. Crimp, 'Sophocles and the War Against Terror'.
38. Gilles Kepel, *The War for Muslim Minds: Islam and the West*, trans. Pascale Ghazaleh (Cambridge, Mass.: Harvard University Press, 2004). As research for *Cruel and Tender*, Crimp also used Jonathan Shay, *Achilles in Vietnam: Combat Training and the Undoing of Character* (New York: Atheneum, 1994); Joshua S. Goldstein, *War and Gender: How Gender Shapes the War System and Vice Versa* (Cambridge: Cambridge University Press, 2001); and René Girard's *Violence and the Sacred*, trans. Patrick Gregory (London: Continuum, 2005), as well as websites about Gulf War syndrome.
39. Crimp, '*Fewer Emergencies*, Vienna'.
40. All references are to *Fewer Emergencies*.
41. See Crimp, *Face to the Wall & Fewer Emergencies*, p. 33. The date was removed when the text was republished in 2005.
42. Crimp, Chaillot.
43. *The Times*, 14 September 2005; *Sunday Times*, 18 September 2005; *Daily Telegraph*, 15 September 2005; *Theatre Record*, Vol. XXV, Issue 19 (2005), p. 1146. See interview with James Macdonald, pp. 216–20.
44. The interpretation of both Macdonald and Crimp, Post-Show Talk about *Fewer Emergencies*, Royal Court Theatre, London, 20 September 2005.

4: 'French Is My film or TV'

1. John Whitley, 'The Enigma That Is Mr Crimp'. But Crimp also said, 'I don't want to be typecast as a translator and I don't want my primary motor to be the thought "Who shall I do next?"'
2. Dominic Cavendish, 'Martin Crimp Talks about *Cruel and Tender*'.
3. Martin Esslin, *The Theatre of the Absurd*, pp. 151, 152.
4. Cavendish, op. cit.
5. Nils Tabert, 'Gespräch mit Martin Crimp', p. 252.
6. *The Times*, 26 November 1997; *Independent*, 26 November

1997; *Theatre Record*, Vol. XVII, Issue 24 (1997), pp. 1524–5.

7. Esslin, op. cit., p. 132.

8. *Financial Times*, 26 November 1997; *Theatre Record*, Vol. XVII, Issue 24 (1997), p. 1526.

9. Gunilla Anderman, *Europe on Stage*, p. 64.

10. The published version is less explicit: 'Well, of course I believe in the inevitability of progress – though not without the occasional hiccup . . .', Crimp, *The Chairs*, p. 39.

11. New European Writers' Season programme.

12. David Bradby, 'Introduction', *Frontline Drama 6: New French Plays*, p. ix. See also interview with Bradby, pp. 209–12.

13. Quoted in Bradby, op. cit., p. x.

14. *Guardian*, 6 December 1997; *Sunday Times*, 23 November 1997; *Financial Times*, 21 November 1997; *Observer*, 23 November 1997; *Theatre Record*, Vol. XVII, Issue 24 (1997), pp. 1501–2.

15. Bernard-Marie Koltès, *Roberto Zucco*, p. 58. See Maria Delgado and David Fancy, 'The Theatre of Bernard-Marie Koltès and the "Other Spaces" of Translation', and interview with James Macdonald, pp. 216–20.

16. *Evening Standard*, 27 November 1997; *The Times*, 28 November 1997; *Daily Telegraph*, 3 December 1997; *Independent on Sunday*, 30 November 1997; *Observer*, 30 November 1997; *Theatre Record*, Vol. XVII, Issue 24 (1997), pp. 1552–4.

17. Bradby, op. cit., p. xli.

18. Ibid., pp. xxxvi, xli.

19. See interview with Katie Mitchell, pp. 197–204.

20. Esslin, op. cit., p. 207.

21. *Guardian*, 10 July 1999æ *Daily Telegraph*, 8 July 1999; *Independent on Sunday*, 11 July 1999; *Independent*, 8 July 1999; *Time Out*, 14 July 1999; *Theatre Record*, Vol. XIX, Issue 14 (1999), pp. 861–3.

22. Sarah Hemming, 'Language of Love', *Financial Times*, 28–29 August 1999.

23. *Daily Mail*, 3 September 1999æ *Guardian*, 4 September 1999; *Financial Times*, 7 September 1999; *Sunday Telegraph*, 5

September 1999; *Observer*, 5 September 1999; *Theatre Record*, Vol. XIX, Issue 17–18 (1999), pp. 1072–5.

24. This piece of business is not in the published playtext.

25. *Sunday Telegraph*, 6 June 2004; *Independent on Sunday*, 6 June 2004; *Mail on Sunday*, 6 June 2004; *Guardian*, 2 June 2004; *Glasgow Herald*, 7 June 2004; *Independent*, 4 June 2004; *Theatre Record*, Vol. XXIV, Issue 11 (2004), pp. 715–18.

26. National Theatre, *June–August 06* [Programme of events] (London: National Theatre, 2006), p. 2. 'Crave' again echoes the title of Kane's 1998 play.

27. Anderman, op. cit., p. 8.

28. Susan Bassnett-McGuire, *Translation Studies*, rev. edn (London: Routledge, 1991), p. 132.

29. Brian Logan, 'Whose Play Is It Anyway?', *Guardian*, 12 March 2003.

30. Dated November 1995. See Crimp, *The Misanthrope*, no page number, reprinted in *Plays Two*, pp. 97–9. The play was revived at Chichester in 2002, with a multiracial cast.

31. Hanna Scolnicov and Peter Holland (eds), *The Play Out of Context: Transferring Plays from Culture to Culture* (Cambridge: Cambridge University Press, 1989), p. 1.

5: 'Dialogue Is Inherently Cruel'

1. Interview dates: 1 February, 15 February and 9 March 2006.

2. The seats in the original Orange Tree Theatre were church pews.

3. 'The first piece of professional theatre I saw was Beckett's *Not I* at the Royal Court Theatre in London in 1975 – it was the day after [15 February] my nineteenth birthday and I still have the text of 11 pages with the ticket tucked inside' (Crimp, Chaillot).

4. Eugene Ionesco's *Macbett* (1972) is a satire on Shakespeare's *Macbeth*; *La Leçon* (1951) and *Le Nouveau Locataire* (1957).

5. Molly Bloom in James Joyce's *Ulysses* (Paris: Shakespeare & Co., 1922); Samuel Beckett, *Happy Days* (1961), *Footfalls* (1976) and *Not I* (1972).

6. Published as *Dealing with Clair* (London: Nick Hern Books, 1988).

7. The new text was used when the play was revived by Connal Orton at the Stephen Joseph Theatre, Scarborough, 29 August–5 October 1996.

8. *Getting Attention*, directed by Christophe Rauck, at Les Abbesses, Théâtre de la Ville, Paris, January–February 2006.

9. Act One, Scene Three and Act Two, Scene Three are both about videoing interviewees in the Masonic Hall. In Act Three, Scene Two, the location is the same but this time the market researchers watch the video of Act Two, Scene Three.

10. Jean Baudrillard, *America*, trans. Chris Turner (London, Verso, 1988).

11. 'Once in a while I have a meeting with a young person like yourself who tells me that my work is old-fashioned. I say to them that's also true of William Shakespeare' (p. 291).

12. 'New Directions' season, MA directing programme at Goldsmiths College, University of London, 20–24 July 1999. Directors Carrie Rossiter and Christine Umpfenbach, designers Miriam Buether and Katja Handt.

13. Harold Pinter, *Old Times* (London: Faber and Faber, 2004), p. 65.

14. Sophocles, *Electra and Other Plays: Ajax, Electra, Women of Trachis, Philoctetes*, trans. E. F. Watling (Harmondsworth: Penguin, 1973).

15. Billie Holiday, 'I Can't Give You Anything but Love', 1928.

16. Jonathan Shay, *Achilles in Vietnam: Combat Training and the Undoing of Character* (New York: Atheneum, 1994).

17. In March 2002. Compare *Face to the Wall & Fewer Emergencies* (2002) and *Fewer Emergencies* (2005).

6: 'Hearing Their Voices'

1. Dominic Dromgoole, *The Full Room*, p. 62.

2. David Greig, 'A Tyrant for All Time', *Guardian*, 28 April 2003. The article is about his experiences of translating Camus', 1945

play *Caligula* for the Donmar Warehouse in London.

3. Ibid.
4. Sierz, interview with Graham Whybrow, 21 February 2006.
5. *Independent on Sunday*, 25 April 1993; *Theatre Record*, Vol. XIII, Issue 8 (1993), p. 433.
6. Dromgoole, op. cit.
7. John O'Mahony, 'Writers' Crimp'.
8. Sierz, interview with Lucy Taylor, 15 March 2005.
9. Stefanie Carp and Stephan Wetzel, 'Nach der Probe: Ein Gespräch zwischen Martin Crimp, Luc Bondy und dem Theater'.
10. *Independent on Sunday*, 2 December 1990; *London Theatre Record*, Vol. X, Issue 24 (1990), p. 1594.
11. *Independent*, 11 March 1991; *Theatre Record*, Vol. XI, Issue 5 (1991), p. 294. The exact words are:

    Carol You want a beer? You asked him if he wants a beer Nick? (*She prods Nick.*) Nick, you asked him if he wants a beer?
    Bob Thanks, but I've, well I've got to get back.
    Carol Why didn't you ask him if he wants a beer? (p. 119)
    Then a little later on:
    Carol You want a beer? (p. 120)
    Also, compare *The Treatment*, pp. 382–3.
12. *Independent*, 18 May 1991; *Theatre Record*, Vol. XI, Issue 5 (1991), p. 604. Nick's actual words are: 'She eat her tea?' (p. 109).
13. *Daily Telegraph*, 18 May 2000; *Theatre Record*, Vol. XX, Issue 10 (2000), p. 616. Stichomythia is an ancient Greek arrangement of dialogue in which lines are spoken by alternate speakers.
14. Pilar Zozaya and Mireia Aragay, 'Interview with Martin Crimp'.
15. Jeremy Kingston, *The Times*, 28 September 1987.
16. I owe this point to Peter Buse.
17. Carp and Wetzel, op. cit.
18. Auriol Smith, 'Reputations: Martin Crimp', TheatreVoice website, 13 May 2005.

19. Reminiscent, surely, of Krapp's memories of the eyes of the women he once knew in Samuel Beckett, *Krapp's Last Tape and Embers* (London: Faber and Faber, 1959), pp. 6, 8, 9.

20. Carp and Wetzel, op. cit.

21. *The Times*, 11 March 1991; *Theatre Record*, Vol. XI, Issue 5 (1991), p. 294.

22. Eleanor Margolies, 'Elements in Contention', *Times Literary Supplement*, 9 June 2000, p. 21.

23. Dan Rebellato, 'Reputations: Martin Crimp', TheatreVoice website, 13 May 2005.

24. O'Mahony, op. cit.

25. Note in *Dealing with Clair*, no page number.

26. Carp and Wetzel, op. cit.

27. Crimp and Joseph Danan, 'The Playwright and the Set Up / L'Auteur et l'Institution', p. 25.

7: 'Viewed with Hostility and Suspicion'

1. Nils Tabert, 'Gespräch mit Martin Crimp', p. 253.

2. Carp and Wetzel, 'Nach der Probe: Ein Gespräch zwischen Martin Crimp, Luc Bondy und dem Theater'.

3. Dominic Dromgoole, *The Full Room*, p. 62.

4. Peter Thomson, 'Crimp, Martin (Andrew)', p. 123.

5. Heiner Zimmermann, 'Images of Woman in Martin Crimp's *Attempts on Her Life*', pp. 70–1.

6. Thomson, op. cit., p. 124.

7. Lindsay Posner, 'Reputations: Martin Crimp', TheatreVoice website, 13 May 2005.

8. Dan Rebellato, 'Reputations: Martin Crimp', TheatreVoice website, 13 May 2005.

9. David Mamet, *Three Uses of the Knife: On the Nature and Purpose of Drama* (London: Methuen, 1998), p. 59. Reminiscent, also, of Nell's 'Nothing is funnier than unhappiness' in Samuel Beckett, *Endgame* (London: Faber and Faber, 1964), p. 64.

10. Auriol Smith, 'Reputations: Martin Crimp', TheatreVoice website, 13 May 2005.

11. Martin Esslin, *The Theatre of the Absurd*, p. 146.
12. Pinter quoted in Martin Esslin, *Pinter the Playwright* (London: Methuen, 2000), p. 27.
13. Posner, interview with Sierz, 3 May 2005.
14. See Peter Buse, 'Sollicitations téléphoniques: *La Campagne* de Martin Crimp'.
15. Anne Tipton, 'Reputations: Martin Crimp', TheatreVoice website, 13 May 2005.
16. John Ginman, '*Cruel and Tender*: Metaphysics and Performance in a Time of Terror', p. 118.
17. John Thaxter, 'Christmas Illusion'.
18. Thomson, op. cit., p. 124.
19. Crimp, '*Fewer Emergencies*, Vienna'.
20. Carp and Wetzel, op. cit.
21. Crimp, op. cit.
22. Ibid.
23. Ibid. And also Clara Escoda Agusti, 'Interview with Martin Crimp'.

8: 'My Plays Emit Criticism'

1. Crimp, Chaillot.
2. Paul Taylor, 'The World According to Crimp'.
3. Nils Tabert, 'Gespräch mit Martin Crimp', p. 262.
4. Dan Rebellato, 'Reputations: Martin Crimp', TheatreVoice website, 13 May 2005.
5. Pilar Zozaya and Mireia Aragay, 'Interview with Martin Crimp'.
6. Ibid.
7. Sierz, interview with Crimp, 16 August 2005. See Jonathan Swift, 'A Modest Proposal for Preventing the Children of Poor People from Being a Burthen to Their Parents or the Country, and for Making Them Beneficial to the Public (1729)', in Angus Ross and David Woolley (eds), *Jonathan Swift: Major Works* (Oxford: Oxford World Classics, 2003), pp. 492–9.
8. Rebellato, op. cit.

9. Sierz, interview with Graham Whybrow, 21 February 2006.
10. Anne Tipton, 'Reputations: Martin Crimp', TheatreVoice website, 13 May 2005.
11. Zozaya and Aragay, op. cit.
12. Lindsay Posner, 'Reputations: Martin Crimp', TheatreVoice website, 13 May 2005.
13. Crimp, op. cit.
14. Dominic Dromgoole, *The Full Room*, p. 62.
15. Zozaya and Aragay, op. cit.
16. Taylor, op. cit.
17. Zozaya and Aragay, op. cit.
18. See Heiner Zimmermann, 'Images of Woman in Martin Crimp's *Attempts on Her Life*', p. 81.
19. Susannah Clapp, 'No Plot, No Characters, No Rules: Martin Crimp Takes the Play Apart', p. 48. She compares Crimp to David Hare.
20. Keith Miller, 'Overkill! Overkill!', *Times Literary Supplement*, 28 March 1997, p. 19.
21. Zimmermann, op. cit., p. 73.
22. Zozaya and Aragay, op. cit.
23. Jack Tinker, *Daily Mail*, 3 November 1988; *Financial Times*, 17 October 1988; *London Theatre Record*, Vol. VIII, Issue 21 (1988), pp. 1443, 1445.
24. Peter Thomson, 'Crimp, Martin (Andrew)', p. 124.
25. Caroline Donald, 'Frozen Pizza and the Search for Happiness'.
26. Zimmermann, op. cit, p. 71.
27. Miller, op. cit.
28. Crimp quoted in Jane Edwardes, 'Kid Gloves'.
29. In February 1993, two ten-year-old boys abducted and killed the two-year-old Jamie Bulger. See Blake Morrison, *As If* (London: Granta, 1997).
30. Crimp, op. cit.
31. Zozaya and Aragay, op. cit.

Conclusion

1. John Thaxter, 'Christmas Illusion'. 'It's written like a piece of music,' said Walters in the same interview.
2. Crimp, interview with Sierz, 16 August 2005.
3. Dominic Cavendish, 'Martin Crimp Talks about *Cruel and Tender*'.
4. Crimp, interview with Sierz, 16 August 2005. 'I, who had been such an ardent subversive, who had so desired the overthrow of the established order, now found myself in the middle of a volcano, and I was afraid' (Luis Buñuel, *My Last Breath*, trans. Abigail Israel [London: Vintage, 2003], p. 153).
5. Harold Pinter, *Old Times* (London: Faber and Faber, 2004), pp. 47–9.
6. Clara Escoda Agusti, 'Interview with Martin Crimp'.
7. Roland Barthes, *A Lover's Discourse: Fragments*, trans. Richard Howard (New York: Hill and Wang, 1978), p. 59.
8. Crimp, interview with Sierz, 9 March 2006. Peter Handke, *The Afternoon of a Writer*, trans. Ralph Manheim (New York: Farrar, Straus & Giroux, 1989).
9. Crimp, 'Questions Aix/Marseille, Théâtre du Gym'.
10. Cavendish, op. cit.
11. Gilbert Adair, *Surfing the Zeitgeist* (London: Faber and Faber, 1997), p. 125. In *La Disparition*, the rule was to write a novel without using the letter e. Georges Perec, *A Void [La Disparition]*, trans. Gilbert Adair (London: Harvill Press, 1994).
12. Carp and Wetzel, 'Nach der Probe: Ein Gespräch zwischen Martin Crimp, Luc Bondy und dem Theater'.
13. Anne Tipton, 'Reputations: Martin Crimp', TheatreVoice website, 13 May 2005.
14. I owe this point to playwright Fin Kennedy. Both *Attempts on Her Life* and *The Country* also feature overlapping conversations.
15. Carp and Wetzel, op. cit.
16. Ibid.
17. Pilar Zozaya and Mireia Aragay, 'Interview with Martin Crimp'.

18. Carp and Wetzel, op. cit.
19. Cavendish, op. cit.
20. Sheila Johnston, 'Tales from Hollywood', cutting in Theatre Museum, no newspaper, no date.
21. Billington, *Guardian*, 22 April 1993; *Theatre Record*, Vol. XIII, Issue 8 (1993), pp. 434.
22. Crimp, '*Fewer Emergencies*, Vienna'.
23. Crimp, interview with Sierz, 16 August 2005.
24. Lindsay Posner, 'Reputations: Martin Crimp', TheatreVoice website, 13 May 2005.
25. See Hans-Thies Lehmann, *Postdramatic Theatre*, trans. Karen Juers-Munby (London: Routledge, 2006).
26. Caroline Egan, 'The Playwright's Playwright'.
27. Dan Rebellato, 'Commentary', in Mark Ravenhill, *Shopping and Fucking* (London: Methuen Student Edns, 2005), p. xxiii.
28. Brooke is also the name of the electioneering politician mercilessly parodied in George Eliot, *Middlemarch* (Oxford: Oxford University Press, 1988), pp. 412–14.
29. 'Sarah Kane' in Heidi Stephenson and Natasha Langridge (eds), *Rage and Reason: Women Playwrights on Playwriting* (London: Methuen, 1997), p. 130.
30. David Hare, *Obedience, Struggle & Revolt: Lectures on Theatre* (London: Faber and Faber, 2005), p. 46.

The Interviews

1. Sam Walters trained as an actor at LAMDA (1962–4), then turned to directing with the formation of the Worcester Repertory Company (1966–7). He created Jamaica's first full-time theatre company, and in 1971 founded the Orange Tree, which he continues to run. His productions have ranged from Shakespeare through Restoration comedy to Feydeau and Brecht, as well as new plays. His awards include an MBE (1999). He is married to Auriol Smith.
2. Act One, Scene 4: Tony and Heather at the temporary bus stop.

3. Anthony Clark is artistic director of the Hampstead Theatre (since 2003). In 1981, he was assistant director at the Orange Tree, where he directed everything from a schools tour of *Macbeth* to new work, including his own plays. He has worked for Tara Arts, Contact Theatre in Manchester (1984–90), and Birmingham Rep, where he launched The Door studio, which stages new work, in 1997.

4. Alain Robbe-Grillet, *In the Labyrinth*, trans. Christine Brook-Rose (London: John Calder, 1970).

5. Auriol Smith is an actor, founder member and associate director of the Orange Tree. She studied drama at Bristol University (1954–8), and helped stage the first production of Pinter's *The Room*. Her acting and directing credits at the Orange Tree are extensive. On television, she has appeared in *Kavanagh QC*, *One Foot in the Grave* and *Peak Practice*, and radio includes Bennett's *Forty Years On*. She is married to Sam Walters.

6. Joe Penhall was born in 1967. His plays include *Some Voices* (1994), *Pale Horse* (1995), *Love and Understanding* (1997), *Blue/Orange* (2000) and *Dumb Show* (2004). He won the John Whiting Award for *Some Voices* and an Olivier Award and *Evening Standard* Award for *Blue/Orange*. He adapted Jake Arnott's *The Long Firm* (BBC, 2004) and Ian McEwan's *Enduring Love* (Paramount, 2004). The reading of *Dealing with Clair* was on 7 July 2004.

7. Jude Kelly is artistic director of the South Bank Centre (since 2005), founder of Metal and also Chair of the Arts, Education and Culture Committee for London 2012, responsible for the cultural and education programme of the Olympics. She has been artistic director of Battersea Arts Centre (1980–8) and West Yorkshire Playhouse, Leeds (1988–2002). Her awards include an Olivier for directing *Singin' in the Rain* (2001) and an OBE (1997).

8. Lindsay Posner was artistic director of the Royal Court Theatre Upstairs (1989–92), and then worked at the RSC. His

many directing credits include Dorfman's *Death and the Maiden* (1992), which won two Olivier Awards. He has a special interest in the work of Pinter and Mamet: *American Buffalo* (1997), *The Caretaker* (2003), *Sexual Perversity in Chicago* (2003), *Oleanna* (2004), *A Life in the Theatre* (2005) and *The Birthday Party* (2005).

9. Tim Albery ran the ICA Theatre in 1980–1. His directing credits include many major theatre and opera productions in Britain, Europe and North America, including *Fidelio* (1994), *From the House of the Dead* (1997), *Katya Kabanova* (1999), *War and Peace* (2001), the *Ring* cycle (2003), *One Touch of Venus* (2004) and *The Merry Widow* (2004).

10. Katie Mitchell set up Classics on a Shoestring in 1990, and ran the RSC's Other Place (1996–9). Her many directing credits include Euripides' *The Women of Troy* (1991), Ibsen's *Ghosts* (1993), Arden's *Live Like Pigs* (1993), Beckett's *Endgame* (1996), Chekhov's *Uncle Vanya* (1998), Aeschylus' *Oresteia* (1999) and Chekhov's *Three Sisters* (2003). She has directed opera for the Welsh National Opera, and is an associate director at the National Theatre.

11. Jean Genet, *Funeral Rites*, trans. Bernard Frechtman (New York: Grove, 1970).

12. Edward Kemp is dramaturg at the Chichester Festival Theatre (since 2003). His adaptations include *The Mysteries* (1998), Faulkner's *As I Lay Dying* (1998), Lessing's *Nathan the Wise* (2003), Bulgakov's *The Master and Margarita* (2004), and his plays include *The Iron and the Oak* (1983), *The Drowned Man* (1984), *A Proper Place* (1986), *5/11* and *Six Pictures of Lee Miller* (both 2005).

13. Georges Perec, *A Void [La Disparition]*, trans. Gilbert Adair (London: Harvill Press, 1994).

14. Jean Baudrillard, *The Spirit of Terrorism and Other Essays*, trans. Chris Turner (London: Verso, 2003).

15. René Girard, *Violence and the Sacred*, trans. Patrick Gregory (London: Continuum, 2005).

16. Susan Sontag, *Regarding the Pain of Others* (Harmondsworth: Penguin, 2004).

17. David Bradby is Professor of Drama and Theatre Studies at Royal Holloway, University of London (since 1988). His books include *Beckett: Waiting for Godot* (2001), *Mise en Scène: French Theatre Now* (with Annie Sparks, 1997). He edited *Koltès Plays: 1* and *2*, and has translated Koltès's *Return to the Desert* and (with Maria Delgado) *Black Battles with Dogs*, and Vinaver's *The Television Programme*.

18. Eugène Ionesco, *The Chairs*, trans. Donald Watson (London: Samuel French, 1958).

19. In the programme text for *The Misanthrope* (1996), it says, 'Forthcoming projects are a new play, **Attempts On Her Life**, and a translation of Koltès' **Roberto Zucco**, both for the Royal Court' (no page number).

20. Gerhard Willert is artistic director of Landestheater Linz, Austria (since 1998). His many directing credits include Koltès's *Roberto Zucco* (1990), Ibsen's *The Master Builder* (1996), Kleist's *The Broken Jug* (2000), Racine's *Phaedra* (2001), Bond's *The Woman* (2003), Brecht's *Mother Courage* (2005), and Vinaver's *Overboard* (2006). In *Martin Crimp: Plays One*, Willert is 'The Director'; photographs of his productions appear on the covers of *Plays One* and *Plays Two*.

21. Sigmund Freud, *Civilization and its Discontents*, trans. James Strachey (New York: W. W. Norton, 1961).

22. James Macdonald is associate director of the Royal Court (since 1992). His many directing credits include opera, classical plays, as well as new writing such as Kane's *Blasted* (1995, 2001), *Cleansed* (1998), *4.48 Psychosis* (2000), and Churchill's *Thyestes* (1994). In Europe and North America, his work includes *4.48 Psychose* (2001) and Churchill's *A Number* (2002). Between 2003 and 2006, he worked on a NESTA fellowship with Katie Mitchell.

BIBLIOGRAPHY

Primary Sources

The work of Martin Crimp

Published plays

Dealing with Clair (London: Nick Hern Books, 1988).

Play with Repeats (London: Nick Hern Books, 1989).

Getting Attention & No One Sees the Video (London: Nick Hern Books, 1991).

The Treatment (London: Nick Hern Books, 1993).

Attempts on Her Life (London: Faber and Faber, 1997).

The Country (London: Faber and Faber, 2000).

Plays One: Dealing with Clair, Play with Repeats, Getting Attention, The Treatment, with author's introduction, 'Four Imaginary Characters' (London: Faber and Faber, 2000).

Face to the Wall & Fewer Emergencies (London: Faber and Faber, 2002).

[After Sophocles], *Cruel and Tender* (London: Faber and Faber, 2004).

Plays Two: No One Sees the Video, The Misanthrope, Attempts on Her Life, The Country, with author's introduction, 'Four Unwelcome Thoughts' (London: Faber and Faber, 2005).

Fewer Emergencies (London: Faber and Faber, 2005).

Radio plays

Three Attempted Acts, in Richard Imison (ed.), *Best Radio Plays of 1985: The BBC Giles Cooper Award Winners* (London: Methuen/ BBC, 1986).

Definitely the Bahamas, unpublished typescript (1986).

Translations

Molière, *The Misanthrope* (London: Faber and Faber, 1996).

Bernard-Marie Koltès, *Roberto Zucco* (London: Methuen, 1997).

Bernard-Marie Koltès, *Roberto Zucco*, in *Plays 1: Black Battles with Dogs, Return to the Desert, Roberto Zucco*, with an introduction by David Bradby (London: Methuen, 1997).

Eugène Ionesco, *The Chairs* (London: Faber and Faber, 1997).

Christophe Pellet, *One More Wasted Year* in David Bradby (ed.), *Frontline Drama 6: New French Plays* (London: Methuen, 1998).

Jean Genet, *The Maids* (London: Faber and Faber, 1999).

Pierre Marivaux, *The Triumph of Love* (London: Faber and Faber, 1999).

Pierre Marivaux, *The False Servant* (London: Faber and Faber, 2004).

Anton Chekhov, *The Seagull* (London: Faber and Faber, 2006).

Unpublished plays

Clang (1976).

British Summer Time Ends, (1980).

Love Games, co-written with Howard Curtis from Jerzy Przezdziecki's original (1981).

Living Remains (1981).

Four Attempted Acts (1984).

A Variety of Death-Defying Acts (1985).

Definitely the Bahamas (1986).

Other writings

Still Early Days, unpublished novel (1980).

An Anatomy, unpublished short-story collection (1982).

'The Statement', winner of *Time Out* short-story competition (1982).

'Stage Kiss' [short story], *London Review of Books*, Vol. 12, No. 14 (1990).

'Stage Kiss', in *Getting Attention & No One Sees the Video* (London: Nick Hern Books, 1991).

'Little Romance: Two Extracts from Work in Progress', in *The Treatment* (London: Nick Hern Books, 1993).

'Mol Flounders', *Observer*, 11 February 1996.

[On Caryl Churchill], in Egan, Caroline, 'The Playwright's Playwright', *Guardian*, 21 September 1998.

'Advice to Iraqi Women', *Guardian*, 10 April 2003; reprinted in the *Independent*, 17 March 2004.

'Sophocles and the War Against Terror', *Guardian*, 8 May 2004.

Unpublished notes

Chaillot [unpublished answers to questions], (January 2004).

'Questions Aix/Marseille, Théâtre du Gym', [unpublished answers to questions] (May 2005).

'*Fewer Emergencies*, Vienna', [unpublished answers to questions] (February 2006).

Interviews with Martin Crimp

Carp, Stefanie, and Stephan Wetzel, 'Nach der Probe: Ein Gespräch zwischen Martin Crimp, Luc Bondy und dem Theater' [After the Rehearsal: A Conversation Between Martin Crimp, Luc Bondy and the Theatre] in *Auf dem Land* programme for Schauspielhaus Zurich, Zurich, September 2001 (English translation by Penny Black).

Cavendish, Dominic, 'Martin Crimp Talks about *Cruel and Tender*', TheatreVoice website, http://www.theatrevoice.com (11 May 2004).

Crimp, Martin, and Joseph Danan, 'The Playwright and the Set Up/L'Auteur et l'Institution', *Franco-British Studies: Journal of the British Institute in Paris*, No. 26 (Autumn 1998), pp. 23–34.

Devine, Harriet, 'Martin Crimp', in *Looking Back: Playwrights at the Royal Court, 1956–2006* (London: Faber and Faber, 2006), p. 81–90.

Donald, Caroline, 'Frozen Pizza and the Search for Happiness', *Independent*, 28 November 1990.

Edwardes, Jane, 'Kid Gloves', *Time Out*, 22–29 May 1991.

Escoda Agusti, Clara, 'Interview with Martin Crimp', unpublished transcript, London, 23 September 2005.

Gallagher, Stephen, 'Crimp and Crave', *Plays International*, June/July 2004.

Jones, Rick, 'Scriptwriters from Hell', *Time Out*, 14–21 April 1993.

Litson, Jo, 'Pardon His French', *The Weekend Australian*, 22 April 2000.

Macdonald, James, and Martin Crimp, Post-Show Talk [about *Fewer Emergencies*], Royal Court Theatre, London, 20 September 2005.

O'Mahony, John, 'Writers' Crimp', *Guardian*, 20 April 1993.

Sierz, Aleks, 'Greek tragedy and the War on Terror', *Sunday Telegraph*, 18 April 2004.

Sierz, Aleks, 'Bondy Comes to London', *Plays International*, May/June 2004.

Sierz, Aleks, 'An Invented Reality', *New Statesman*, 5 September 2005.

Sierz, Aleks, 'Crimp's Political Theatre', *Plays International*, Autumn 2005.

Tabert, Nils, 'Gespräch mit Martin Crimp' [Conversation with Martin Crimp], in Nils Tabert (ed.), *Playspotting: Die Londoner Theaterszene der 90er* (Reinbek bei Hamburg: Rowohlt Taschenbuch Verlag GmbH, 1998), pp. 251–62 (English translation by Penny Black).

Taylor, Paul, 'The World According to Crimp', *Independent*, 10 May 2000.

Thaxter, John, 'Sex and Suffering', *Richmond and Twickenham Times*, 12 October 1984.

Thaxter, John, 'Christmas Illusion', *Richmond and Twickenham*

Times, 13 December 1985.

Whitley, John, 'The Enigma That Is Mr Crimp', *Daily Telegraph*, 11 May 2000.

Zozaya, Pilar, and Mireia Aragay, 'Interview with Martin Crimp', unpublished transcript, Barcelona, 14 February 2005.

Secondary sources

Programme notes

Sierz, Aleks, 'The Treatment', programme note for Martin Crimp's *The Treatment*, Rozmaitosci Theatre, Warsaw (September 2002).

Sierz, Aleks, 'The Masks of Heracles', programme note for Martin Crimp's *Cruel and Tender*, National Theatre of Slovenia, Ljubljana (October 2005).

Newspaper and magazine articles

Christopher, James, 'Murder without a Moral', *The Times*, 25 November 1997.

Clapp, Susannah, 'No Plot, No Characters, No Rules: Martin Crimp Takes the Play Apart', *New Statesman*, 21 March 1997.

Egan, Caroline, 'The Playwright's Playwright: Who's Best at Making Drama Out of a Crisis?' [Sarah Kane on Martin Crimp], *Guardian*, 21 September 1998.

Journal articles and book chapters

Angel-Perez, Elisabeth, 'Martin Crimp: *The Treatment* (1993) et *Attempts on Her Life* (1997): Tricotage du Texte et Auto-Engendrement', *Ecritures Contemporaines* 5 (2002), pp. 99–110.

Angel-Perez, Elisabeth, 'Martin Crimp et la Spectropoétique de la Scène', in her *Voyages au Bout du Possible: Les Théâtres du traumatisme de Samuel Beckett à Sarah Kane* (Paris: Klincksieck, 2006), pp. 197–212.

Buse, Peter, 'Sollicitations téléphoniques: *La Campagne* de Martin

Crimp', in Elisabeth Angel-Perez and Nicole Boireau (eds), *Le Théâtre contemporain anglais (1985–2005)* (Paris: Klincksieck, forthcoming 2006).

Dromgoole, Dominic, 'Martin Crimp', in his *The Full Room: An A–Z of Contemporary Playwriting*, rev. edn (London: Methuen, 2002), pp. 61–3.

Escoda Agusti, Clara, '"head green water to sing": Minimalism and Indeterminacy in Martin Crimp's *Attempts on her Life* (1997)'. Paper given at the 'Drama and/after Postmodernism' conference, Augsburg University, Augsburg, 25–28 May 2006.

Ginman, John, '*Cruel and Tender*: Metaphysics and Performance in a Time of Terror', *Western European Stages*, Vol. 16, No. 3 (Fall 2004), pp. 113–18.

Luckhurst, Mary, 'Political Point-Scoring: Martin Crimp's *Attempts on Her Life*', *Contemporary Theatre Review*, Vol. 13 (1) (February 2003), pp. 47–60.

Rebellato, Dan, 'Crimp, Martin [Andrew]', in Colin Chambers (ed.), *The Continuum Companion to Twentieth Century Theatre* (London: Continuum, 2002), pp. 182–3.

Spengler, Rachel, 'Une Dramaturgie du Décentrement: Étude de *Atteintes à sa vie*, *Tout va mieux* et *Face au mur* de Martin Crimp', *L'Annuaire Théâtral*, No. 38 (Autumn 2005), pp. 53–67.

Thomson, Peter, 'Crimp, Martin (Andrew)', in Thomas Riggs (ed.), *Contemporary Dramatists*, 6th edn (Detroit/New York: St James Press, 1999), pp. 123–4.

Zimmermann, Heiner, 'Images of Woman in Martin Crimp's *Attempts on Her Life*', *European Journal of English Studies*, Vol. 7 (1) (April 2003), pp. 69–85.

Zimmermann, Heiner, 'Martin Crimp, *Attempts on Her Life*: Postdramatic, Postmodern, Satiric?' in Margarete Rubik and Elke Mettinger-Schartmann (eds), *(Dis)Continuities: Trends and Traditions in Contemporary Theatre and Drama in English*, Contemporary Drama in English 9 (Trier: Wissenschaftlicher Verlag Trier, 2002), pp. 105–24.

Websites

Sierz, Aleks, 'Martin Crimp', *The Literary Encyclopedia*, http://www.LiteraryEncyclopedia.com (November 2004).

Sierz, Aleks, panel discussion, with Lindsay Posner, Dan Rebellato, Auriol Smith and Anne Tipton, 'Reputations: Martin Crimp', http://www.theatrevoice.com (13 May 2005).

Urban, Ken, 'Review of *Attempts on Her Life* by Martin Crimp at Soho Rep, New York', http://www.nytheatre.com/nytheatre/archweb/arch_024.htm (April 2002).

Urban, Ken, 'Interview with Director Steve Cosson', http://www.nytheatre.com/nytheatre/archweb/arch_024.htm (April 2002).

Background

Books

Anderman, Gunilla, *Europe on Stage: Translation and Theatre* (London: Oberon Books, 2005).

Billington, Michael, *One Night Stands: A Critic's View of Modern British Theatre* (London: Nick Hern Books, 1993).

Boireau, Nicole, *Théâtre et Société en Angleterre des Années 1950 à Nos Jours* (Paris: Presses Universitaires de France, 2000).

Bradby, David (ed.), *Frontline Drama 6: New French Plays* (London: Methuen, 1998).

Buchan, Norman, and Tricia Sumner (eds), *Glasnost in Britain? Against Censorship and in Defence of the Word* (London: Macmillan, 1989).

Bull, John, *Stage Right: Crisis and Recovery in British Contemporary Theatre* (London: Macmillan, 1994).

Chambers, Colin, *Inside the Royal Shakespeare Company: Creativity and the Institution* (London: Routledge, 2004).

Clark, Peter, *Hope and Glory: Britain 1900–2000*, 2nd edn (Harmondsworth: Penguin, 2004).

Edgar, David, *State of Play: Playwrights on Playwriting* (London:

Faber and Faber, 1999).

Esslin, Martin, *Pinter the Playwright*, 6th edn (London: Methuen, 2000).

Esslin, Martin, *The Theatre of the Absurd*, 3rd edn (London: Methuen, 2001).

Eyre, Richard, and Nicholas Wright, *Changing Stages: A View of British Theatre in the Twentieth Century* (London: Bloomsbury, 2000).

Ghilardi, Lia, *The Creative City: Artists and the Creative City* (Stroud: Comedia, 1995).

Gottlieb, Vera, and Colin Chambers (eds), *Theatre in a Cool Climate* (Oxford: Amber Lane Press, 1999).

Hewison, Robert, *Culture and Consensus: England, Art and Politics Since 1940*, rev. edn (London: Methuen, 1997).

Kershaw, Baz (ed.), *The Cambridge History of British Theatre: Volume 3 – Since 1895* (Cambridge: Cambridge University Press, 2004).

Lesser, Wendy, *A Director Calls: Stephen Daldry and the Theatre* (London: Faber and Faber, 1997).

Marwick, Arthur, *British Society Since 1945*, 2nd edn (Harmondsworth: Penguin, 1990).

Morley, Sheridan, *Spectator at the Theatre* (London: Oberon Books, 2002).

Nightingale, Benedict, *The Future of Theatre* (London: Phoenix, 1998).

Peacock, Keith D., *Thatcher's Theatre: British Theatre and Drama in the Eighties* (Westport, Conn.: Greenwood Press, 1999).

Rabey, David Ian, *English Drama Since 1940* (London: Longman, 2003).

Reitz, Bernhard, and Mark Berninger (eds), *British Drama of the 1990s* (Heidelberg: Universitätsverlag C., Winter, 2002).

Roberts, Philip, *The Royal Court Theatre and the Modern Stage* (Cambridge: Cambridge University Press, 1999).

Saunders, Graham, *'Love Me or Kill Me': Sarah Kane and the Theatre of Extremes* (Manchester: Manchester University Press, 2002).

Shellard, Dominic, *British Theatre Since the War* (New Haven: Yale University Press, 1999).

Sierz, Aleks, *In-Yer-Face Theatre: British Drama Today* (London: Faber and Faber, 2001).

Smith, Chris, *Creative Britain* (London: Faber and Faber, 1998).

Wardle, Irving, *The Theatres of George Devine* (London: Eyre Methuen, 1979).

Chapters and articles

Asquith, Rosalind, 'Subversion at Lunchtime or Business as Usual?', in Sandy Craig (ed.), *Dreams and Deconstructions: Alternative Theatre in Britain* (Ambergate: Amber Lane Press, 1980), pp. 145–52.

Delgado, Maria, and David Fancy, 'The Theatre of Bernard-Marie Koltès and the "Other Spaces" of Translation', *New Theatre Quarterly*, 66 (May 2001), pp. 141–60.

Dennewald, Martine, 'An der Rändern der Identität: Überindividuelle Figurenkonzeptionen bei Crimp, Kane, Abdoh und Foreman', *Forum Modernes Theater*, No. 19 (1) (2004), pp. 43–71.

Pankratz, Annette, 'Signifying Nothing and Everything: The Extension of the Code and Hyperreal Simulations', in Hans-Ulrich Mohr and Kerstin Mächler (eds), *Extending the Code: New Forms of Dramatic and Theatrical Expression*, Contemporary Drama in English 11 (Trier: Wissenschaftlicher Verlag Trier, 2004), pp. 63–78.

Tönnies, Merle, 'The "Sensationalist Theatre of Cruelty" in 1990s Britain, Its 1960s Forebears and the Beginning of the 21st Century', in Margarete Rubik and Elke Mettinger-Schartmann (eds) *(Dis)Continuities: Trends and Traditions in Contemporary Theatre and Drama in English*, Contemporary Drama in English 9 (Trier: Wissenschaftlicher Verlag Trier, 2002), pp. 55–71.

Websites

Almeida Theatre: http://www.almeida.co.uk

Chichester Festival Theatre: http://www.cft.org.uk
National Theatre: http://www.nationaltheatre.org.uk
Orange Tree Theatre: http://www.orangetreetheatre.co.uk
Royal Court Theatre: http://www.royalcourttheatre.com
Royal Shakespeare Company: http://www.rsc.org.uk
West Yorkshire Playhouse: http://www.wyplayhouse.com
Young Vic Theatre: http://www.youngvic.org

Interview dates
Luc Bondy: 31 March 2004.
Joe Penhall: 1 October 2004.
Anthony Clark: 24 November 2004.
David Farr: 26 November 2004.
Sam Walters: 25 February 2005.
Lucy Taylor: 15 March 2005.
Lindsay Posner: 3 May 2005.
Anne Tipton: 4 May 2005.
Auriol Smith: 10 May 2005.
Katie Mitchell: 27 May 2005.
Edward Kemp: 23 June 2005.
David Bradby: 6 July 2005.
Jude Kelly: 9 August 2005.
Gerhard Willert: 18 September 2005.
James Macdonald: 30 September 2005.
Tim Albery: 31 October 2005.
Graham Whybrow: 21 February 2006.
Martin Crimp: 1 February, 15 February and 9 March 2006.

INDEX

Note: Works (including translations) by Martin Crimp are listed in the index under their titles; works by other writers are listed under the writers' names.